Maternity Policy and the Making of the Norwegian
Welfare State, 1880–1940

Anna M. Peterson

Maternity Policy and the Making of the Norwegian Welfare State, 1880–1940

palgrave
macmillan

Anna M. Peterson
Luther College
Decorah, IA, USA

ISBN 978-3-319-75480-2   ISBN 978-3-319-75481-9   (eBook)
https://doi.org/10.1007/978-3-319-75481-9

Library of Congress Control Number: 2018936144

© The Editor(s) (if applicable) and The Author(s) 2018
This work is subject to copyright. All rights are solely and exclusively licensed by the
Publisher, whether the whole or part of the material is concerned, specifically the rights of
translation, reprinting, reuse of illustrations, recitation, broadcasting, reproduction on
microfilms or in any other physical way, and transmission or information storage and retrieval,
electronic adaptation, computer software, or by similar or dissimilar methodology now
known or hereafter developed.
The use of general descriptive names, registered names, trademarks, service marks, etc. in this
publication does not imply, even in the absence of a specific statement, that such names are
exempt from the relevant protective laws and regulations and therefore free for general use.
The publisher, the authors, and the editors are safe to assume that the advice and information
in this book are believed to be true and accurate at the date of publication. Neither the
publisher nor the authors or the editors give a warranty, express or implied, with respect to
the material contained herein or for any errors or omissions that may have been made. The
publisher remains neutral with regard to jurisdictional claims in published maps and
institutional affiliations.

Cover credit: © WS Collection / Alamy Stock Photo

Printed on acid-free paper

This Palgrave Macmillan imprint is published by the registered company Springer International
Publishing AG part of Springer Nature.
The registered company address is: Gewerbestrasse 11, 6330 Cham, Switzerland

For Nina

ACKNOWLEDGEMENTS

My profound thanks go to the many people who made this book possible. This book began as a Ph.D. dissertation at Ohio State University, where Birgitte Søland nurtured the scholar in me and offered me guidance and support along the way. I'm grateful for her continued advice and counsel.

In Norway, a community of scholars and friends created a warm and inclusive environment that encouraged historical inquiry and interdisciplinary and intercultural exchange. The Centre for Gender Research at the University of Oslo introduced me to colleagues both supportive and engaging during a year-long research stay. I am thankful for many enriching conversations with Gro Hagemann and Inger Elisabeth Haavet. The coffee breaks, glasses of wine and dinners I shared with Unn Conradi Andersen, Anne Bitsch, Greta Gober, Trine Rogg Korsvik, Joana Serrado, Stina Hansteen Solhøy and Rannveig Svendby made my stay in Norway not only productive but enjoyable. Thank you as well to Gitte Moen, Ingolf Grønvold, and Birgitte and Anders Hartmann who kindly opened their homes to me while I conducted preliminary research in Oslo.

I am indebted to the generous financial support of the American-Scandinavian Foundation that enabled me to research this topic. I am also thankful for numerous travel grants and funding provided by Ohio State University, Luther College, and the Royal Norwegian Embassy.

My research abroad was also facilitated by the generosity of archivists and librarians. Staff at the National Archives, National Library, Oslo City Archives, and various regional archives greeted my project with enthusiasm and helped me identify key sources that strengthened and informed

viii ACKNOWLEDGEMENTS

this project. I am also grateful for the warm welcome I received from the staff at the Norwegian Association of Midwives who not only shared their organizational records with me, but also friendly conversation and numerous cups of coffee. Lastly, I am indebted to Joron Pihl for graciously granting me access to Katti Anker Møller's personal papers housed in the Manuscript Collection at the National Library.

The book has benefitted from assistance from numerous hands and eyes during the production stages. I am grateful to Sharla Plant at Palgrave Macmillan for first recognizing the potential in this project and for placing me in the excellent care of editor Emily Russell and her assistant, Carmel Kennedy. Their keen eyes and observations have helped take this manuscript from dissertation to book. Two Luther College students, Race Fisher and Katie Patyk, also provided invaluable assistance. Thank you.

My family, friends, and colleagues also deserve special thanks. They gave me the love and understanding necessary for undertaking and completing such a project. In particular, Sri Thakkilapati, Edward Tebbenhoff, Kate Elliott, Holly Moore, Pedro dos Santos, Maryna Bazylevych, and Angela Kueny all expressed interest in this project and invested their time and energy in it at difficult stages of the writing process. My family, especially my mother, Diane Peterson, has continuously offered unconditional love and a sympathetic ear. My partner, Dalton Little, has never wavered in his belief in me and my abilities even when my own faith in myself has faltered. Our daughter, Nina, has enriched my understandings of motherhood and given me perspective on the enormous challenges and opportunities it presents. This book is dedicated to her.

Portions of this book were previously published. Some material from Chap. 4 originally appeared in "Maternity and the Castberg Children's Rights Laws: Legislative Framing and Outcomes, 1900–1915," *Tidsskrift for velferdsforskning*, no. 4, 2015. (Published in Norwegian: "Maternitet og de castbergske barnelover.") Some material from Chap. 5 originally appeared in "'Et skjærende misforhold mellom lovens hensikt og dens virkninger:' Single Mothers and Midwives Respond to the Castberg Laws, 1916–1940," *Historisk tidsskrift*, vol. 94, no. 2, 2015.

CONTENTS

1   Introduction   1

2   "What Nature Itself Demands:" The Development of Maternity Legislation at the End of the Nineteenth Century   25

3   "For the Health of the People:" Public Health and the Compensation of Maternity Leave in the 1910s   61

4   "Protecting Mothers and Children:" The Castbergian Children's Laws and Maternity Assistance for Single Mothers in the 1910s   101

5   "Getting the Most Money Possible:" Women's Responses to the Implementation of Maternity Laws, 1916–1930   123

6   "Mothers' Freedom Is the Key to Women's Emancipation:" Feminist Efforts to Expand Maternity Legislation in the Interwar Period   163

7   Conclusion   203

Index   211

LIST OF ABBREVIATIONS

AKF   The Women's Federation of the Norwegian Labor Party, *Arbeiderpartiets kvindeforbund*

CCL   Castbergian Children's Laws, *De Castbergske barnelover*

DNJ   The Norwegian Association of Midwives, *Den norske jordmorforening*

NKF   The Norwegian Association for Women's Rights, *Norsk kvinnesaksforening*

NKN   Norwegian National Women's Council, *Norske kvinners nasjonalråd*

LIST OF FIGURES

Fig. 2.1 Betzy Kjelsberg at a loom with shuttle in hand and wearing an apron (work clothes). In the background there stands the sign "Do not spit on the stairs." 1914. Courtesy of the Norwegian Museum of Science and Technology — 49

Fig. 3.1 Portrait of Katti Anker Møller by Eivind Enger, 1916. Courtesy of the Norwegian Museum of Science and Technology — 63

Fig. 3.2 Portrait of Johan Castberg by Ernest Rude, 1921. Courtesy of the Oslo Museum — 64

Fig. 3.3 Photograph of Midwife with a newborn baby, by Martin Evensen, 1920. Courtesy of Domekirkeodden Museum — 84

Fig. 4.1 Sick mother with 7 children, 1910. Courtesy of the Norwegian Museum of Science and Technology — 107

Fig. 5.1 "The misery room," Arbeiderhjem på Sagene, Oslo. Courtesy of the Norwegian Museum of Science and Technology — 129

Fig. 5.2 Two bureaucrats working at the welfare office in Hedmark county, 1923. Courtesy of Domekirkeodden Museum — 135

Fig. 5.3 Dr. Randers examines an infant at an infant control station, 1914. Courtesy of the Norwegian Museum of Science and Technology — 143

Fig. 6.1 Reception Hall at the Oslo Social Welfare Office, 1945–1950. Courtesy of Oslo Museum — 190

xiii

CHAPTER 1

Introduction

Norway is upheld as the best place to live on Earth. It boasts high levels of social cohesion, standards of living, and gender equality and consistently ranks at the top of international reports that measure quality of life.[1] Many interested in understanding why this is the case have turned to studying Norway's social policies. When *New York Times* journalist, Katrin Bennhold, toured Norway in 2011 in search of the key to its success she initially believed that Norway's oil money would be the reason behind its generous cradle-to-grave social benefits and ability to run a budget surplus. Mie Opjordsmoen, then leader of the Norwegian National Trade Union, corrected her: "Women. Norwegian women work, pay taxes and have babies. That's our secret."[2] Opjordsmoen was referring to the fact that Norway currently has one of the highest birth rates and percentage of women's labor market participation in Europe.[3] Many credit this to the comprehensive parental leave policies that are in place.[4] Norwegian parents may take 49 weeks of leave from work at 100% pay, or alternatively 59 weeks at 80% pay. Maternal and paternal quotas designate 10 weeks of the leave to each parent.[5] These Norwegian policies are some of the most generous in the world, and scholars have found them instrumental in promoting gender equality.[6]

Women's ability to combine paid work with motherhood, credited by Opjordsmoen as the "secret" to Norwegian success, originated in the late nineteenth century. During this time, a number of Western European

© The Author(s) 2018

A. M. Peterson, *Maternity Policy and the Making of the Norwegian Welfare State, 1880–1940*, https://doi.org/10.1007/978-3-319-75481-9_1

countries scrambled to pass legislation that would protect women's and children's health from the adverse effects of mass industrialization and prevent social revolution.[7] Norwegian maternity legislation developed within, and was influenced by, this European-wide push for social reform. Yet even in the early twentieth century, Norwegian maternity policy was more generous and comprehensive than its European counterparts and included paid leave from work, medical assistance, increased workplace rights, and financial assistance for both unmarried and married mothers.

To understand the reasons behind this adherence to, and deviation from, European precedents, this book details the development of Norwegian maternity policies from the end of the nineteenth century to the Nazi invasion of 1940. I analyze the interactions between state authorities, medical professionals, and women in the development, implementation, and revision of policies and reveal a process of welfare state development in which women played a central part. As the first book-length history of Norwegian maternity policies, this study significantly increases our understanding of the Scandinavian welfare state model and women's involvement in the creation of social policies.

Norwegian Historical Context

The particularities of the Norwegian historical context, including Norway's recent independence, women's early enfranchisement, and tradition of democratic policymaking, was crucial to women's ability to shape maternity policy to their particular needs and interests. Norwegian culture, geography and social make-up differed from its Scandinavian neighbors and influenced the political climate that developed in Norway. This difference not only affected the types of policies pursued by the Norwegian government, but also the role feminists, midwives, and the intended policy recipients played in the process.

The political situation in Norway at the end of the nineteenth century was conducive to the growth of democratic, grass-roots initiatives. Since 1814 it had operated under a liberal Constitution modeled after the one written in the United States following the Revolutionary War. The Norwegian constitution was based on a democratic structure of government with a one-chambered parliament, the Storting. Also in 1814, Norway entered into a union with Sweden as a part of the political fallout following the Napoleonic Wars. Prior to this, Norway had been under Danish rule. The new political union with Sweden entailed joint rule under one (Swedish) king and joint foreign policy. Norway controlled its own domestic policy, which after 1884 was decided by a system of parliamentary democracy, making Norway one of the first countries in Europe to have a parliamentary democracy.

Norwegian politics were never dominated by an autocratic class, but rather by coalitions of farmers and the urban middle classes. In 1900, Norway was a country of just over 2.2 million people, and the majority of Norwegians still lived in rural areas and free landholders were numerous. Industrialization came very late to Norway and small-scale, family-based industries remained prevalent long into the twentieth century.[8] This contributed to the lack of an aristocratic or strong bourgeois class in Norway. Instead, the political elite in Norway were largely civil servants with academic training and liberal ideas.[9] As a result, even the conservative party in Norway was much more liberal than conservative parties elsewhere.

When parliamentary democracy was adopted in 1884 it was an alliance of farmers and members of the urban lower middle classes who pushed through this reform and established the first political party, *Venstre* (The Liberal Party). The opponents of parliamentary democracy, mainly the existing political elite and bourgeois class, formed *Høyre* (The Conservative Party). These two parties would dominate parliamentary politics until the Norwegian Labor Party came to power in the late 1920s.

In spite of the fact that Norway's union with Sweden allowed Norwegians a great deal of autonomy, it inspired the growth of nationalistic feelings in Norway. A flourishing national movement developed in Norway over the course of the nineteenth century and focused on cultivating a distinct Norwegian culture and identity. The strength of this nationalist movement eventually led to the abolition of the Swedish-Norwegian union in 1905.

The development of a nationalist movement in Norway coincided with the creation of feminist movements across Scandinavia in the late-nineteenth century. While early Scandinavian feminist movements were quite small in scope and established later than in other European countries, they were able to achieve many of their goals.[10] In fact, Richard Evans has referred to Scandinavian feminist movements as the "most successful in Europe before the First World War."[11] Evans' claim is largely based on the fact that Scandinavian feminists succeeded in getting important legal and educational reforms for women, and perhaps most important, women's suffrage, passed prior to most other European countries.

In Norway, women's rights activists were able to use the political and social climate to win universal voting rights for women prior to any other sovereign nation. Certain groups of Norwegian men had received suffrage following the signing of the constitution in 1814 and again after the adoption of parliamentary democracy in 1884. Feminists worked to get equal voting privileges for women as well. In the lead up to Norwegian independence in 1905, women mobilized in support of Norwegian sovereignty. Their efforts bolstered their claims for citizenship in the new nation and helped push through suffrage rights for certain groups of women in 1907.[12] Feminists were not satisfied with this victory and continued to press for universal voting rights for women. This was actualized in 1913 when all Norwegian women gained the right to vote.

Norwegian feminists were also able to achieve many other reforms in the early twentieth century. They won not only voting rights, but they also saw to the liberalization of divorce laws and gained access to civil service positions. Norwegian feminist organizations prevented restrictive legislation for women workers from being passed as well. Norway's rejection of international conventions on the prohibition of women's night work, for example, was a major triumph for middle-class feminists and demonstrated the influence and power they had over policy decisions.[13]

Norway's lack of aristocracy and reliance on a more democratic, unicameral system of parliament can partially explain Norway's early implementation of women's suffrage and the feminist achievement of other liberal reforms.[14] Not all politicians supported women's rights and many fought to restrain feminist influence over politics. Yet feminists found allies for their causes from a diverse group of political actors, including many from the Liberal Party and even members of the rural opposition.[15] The lack of social and political tensions created political conditions that were more amenable to feminist demands.

Due to the small size of the Norwegian population and government, many feminists also had personal connections to men who sat in Parliament. In 1910 Kristiania, the capital (later renamed Oslo), was a city of just under 250,000 people.[16] The size of the Norwegian middle class at this time was also quite small. As a result, many bourgeois feminists had personal and/or family ties to men who sat in Parliament. Katti Anker Møller, for example, was the sister-in-law of Johan Castberg, a politician who would be appointed Minister of Social Affairs, Minister of Justice, and Supreme Court Justice during the same period of time that Møller worked to achieve greater rights for mothers. Møller's uncle, Wollert Konow, was also a high-ranking politician who served as Minister of the Interior, Minister of Agriculture, President of the Storting, and

Prime Minister during the course of his career. Møller was just one of many Norwegian feminists who had family connections to prominent politicians. These close relationships helped Norwegian feminists in their efforts to shape the political agenda.

Even women who did not belong to organized feminist movements were able to have their voices and opinions heard in Norway. It had a democratic, cooperative system of government that relied on the input of interest groups as a part of the legislative process. For example, when a law on industry was to be debated, the government asked for pertinent organizations including employers' associations, workers' associations, and health councils, to provide an opinion on the proposed law. In many ways this allowed groups further removed from the center of political power to participate in legislative development. When it came to maternity legislation, groups such as the Norwegian Association of Midwives and feminist organizations got the chance to formulate and articulate a stance on the issue.[17] These opinions were then taken into account when Parliament crafted and voted on the piece of legislation. In this political context, women were more readily able to access channels of political power even prior to their enfranchisement or election to political bodies.

NORWEGIAN MATERNITY POLICIES WITHIN THE GREATER CONTEXT OF EUROPEAN MATERNITY LEGISLATION

Maternity policies—including maternity leave, free midwifery services and public assistance for new mothers—were some of the first welfare policies enacted in Western Europe. These pieces of legislation almost exclusively targeted women, and in Norway, feminists, midwives, and the intended policy recipients negotiated the effects this legislation had on their lives. They also actively lobbied the state for the revision of maternity policies. These concerted efforts led to a significant alteration of the content and scope of maternity leave between 1880 and 1940.

Women's interactions with the state at the national and local level was largely responsible for the transformation of maternity policy from a mandatory, restrictive form of state control over women's reproduction to a benefit all women had a right to receive. Under Norway's first maternity leave law in 1892 women in the industrial workforce were required to take an unpaid leave of absence after giving birth, but their jobs were not protected if they complied with the law. By 1940 maternity policies had increased in number, content, and scope, and the intended recipients perceived them as benefits and rights to which they were entitled. A greater number of working women could now chose whether or not to take a paid maternity leave and the state protected their right to return to work afterward. Women who did not work outside the home were also eligible to receive maternity benefits, including medical assistance and financial support.

Maternity legislation became an important part of discussions about workers' rights and women's rights at the end of the nineteenth century throughout Europe. At the turn of the twentieth century men, and some women, from across the European continent met at international labor conferences in Berlin, Zurich, Brussels, Paris, Berne and Basel.[18] These conferences sought to tackle some of the worst effects of industrialization and to set a European standard of industrial regulations and social reform. Whether it was through prohibitions on night work or limiting women's working hours, labor activists and politicians often targeted women's labor in their efforts to create modern labor policies. These areas of restrictive labor policies for women were often contentious and created rifts between political parties, and bourgeois and working-class women's rights activists. In contrast, proposals concerning maternity leave often passed without debate in the nineteenth century. Even radical opponents of protective legislation believed that women should receive special protection during the time surrounding childbirth.[19]

The incorporation of maternity into labor policy involved defining the length of time a woman should abstain from work during pregnancy and childbirth. Out of a stated concern for women's reproductive health, the 1890 International Labor Conference in Berlin concluded that a woman should refrain from work for four weeks following childbirth. The recommendations of these international bodies influenced the development of maternity legislation in many European states.

Some of the earliest efforts to restrict women's labor in the weeks surrounding childbirth were introduced in Central Europe. Switzerland may have been the first country to legislate mandatory maternity leave in 1877, but German maternity policy became the model to follow in the nineteenth century. Similar to Bismarck's other innovative social insurance schemes, maternity leave also became a tool of the German state in its efforts to quell social unrest. In general, these early policies limited women's ability to work for four to six weeks following childbirth, but did not provide any type of compensation for lost wages. Philanthropic and women's rights organizations, such as the German *Bund for Muttershutz* helped alleviate some of the problems associated with this situation. They helped mothers, particularly unmarried mothers, by providing financial support.[20] Other countries such as Belgium, Norway and Denmark passed similar maternity leave laws in 1889, 1892 and 1901.[21]

Scholars have described the First World War as a watershed event in the development of publicly funded maternity policies.[22] Prior to the war, France passed a comprehensive set of maternity policies in 1913.[23] This legislation aimed to keep new mothers at home during the time surrounding childbirth and provided these women with compensation for wages lost.[24] French anxiety about depopulation and the *crise de natalité* helped fuel debates about these laws and ultimately framed maternity legislation in terms of mutual benefit to the child and the state.[25] The 1913 French law stipulated that a pregnant worker must take leave from work for four weeks following childbirth, but she could obtain a daily allowance for up to eight weeks before and after birth. This benefit hinged on the fulfillment of certain criteria, with breast-feeding being an elemental part of compliance, but in general women did not have to obtain medical certification of inability to work in order to receive postpartum allowances.[26]

Increasingly in the interwar period, European maternity policies began to provide a growing number of mothers with financial support through mother allowances, free childbirth clinics and comprehensive maternity benefits. Typically these benefits fell outside of private organizations or insurance schemes. Instead, the state became the ultimate provider of maternity insurance covered under the ever-expanding umbrella of social welfare. As women's historians have argued, these reproductive policies became the backbone of the modern welfare state.[27]

In many European countries, moral concerns limited the types of maternity legislation implemented prior to the Second World War. While unmarried mothers stood to benefit the most from the passage of comprehensive maternity benefits, they were often excluded from maternity policies. For example, in the Netherlands maternity leave was not compensated until 1929 and even then only married women workers were eligible to receive the benefit. Catholic and Protestant politicians exerted considerable influence over this outcome.[28] In the United States, the meager mothers' pensions that were implemented in the 1920s applied only to "worthy" women such as widows.[29] Efforts to discourage immorality, including sex outside of marriage, also prevented the creation of systems of support for unmarried mothers, including child support from fathers of illegitimate children.

Norway followed the general pattern of maternity policy development, but Norwegian maternity benefits tended to be more generous and comprehensive than other European nations.[30] Compensation for the mandated maternity leave came quite early compared to other European countries. Also, the benefits women could receive in conjunction with maternity were not confined to one law. Women could use a variety of different policies, including the sickness insurance law and the Castbergian Children's Laws, to ensure they received the compensation and birthing assistance they needed. In addition to this, unmarried women were covered by maternity policies. Arguments about morality did not prevent the government from including unmarried women in their legislative initiatives. In fact, unmarried women were often the main beneficiaries of maternity policies until this was expanded to include married women. Norway's relatively unique approach to maternity legislation can be partly explained by the social and political climate in Norway at the turn of the twentieth century. These conditions made it possible for different groups of women to shape Norwegian maternity policy.

THE SCANDINAVIAN MODEL OF WELFARE

By focusing on the creation of maternity policies in Norway, this book sheds light on foundational aspects of Scandinavian welfare state development.[31] The case of Norway is situated within the broader European context, demonstrating how, when, and why Norwegian policy deviated from or imitated non-Scandinavian models of welfare. This research significantly adds to discussions of whether or not Scandinavia followed its own *sonderweg* in regards to the development of welfare policies.[32]

Typically, welfare state scholars consider the Scandinavian states of Norway, Denmark and Sweden a distinct and cohesive model characterized, among other things, by universal entitlements and high levels of gender equality.[33] Welfare state scholars, however, disagree over what contributed to the development of these characteristics. Peter Baldwin has argued that the push for universal welfare policies was due in large part to the tension between rapid industrialization and the power of the Scandinavian farmers' movement.[34] Others have focused on a different causal dynamic, arguing that the presence of homogenous Lutheran state churches in Scandinavian countries led to the absence of substantial religious conflicts and this increased the ability state actors had to push through progressive social reforms.[35]

My research adds to this scholarly conversation and demonstrates that women's participation in the crafting of Scandinavian welfare states also contributed to the universal nature of policies. Women pushed for the broad application of universal social policy. Feminists in particular wanted maternity policies that would benefit middle-class, married women like themselves as well as industrial women workers. Their efforts to expand maternity policy in the interwar period benefitted from the growth of the social democratic Labor Party and were a part of a greater trend toward universal welfare benefits, but were shaped by their particular concerns about women's political and economic rights.

Within the literature on Scandinavian welfare states, Norway is often seen as an exception to the Scandinavian model especially in regards to family policies.[36] Many Scandinavian scholars have identified this in their attempts to problematize the notion of a cohesive Scandinavian model of welfare. These scholars argue that Norwegian policies are more conservative and encouraging of a traditional family structure than Swedish or Danish policies. They base this argument on married women's lower rates of full-time employment, benefit arrangements for single mothers, and the comparatively late passage of childcare policies in Norway.[37] Yet in spite of Norway's seemingly conservative approach to these issues, it has also been able to achieve high levels of gender equality. I believe this equality is related to the fact that the Norwegian state promoted dual paths to economic support for motherhood early in its welfare state development.[38]

My findings complicate the idea that Norway was ambivalent towards mothers' employment outside the home and only pursued policies that supported traditional family structures.[39] Norwegian politicians may have developed childcare policies later than its Scandinavian neighbors, but they also created more generous and comprehensive maternity leave policies for working women at an earlier period in time than in Denmark and Sweden. Instead of being hostile towards the gainful employment of mothers, early Norwegian welfare legislation incorporated the demands of feminists, midwives and working women, and ultimately supported women's work both inside and outside the home.[40] During the formative period of policy development, a diverse group of feminists, midwives and working women concurrently articulated demands for women's increased rights in the home and in the workforce. These demands led to the creation of policies that bolstered women's ability to stay at home with their children, including public assistance for single mothers and municipal mothers' pensions. During the same period of time, legislation was also passed to help strengthen women's ability to combine motherhood and waged labor. This included worker protection acts and sickness insurance laws.

WOMEN AND THE WELFARE STATE

By highlighting the extensive participation of women in Norwegian policy making, I further untangle the relationship between what feminist scholar Helga Marie Hernes has termed "welfare state and woman power."[41] In this book, I integrate a national analysis of women's influence on the political development of maternity laws with a study of how the implementation of these policies operated at the local level. This approach connects everyday life and local medical and bureaucratic practices with national policy. It examines the relationship between rural and urban political contexts, which in Norway were fraught with tension. It also incorporates a broad range of historical actors, including the very women targeted by welfare legislation, in its effort to examine the influence women had on the development of maternity laws.

After laws were passed they were interpreted and implemented by state bureaucrats in local welfare offices throughout Norway. Varying regional conditions significantly altered the way maternity policies were applied in local contexts. By examining exchanges between welfare officials and recipients at the local level, working and poor women's involvement in the development of welfare policy come to light. Working and poor women's negotiations with bureaucrats at this level demonstrate that these women were far from passive recipients of state-controlled welfare. As Linda Gordon found in her study of women's interactions with child welfare caseworkers, these welfare "clients" were "heroes of their own lives."[42]

Through one-on-one interactions and on an everyday basis, women at the local level inspired and instigated large-scale policy changes at the national level. Their dogged determination to receive what they believed was theirs, their creative use of policies in ways unintended by lawmakers—alongside their refusal to apply for maternity services they did not find beneficial—had an impact on policy discussions at all political levels that is imperative to our understanding of welfare state development.

Just as examining the laws or the parliamentary record alone obscures the dynamism of the legislative process and the diverse number of people involved in policy making, the same is true of trying to understand the role women played in welfare state development. Focusing on feminists alone masks the involvement of women in politics across classes, occupations and locales. Maternity policy was of interest to a great number of women, including the intended policy recipients, midwives, and feminists of multiple ideological persuasions.

INTRODUCTION 11

Labor historians have often viewed much of maternity legislation as detrimental to women's equality efforts because it restricted women's right to participate in the workplace on an equal footing with men.[43] Others have argued that welfare policies concerning mothers and children offered a way for women to solve the "maternal dilemma" of balancing motherhood with individualism.[44] The idea that women have benefitted from welfare policies has also been criticized for romanticizing women's relationship to the state and ignoring the fact that the Scandinavian model of welfare reinforced women's "client" status and men's productive roles.[45] Yet scholars generally agree that in Scandinavia, the welfare state has been beneficial to women and has helped them achieve greater economic and social rights.[46]

My research supports the argument that women's involvement in the writing of policy made policies more beneficial to women, but also complicates it by looking at different groups of women. Due to their power relative to the intended policy recipients, I find that Norwegian middle class and professional women were better able to shape policies to their particular needs and interests.[47] I argue that women's participation in the creation of welfare policies can lead to policies more amenable to women's interests, but not for all women all the time.

Previous research on women's influence on welfare state development has too often focused on women as a monolithic category synonymous with middle-class feminists.[48] I detail women's private lives and public efforts in order to convey the complexity of the process involved in developing maternity legislation. Women's direct involvement in crafting legislation, such as that evidenced in Katti Anker Møller's hand-drafted legislative proposals, are studied alongside the way the laws influenced poor and working women's daily lives. Their determination to benefit from maternity policies in ways that suited the particulars of their personal lives is equally important to the history of maternity legislation as feminist lobbying of the state. It is only through looking at women's participation in the crafting of welfare states in all of its subtleties and complexities that a richer understanding of welfare states and women's empowerment can be gained.

While feminists may have had the most direct influence on politicians, and thus legislative outcomes, midwives and the intended recipients of maternity policy also eagerly discussed policy particulars. Maternity legislation affected midwives' and poor and working-class women's occupational and personal lives much more intimately than women's rights

12   A. M. PETERSON

activists and they fought to make policy as beneficial to their diverse situations as possible. Looking at the diversity of women's participation in the development of maternity legislation demonstrates that women did not act as a monolithic group and that their disparate needs and interests affected policy outcomes.

MATERNITY POLICIES AND THE MEDICALIZATION OF CHILDBIRTH

This book's focus on maternity policy also contributes to scholarship on the history of medicine, particularly research on the medicalization of childbirth. Much of the earlier work on this topic has focused on how modern medical definitions of pregnancy and childbirth led to a reduction in women's reproductive choices and agency.[49] Researchers found that in addition to the birthing woman herself, midwives also experienced a significant loss in power as a result of the medicalization of childbirth.[50]

My findings reinforce the work of recent scholars who have aimed to discover the ways in which birthing women and midwives negotiated and perhaps even encouraged the increased medical management of childbirth.[51] By engaging in debates about maternity policy, Norwegian women not only affected the development of laws, they also participated in, and responded to, the medicalization of childbirth.

Maternity legislation reflected the state's increased interests in protecting the health of women and children. This went hand-in-hand with changes in the medical management of maternity. In many cases, medical developments shaped the creation of maternity policies. Practitioners of medicine, which included midwives, tried to use the state's focus on maternal and infant health to bolster their efforts to professionalize. Both doctors and midwives wanted the state to recognize them as the experts on issues of maternity and childbirth. They emphasized that their knowledge of modern hygienic medical practices would help the state in its efforts to increase the overall health and vitality of the nation. As a result, these medical practitioners encouraged the institutionalization of birth.

At times, this professional jockeying for power led to struggles between midwives and others.[52] This was certainly the case in regard to doctors and midwives in Norway, though geography and social conditions necessitated the use of midwives and muted some of these tensions. Midwives also clashed with feminists who claimed to represent the interests of all women in their drive to medicalize and institutionalize childbirth. Midwives encouraged the medicalization of birth, but were careful to do so in a way that enhanced and protected their positions. Their successful management of the medicalization of birth in spite of this competition reveals much about the status of Norwegian midwives.

Poor and working-class women were also active agents in the process that led to the medicalization of birth. They did not passively accept medical dictates of where and how they should give birth. Women embraced, rejected, and adapted medical ideas regarding pregnancy and childbirth depending on their individual circumstances. Even when the state tried to encourage the institutionalization of birth by tying maternity benefits to hospital stays, not all women accepted these new norms of childbirth. The history of reproduction demands a combined analysis of ideas and practice, and this study points to the importance of examining shifting cultural beliefs and habits surrounding childbirth in order to understand the development of maternity policy.

DEFINING FEMINISTS, MIDWIVES AND WORKING WOMEN

Understanding women as a diverse category of actors involved in the creation of welfare policies is a primary consideration of this study. Women from divergent political, social, and economic backgrounds all had much to gain and lose from the enactment of maternity legislation. While a great number of people formed opinions on this issue, the women most directly involved in the development of maternity policy in Norway fall into three broad categories: feminists, midwives, and the intended recipients of the policies. These categories are not perfectly delineated and separate. My intention with studying these subcategories of women is to further untangle what we mean by women when we discuss women's influence on welfare policy, but my own definition of categories deserves discussion.

In this book the word "feminist" is employed to describe a diverse set of women and organizations who worked for the achievement of greater rights for women and who saw this work as distinctly political. I use the word "feminist" to communicate to the reader the individuals and organizations who engaged in maternity policy discussions across ideological divides in their struggle to challenge women's subordination to men. The terms "feminist" and "feminism" first came into usage by Hubertine Auclert in late-nineteenth-century France. Since that time, scholars and activists have debated the meaning of these designations.

One of the flashpoints in this debate occurred in the early 1990s when historians argued over how best to describe the varied and competing nature of women's protests against male domination. To counter what she saw as a pervasive trend in Anglo-American scholarship to only apply the words "feminist" and "feminism" to individuals and movements who sought rights for women equal to those of men, Karen Offen offered a broader framework that included feminist arguments grounded in women's difference. She divided feminism into two distinct types of argumentation: "individualist," which asserted women's rights as individual rights and "relational," which demanded "women's rights as women in relation to men."[53]

Seth Koven and Sonya Michel further explored what Offen called "relational" feminism in their work on maternalism. Koven and Michel outlined how maternalist efforts to achieve greater rights for women and children were predicated on practices of othering that denigrated and silenced the poor and working-class populations they claimed to represent. While some scholars prefer to use the term maternalist as a way to discuss women's political and organizational activities without getting bogged down in the debate about what can and cannot be properly considered "feminist," I follow the practice of other historians who define maternalism as a form of feminism.[54] To do so heeds Offen's warning that excluding this type of feminist thought from the label "feminist" is to "miss the rich historical complexity of protest concerning women's subordination."[55]

The women and organizations I include in this study are diverse and do not fall neatly into a dualistic understanding of feminism as either individualist or relational. For some Norwegian women, including Katti Anker Møller, the labels of "relational" and "maternalist" work quite well to describe their focus on women's biological and social roles as mothers as the locus of their claim to political, economic, and social rights. Others, including Gina Krog, had ideologies that fit much more in-line with individualist or equality-based arguments for women's claim to rights as individuals. Given the nature of maternity policy, it often required much of feminists of all types in that it involved women's rights as individuals and their specific rights as women. Maternity laws mixed dependency with autonomy and complicated visions of women as either fully independent or fully dependent. As Ann Taylor Allen has argued, feminists were often conflicted between the social and individualist aspirations of motherhood.[56] This book examines the fault lines feminists walked in regard to maternity policy and how contrastive feminist activities diverged and intersected with one another over issues of maternity.

INTRODUCTION 15

Other methods of differentiating types of feminism often involve coupling the term feminism with a political ideology: conservative feminism, liberal feminism (most often aligned with individualist feminism), and socialist feminism. You will find organizations and women in this book that fall under all of these additional categories. The *Norske kvinners nasjonalråd*, or Norwegian National Council of Women (NKN), comprised upper-middle-class and elite women who espoused conservative takes on furthering women's rights in politics and society. The *Arbeiderpartiets kvinneforbund*, or Women's Federation of the Norwegian Labor Party (AKF), contained active and outspoken women of socialist persuasions who believed the dual oppressors of gender and class key to women's emancipation. The *Norsk kvinnesaksforening*, or Norwegian Association for Women's Rights (NKF), was a feminist organization closely connected to the Liberal Party. All of these women and the organizations they operated within were concerned with the development of maternity policies and all of them played a role in their creation and revision between 1880 and 1940. While they might not have agreed on ideology or approach, these women involved themselves in maternity policy discussions and developments because they saw maternity as key to their larger goal of advancing women's rights as citizens.

Feminists approached maternity policy from a distinct perspective as compared to the professionally oriented midwives and the economically oriented intended recipients of policy. Midwives are perhaps the group most easily defined as these women belonged to the same occupational category. If we consider the range of women involved in childbirth assistance, particularly in the nineteenth century and in rural areas of the country, the category of midwife is quite diverse and includes untrained midwives, referred to as "helping wives" or *hjelpekoner*. These women most often fulfilled their callings as individuals and did not form a collective with other untrained midwives. They were not organized and as such did not involve themselves in political matters such as maternity policy. Professional midwives who were educated and trained in midwifery schools did form professional organizational bodies, such as The Norwegian Association of Midwives, or *Den norske jordmorforening*, (DNJ) and participated in the development of maternity policy at both the individual and collective level. These midwives, most often publicly employed district midwives, are the primary focus of this study.

The third and final group of women most directly involved in the creation of maternity policy in Norway was the intended recipients of maternity policy.

16   A. M. PETERSON

This subcategory of women is perhaps the most difficult to define as the imagined targets or beneficiaries of policies changed over time and varied according to the policy under discussion. I refer to them broadly as "working women" as maternity policy was closely related to work and factory legislation throughout this period of welfare state development and policymakers most often envisioned employed women as the objects of maternity policy. Yet in some cases "working women" is not the best or most precise terminology. For example, the Castbergian Children's Laws primarily affected mothers who were not married regardless of their occupational status. In this case, I refer to the women who responded to maternity policy as "single mothers" to best describe their position in relation to the policy. When referring to this group of women, I try whenever possible to identify the particular socioeconomic or occupational group of women defined in maternity policies. When this is not possible or when doing so obscures the meaning of the relationship between the policy and the person affected by the policy, I will use the less precise designation of "intended recipient" of maternity policy.

SOURCE MATERIAL & ORGANIZATION

The book's innovative study of poor, rural women alongside urban middle-class feminists is rooted in an inclusive archival source base. As the political and cultural center of the country, much of my analysis of the history of Norwegian maternity policies focuses on Oslo. Governmental records, most notably parliamentary debates, laws, and ministerial paperwork make up the formation of my research on the national legislative process that took place there. The involvement of feminists and midwives in this process is chronicled in sources such as women's organizational records, periodicals, manuscript collections, and personal correspondence. In order to survey the laws' implementation at the local level, I investigated welfare case records, hospital records, and transcripts from criminal trials at regional archives located in Bergen, Hamar, Kongsberg, Kristiansand and Trondheim. These local archival sources allowed me access to poor and working women's responses to maternity policies. Additionally, I examined other sources that speak to shifting cultural attitudes toward maternity, including newspapers, medical tracts, popular periodicals and literature.

The book examines the development of maternity policy in Norway as compared to its European counterparts from the earliest law passed in 1892 to the last law implemented before the start of World War Two. It demonstrates that midwives, feminists, and working women transformed the 1892 law from a restriction on women's working and reproductive lives to a more generous policy that benefitted women economically and occupationally. Periodization is important to understanding this process and the book's structure is chronological in nature.

Chapter 1 examines Norway's first maternity leave law in 1892 and the reasons why women were largely absent from the policymaking process at this time. Chapter 2 traces women's success in incorporating compensatory maternity leave coverage in Norway's 1909 and 1915 sickness insurance laws. It demonstrates how feminists and midwives directly engaged policymakers in their efforts to institute a maternity benefit that included free midwifery, maternity home stays, and covered not only women factory workers, but also the wives of men who worked in industry. Many Norwegian women did not qualify for maternity benefits under the sickness insurance law. Chapter 3 outlines Møller's and Castberg's efforts to gain support for legislation in 1915, the Castbergian Children's Laws, which contained maternity assistance that was more comprehensive and expansive in coverage than the provisions outlined under the sickness insurance laws. Chapter 4 looks at women's varied responses to the implementation of maternity policies from 1916–1930. It demonstrates the broad effects of social policy at the local and individual level and shows how women's responses to these effects often led to revisions in welfare policy and implementation. Situated within the larger history of European feminist struggles for economic rights in the interwar period, Chap. 5 examines feminist efforts to transform maternity support from a form of economic protection, one that in many cases was tainted by a rhetoric of dependence and included means testing, to an economic right.

I find the actions of feminists, midwives, and intended welfare recipients instrumental in understanding the massive transformation of Norwegian maternity policy that occurred from 1892 and 1940. The policies grew in size and scope. They went from affecting a relatively small portion of the population to encompassing a majority of women in their childbearing years. The policies shifted from a predominantly industrial focus to take on greater social, medical and political meaning. These reproductive policies were at the core of the developing welfare state. Following their development reveals how feminists, midwives, and intended welfare recipients played a role in the creation of maternity policies. Doing so also speaks to women's diverse influence in the making of the Norwegian welfare state more broadly. Feminists, midwives, and intended policy recipients helped design policy and interpreted and adjusted policies to suit their daily lives and goals. Their influence on policy demonstrates the ability of women to assert agency and power at multiple levels of the policymaking process and help to explain the origins of Norway's secret to welfare state success.

NOTES

1. See, for example, United Nations Development Programme, "Inequality-adjusted Human Development Index," Human Development Reports. United Nations Development Programme, 2016, http://hdr.undp.org/en/composite/IHDI; United Nations Development Programme, "Gender Inequality Index," Human Development Reports. United Nations Development Programme, 2016, http://hdr.undp.org/en/composite/GII; and Organisation for Economic Co-operation and Development, OECD Better Life Index, OECD, 2016, http://www.oecdbetterlifeindex.org.
2. Katrin Bennhold, "Working Women are the Key to Norway's Prosperity," *New York Times*, June 28, 2011, accessed July 19, 2017, http://www.nytimes.com/2011/06/29/world/europe/29iht-letter29.html.
3. In 2010, 73% of women of working age participated in the Norwegian labor market. Only Iceland had higher rates of women's participation in the labor market with 77% of women of working age employed. Iceland and Norway are also the two countries with the highest birth rates in Europe. Norway's birth rate hovers around 1.9 and Iceland's birth rate around 2.0. Organisation for Economic Co-operation and Development, "OECD Family Database," OECD: Better Policies for Better Lives, OECD, 2010, accessed June 12, 2013, http://www.oecd.org.
4. See, for example: Organisation for Economic Co-operation and Development, "Can Policies Boost Birth Rates," OECD Family Database, OECD, 2007, accessed June 12, 2013, www.oecd.org.
5. Norwegian Welfare and Labour Administration, "Parental Benefit," NAV, Arbeids- og velferdsetaten, 2017, accessed July 19, 2017, https://www.nav.no/internett/en/Home/Benefits+and+services/Relatert+informasjon/parental-benefit;cmsnavno_JSESSIONID=xzuzNHwkkgY2r1b9cfpg+qQt.
6. Alyson Hurt, Erin Killian, and JoElla Straley, "Time with a Newborn: Maternity Leave Policies Around the World," National Public Radio, NPR, August 8, 2011, accessed June 12, 2013, https://www.npr.org/2011/08/09/137062676/time-with-a-newborn-maternity-leave-policies-around-the-world.
7. For a discussion of factory legislation that targeted women specifically, see: Ulla Wikander, Alice Kessler-Harris, Jane Lewis, eds., *Protecting Women: Labor Legislation in Europe, the United States, and Australia, 1880–1920* (Urbana, IL: University of Illinois Press, 1995).

INTRODUCTION   19

8. Statistisk sentralbyrå, "Folketelling 1900," Statistisk sentralbyrå, accessed February 12, 2013, http://www.ssb.no/a/folketellinger/fob1900.html; Francis Sejersted, *Sosialdemokratiets tidsalder Norge og Sverige i det 20. århundre* (Oslo: Pax, 2005).

9. Gro Hagemann, "Maternalism and Gender Equality: Tracing a Norwegian Model of Welfare," in *Reciprocity and Redistribution: Work and Welfare Reconsidered*, ed. Gro Hagemann (Pisa, Italy: Pisa University Press, 2007), 69.

10. See: Drude von der Fehr, Anna G. Jonasdottir and Bente Rosenbeck, eds., *Is there a Nordic Feminism?: Nordic Feminist Thought on Culture and Society* (London: UCL Press Limited, 1998); Richard J. Evans, *The Feminists: Women's Emancipation Movements in Europe, America and Australasia, 1840–1920* (New York: Routledge, 2012).

11. Evans, *The Feminists*, 69.

12. Only women who were at least 25 years old and met certain tax-paying thresholds had the right to vote. Ida Blom, "Structures and Agency: A Transnational Comparison of the Struggle for Women's Suffrage in the Nordic Countries during the Long 19th Century," *Scandinavian Journal of History* 37, no. 5 (2012): 608.

13. Gro Hagemann, "Maternalism and Gender Equality," 78.

14. Norway was the first independent country to implement universal voting rights for women in 1913. See Karen Offen, *European Feminisms, 1700– 1950* (Stanford: Stanford University Press, 2000).

15. Hagemann, "Maternalism and Gender Equality," 76.

16. "Folketall – Oslo, 1910" Byarkivet.

17. Housewives' organizations were also perceived to be representative of women's interests, but in contrast to feminist organizations, the government does not appear to have asked these groups for their opinions on maternity legislation. Housewives' organizations were interested in the issue of maternity provisions and discussed it in their periodicals, but they did not offer unsolicited opinions to the government on the topic. As such, they were not directly involved in the development of maternity policies and are not included in the scope of this study.

18. Ulla Wikander, "Some Kept the Flags of Feminist Demands Waving': Debates at International Congresses on Protecting Women Workers," in *Protecting Women: Labor Legislation in Europe, the United States, and Australia, 1880–1920*, eds. Ulla Wikander, Alice Kessler-Harris, and Jane Lewis (Urbana, IL: University of Illinois Press, 1995), 54–55.

19. Wikander, "Some Kept the Flags of Feminist Demands Waving," 37.

20. Ann Taylor Allen, *Feminism and Motherhood in Western Europe, 1890– 1970: The Maternal Dilemma* (New York: Palgrave Macmillan, 2005), 72.

21. Allen, *Feminism and Motherhood*, 71.

20   A. M. PETERSON

22. Deborah Dwork, *War is Good for Babies and Other Young Children: A History of the Infant and Child Welfare Movement in England, 1898–1918* (New York: Tavistock Publications, 1987); Harry Hendrick, *Child Welfare: Historical Dimensions, Contemporary Debate* (Bristol: The Policy Press, 2003), 64; Susan R. Grayzel, *Women's Identities at War: Gender, Motherhood, and Politics in Britain and France During the First World War* (Chapel Hill, NC: University of North Carolina Press, 1999).
23. Allen, *Feminism and Motherhood*, 71.
24. Mary Lynn Stewart argues that the comparatively late legislation of maternity leave in France was due to the government's reluctance to require women to miss work without pay, while simultaneously being unable to come to agreement over what compensation would entail. Mary Lynn Stewart, *Women, Work and the French State: Labour, Protection and Social Patriarchy, 1879–1919* (London: McGill-Queen's University Press, 1989).
25. Rachel Fuchs, "The Right to Life: Paul Strauss and the Politics of Motherhood," in *Gender and the Politics of Social Reform in France, 1870–1914*, eds. Elinor Ann Accampo, Rachel Ginnis Fuchs, and Mary Lynn Stewart (Baltimore: John Hopkins University Press, 1995).
26. Stewart, *Women, Work and the French State*, 189.
27. Some examples of this include Gisela Bock and Pat Thane, eds., *Maternity and Gender Policies, Women and the Rise of the European Welfare States, 1880s–1950s* (London: Routledge, 1991); Seth Koven and Sonya Michel, eds., *Mothers of a New World: Maternalist Politics and the Origins of Welfare States* (New York: Routledge, 1993); Kathleen Uno, *Passages to Modernity: Motherhood, Childhood, and Social Reform in Early Twentieth Century Japan* (Honolulu: University of Hawai'i Press, 1999).
28. Marian van der Klein, Rebecca Jo Plant, Nichole Sanders and Lori R. Weintrob, eds., *Maternalism Reconsidered: Motherhood, Welfare and Social Policy in the Twentieth Century* (New York: Berghahn Books, 2012), 54. As Kimberly Morgan has shown, the presence of religious cleavages in a society often leads to more conservative family policies. She finds that the higher the degree of religious homogeneity or secularization, the greater the likelihood generous family policies will be implemented. See: Kimberly Morgan, *Working Mothers and the Welfare State: Religion and the Politics of Work-Family Policies in Western Europe and the United States* (Stanford: Stanford University Press, 2006).
29. Molly Ladd-Taylor, *Mother-Work: Women, Child Welfare, and the State, 1890–1930* (Urbana, IL: University of Illinois Press, 1994); Linda Gordon, *Pitied But Not Entitled: Single Mothers and the History of Welfare, 1890–1935* (New York: Free Press, 1994); Theda Skocpol, *Protecting Soldiers and Mothers: The Political Origins of Social Policy in the United States* (Cambridge, MA: Harvard University Press, 1995).

INTRODUCTION   21

30. This is true even in relation to other Scandinavian countries. For example, Danish women did not receive compensation for mandatory maternity leave through the health insurance mechanism until 1915, and then for only 10 of the 48 days required. For a discussion of the Danish case see Anette Borchorst and Magtudredingen (projekt), *Køn, magt og beslutninger: Politiske forhandlinger om barselsorlov, 1901–2002* (Århus, Denmark: Magtutredningen, 2003). In Sweden, politicians could not agree as to what form paid maternity leave should take and this delayed its implementation until late into the interwar period. See: Anne Karine Sørskår, "Fra mors plikt til fars rettighet: Om betalt fødselspermisjon i Norge og Sverige, 1892–1987" (master's thesis, University of Bergen, 1988).

31. The origin of the term "welfare state" developed in the 1930s to distinguish liberal democratic countries from the "warfare state" of Nazi Germany. The term welfare state has become *the* way to designate states that secure social provisions for their citizens, but which states are characterized by this term, and to what extent, is under constant dispute. In this book, a "welfare state" describes a country where the state is the primary provider of social goods, including education, health care, social security, housing and social services. For some reflections on this subject see: Christopher Pierson and Francis G. Castles, eds., *The Welfare State: A Reader*, 2nd ed. (Cambridge, England: Polity Press, 2006).

32. The term *sonderweg* was originally used to describe the "special path" of Germany's history. For a recent reflection on this debate in German historiography see: Helmut Walser Smith, "When the Sonderweg Debate Left Us," *German Studies Review* 31, no. 2 (2008): 225–240.

33. Most famously Gøsta Esping-Andersen argued for a distinct Scandinavian model of welfare and credited it with the highest level of decommodification, largely because of the historical power of the Social Democratic Party. See: Gøsta Esping-Andersen, *The Three Worlds of Welfare Capitalism* (Princeton, NJ: Princeton University Press, 1990), 3.

34. Baldwin credits this with farmers' growing economic and political importance in Scandinavia, which allowed them to exert pressure on the government to enact universalist, tax-based policies that would benefit farmers as well as urban workers. See: Peter Baldwin, *The Politics of Social Solidarity: Class Bases of the European Welfare State, 1875–1975* (Cambridge: Cambridge University Press, 1990).

35. Kimberly Morgan argues that, among other things, this contributed to the creation of a universalized breadwinner model in Scandinavia in the postwar period. See: Kimberly Morgan, *Working Mothers and the Welfare State*; Kari Melby, Anu Pylkkänen, Bente Rosenbeck, and Christina Carlsson Wetterberg, eds., *The Nordic Model of Marriage and the Welfare State* (Copenhagen: Nordic Council of Ministers, 2000).

36. For a detailed discussion of the particulars of the Norwegian case see: Anne-Lise Seip, *Sosialhjelpstaten blir til: norsk sosialpolitikk, 1740–1920* (Oslo: Gyldendal Norsk Forlag, 1984); Anne-Lise Seip, *Veiene til velferdsstaten: norsk sosialpolitikk, 1920–1975* (Oslo: Gyldendal, 1994).

37. Niels Finn Christiansen, Klaus Petersen, Nils Eding, Per Haave, *The Nordic Model of Welfare – A Historical Reappraisal* (Copenhagen: University of Copenhagen Press, 2006); Kari Melby, et al., eds., *Inte ett ord om Karlek: aktenskap och politik I Norden ca. 1850–1930* (Göteborg: Makadam I Samarbete Med Centrum För Danmarksstudier Vid Lunds Universitet, 2006); Francis Sejersted, *Sosialdemokratiets tidsalder: Norge og Sverige i det 20. århundre* (Oslo: Pax, 2005); Arnlaug Leira, *Welfare States and Working Mothers: The Scandinavian Experience* (Cambridge: Cambridge University Press, 1992); Anne Lise Ellingsæter and Arnlaug Leira, eds., *Politicising Parenthood in Scandinavia: Gender Relations in Welfare States* (Bristol: The Policy Press, 2006); Christina Bergqvist, et al., eds., *Equal Democracies?: Gender and Politics in the Nordic Countries* (Oslo: Scandinavian University Press, 1999).

38. My research confirms Gro Hagemann's and Inger Elisabeth Haavet's findings that Castberg and Møller successfully incorporated maternalist policy ideas into the Norwegian welfare state, and examines their actions in relation to other policy actors. The focus on mothers and children was very strong in Norway at the turn of the twentieth century, not least because feminists and other women used this strategically to gain concessions from the government. See: Gro Hagemann, "Maternalism and Gender Equality"; Inger Elisabeth Haavet, "Milk, Mothers and Marriage: Family Policy Formation in Norway and its Neighbouring Countries in the Twentieth Century," in *The Nordic Model of Welfare: A Historical Reappraisal*, eds. Niels Finn Christiansen, Klaus Petersen, Nils Edling, and Per Haave (Copenhagen: Museum Tusculanum Press, 2006). I look at how the involvement of equal-rights feminists, alongside radical maternalists, participated in the creation of maternity legislation and influenced the shape of nascent family policies.

39. Arnlaug Leira, "Updating the 'Gender Contract'? Childcare Reforms in the Nordic Countries in the 1990s," *Nora-Nordic Journal of Feminist and Gender Research* 10, no. 2 (2002):81–89; Ellingsæter and Leira, *Politicising Parenthood in Scandinavia*.

40. This continues to be one of the defining characteristics of the Norwegian welfare state. For example, Norwegian women have the highest rate of women's part-time employment of all the Scandinavian countries, and Norway is also the only Scandinavian country to offer benefit arrangements for single mothers. For more information on women's part time employment, see: Organisation for Economic Co-operation and Deveopment, "Gender Differences in Employment Outcomes," OECD

INTRODUCTION   23

Family Database, OECD, accessed June 12, 2013, www.oecd.org. Arnlaug Leira credits Norway's reluctance to prioritize a universal breadwinner model with giving women more flexibility to fulfill their dual roles as earners and carers. See: Leira, *Welfare States and Working Mothers.*

41. Helga Marie Hernes, *Welfare State and Woman Power: Essays in State Feminism* (Oslo: Norwegian University Press, 1987).

42. Gordon's scholarship on the American context, including *Heroes of Their Own Lives: The Politics and History of Family Violence: Boston 1880–1960* (New York: Penguin Books, 1989) and *Pitied But Not Entitled: Single Mothers and the History of Welfare, 1890–1935* (New York: Free Press, 1994) helped inspire my decision to examine welfare recipients' role in the development of maternity legislation in Norway.

43. Ulla Wikander, Alice Kessler-Harris, Jane Lewis, eds., *Protecting Women: Labor Legislation in Europe, the United States, and Australia, 1880–1920* (Urbana, IL: University of Illinois Press, 1995).

44. Allen, *Feminism and Motherhood.*

45. Birte Sum, "The Scandinavian Welfare States – Towards Sexual Equality or a New Kind of Male Domination?" *Acta Sociologica* 30, no. ¾ (1987): 255–270.

46. Kari Melby, Christina Carlsson Wetterberg and Anna-Birte Ravn, eds., *Gender Equality and Welfare Politics in Scandinavia: The Limits of Political Ambition?* (Bristol, UK: The Policy Press, 2009).

47. This debate originated in women's and gender historians' critique of Gøsta Esping-Andersen and other theorists for ignoring the gendered aspects of welfare policies. These feminist scholars drew attention to the fact that many early welfare legislative initiatives targeted women, and they set out to uncover the impact gender had on the creation of welfare states and on welfare outcomes. Some of these early criticisms include: M. Langan and I. Ostner, "Gender and Welfare: Towards a Comparative Framework," in *Towards a European Welfare State?*, ed. Graham Room (Brisol: SAUS, 1991); Jane Lewis and G. Astrom, "Equality, Difference and State Welfare: The Case of Labour Market and Family Policies in Sweden," *Feminist Studies* 18, no. 1 (1992): 59–87.

48. Gisela Bock and Pat Thane, eds., *Maternity and Gender Policies: Women and the Rise of the European Welfare States, 1880s–1950s* (London: Routledge, 1991); Seth Koven and Sonya Michel's introduction of the concept of "maternalism" has been hugely influential on the study of this topic. See: "Womanly Duties: Maternalist Politics and the Origins of Welfare States in France, Germany, Great Britain, and the United States, 1880–1920," *American Historical Review* 95, no. 4 (1990): 1076. Koven and Michel further explored these ideas and examined the correlation between the strength or weakness of the state apparatus and women's ability to influence welfare policies in the anthology they edited: *Mothers of a*

New World: Maternalist Politics and the Origins of Welfare States (New York: Routledge, 1993). Many scholars have been interested in the concept of maternalism and analyzed its usefulness in a number of essays. See, for example: Lynn Y. Weiner, "Maternalism as a Paradigm: Defining the Issues," *Journal of Women's History* 5, no. 2 (1993): 96–98; Felicia A. Kornbluh, "The New Literature on Gender and the Welfare State: The U.S. Case," *Feminist Studies* 22, no. 1 (1996): 171–197; Jane Lewis, "Women's Agency, Maternalism and Welfare," *Gender & History* 6, no. 1 (1994): 117–123. For a recent evaluation of the idea of maternalism see van der Klein, et al., eds., *Maternalism Reconsidered*. Other works inspired by Koven and Michel and Thane and Bock's anthologies include: Ladd-Taylor, *Mother-Work*; Linda Gordon, *Pitied but Not Entitled: Single Mothers and the History of Welfare, 1890–1935* (New York: Free Press, 1994); Theda Skocpol, *Protecting Soldiers and Mothers: The Political Origins of Social Policy in the United States* (Cambridge, MA: Harvard University Press, 1992).

49. An excellent example of this can be found in: Ann Oakley, *Women Confined: Towards a Sociology of Childbirth* (Oxford: Martin Robertson & Company, 1980).

50. Jean Donnison, *Midwives and Medical Men: A History of Inter-Professional Rivalries and Women's Rights* (London: Heinemann, 1977).

51. Judith Leavitt, *Brought to Bed: Childbearing in America, 1750 to 1950* (New York: Oxford University Press, 1986); Regina Kunzel, *Fallen Women, Problem Girls: Unmarried Mothers and the Professionalization of Social Work, 1890–1945* (New Haven: Yale University Press, 1993); Charlotte G. Borst, *Catching Babies: The Professionalization of Childbirth, 1870–1920* (Cambridge, MA: Harvard University Press, 1995). For the Norwegian context, see: Ida Blom, *"Den haarde dyst": Fødsler og fødselshjelp gjennom 150 år* (Oslo: Cappelen, 1988); Tora Korsvold, *Sykehusfødselen tar form: med en nærstudie av E.C. Dahls stiftelse* (Oslo: Abstrakt, 2001).

52. This has been the topic of many previous studies conducted by women's historians. For a discussion of this, see: Donnison, *Midwives and Medical Men*.

53. Karen Offen, "Defining Feminism: A Comparative Historical Approach," *Signs* 14, no. 1 (1988): 136.

54. van der Klein, et al., eds., *Maternalism Reconsidered*, 4.

55. Offen, "Defining Feminism," 138.

56. Allen, *Feminism and Motherhood*, 5.

CHAPTER 2

"What Nature Itself Demands:"
The Development of Maternity Legislation
at the End of the Nineteenth Century

In 1914, M.P. Dr. Ludvig Larsen Kragtorp (*Venstre*, Liberal Party) conjured up the image of a North American Indian corralling livestock on horseback minutes after giving birth to open the parliamentary debate on paid maternity leave.[1] Kragtorp used this vivid example to argue that while primitive women might be able to "ride into the nearest bush, [give birth] alone and throw themselves upon the back of a horse … with their newborn baby in their arms" such could not be expected of "cultured peoples."[2] Through this example, Kragtorp referenced an idea that had been established in many European countries at the end of the nineteenth century; namely, that maternity leave was one of the markers of a modern, civilized society.

Mandatory maternity leave had been enacted in many European countries at the end of the nineteenth century. Coinciding with efforts to define maternity as a condition in need of protection, maternity leave policies addressed European state concerns with rapid industrialization and "the social question."[3] Governments across Western Europe responded to assertions that women needed rest after giving birth by integrating mandatory maternity leaves into factory regulations. In 1877 Switzerland became the first country to require women to take leave of industrial work after giving birth. Germany (1878), Holland (1889), and Great Britain (1891) followed suit, and by 1900 over ten European countries had enacted compulsory maternity leave. The leaves varied in length from two to eight weeks, with only Switzerland requiring women to take some of

© The Author(s) 2018

25

A. M. Peterson, *Maternity Policy and the Making of the Norwegian Welfare State, 1880–1940*, https://doi.org/10.1007/978-3-319-75481-9_2

26 A. M. PETERSON

this leave prior to the birth.[4] Germany and Austria-Hungary were the only two countries to provide compensation during this period, paid through contributory insurance systems. France was noticeably delayed in enacting maternity leave laws. Though infant mortality was a point of deep concern for French politicians, so too was government intervention in family life.

The enactment of Norwegian maternity leave legislation in 1892 took place within this general European trend toward mandating women take time off from industrial work after giving birth. In line with other European countries, Norwegian policy required women take six weeks off of industrial work after giving birth without pay. Compared to the other Scandinavian countries of Sweden and Denmark, Norway instituted maternity leave much earlier and required women to take longer leaves. Sweden created its first maternity leave law in 1900 and Denmark in 1901. The Swedish and Danish policies were only four weeks in length and were also unpaid.[5] The discrepancy in the timing and the length of maternity leave policy between Norway and its Scandinavian neighbors may be attributed to Norwegian politicians' greater propensity for reform, and perhaps is also due to its lower level of industrialization. It may have been easier to pass factory regulations in Norway than in Denmark and Sweden because the legislation would have affected fewer workers.

European women did not play a large role in the shaping of maternity-leave policy at the end of the nineteenth century. While feminists actively participated in debates about maternity and advocated for state support of pregnant and postpartum women, they did not initiate discussions of maternity leave legislation or contribute to the policymaking process in the 1880s and 1890s.[6] Rather, women responded to the laws after they were passed and worked in subsequent decades to get maternity leave compensated and applied to larger groups of women.

In Norway, feminists, midwives and working women were also largely uninvolved in the maternity leave legislation passed in 1892. These groups of women were focused instead on lobbying for other issues that appeared more pressing to them at the time: women's suffrage, midwifery reform, and unionizing. After maternity leave was implemented and the effects of the legislation were known, feminists, midwives, and working women would seize opportunities in the early twentieth century to shape the policy to their benefit. But at the end of the nineteenth century, women's lack of participation in crafting Norway's first maternity leave law led to a narrowly defined, restrictive policy that would take feminists, midwives, and working women decades to improve upon.

While women were markedly absent from the policymaking process in 1892, discussions of maternity leave were punctuated by tensions between lawmakers' desire to restrict women's labor for the sake of the nation and their recognition of women's rights. Whether it was through prohibitions on night work or limiting women's working hours, European labor activists and politicians frequently targeted women's labor in their efforts to create modern labor policies. These gender-specific labor policies were often contentious because they inhibited women's right to work. When it came to imposing a ban on women's night work, Norwegian reformers consistently refused to follow the lead of other European countries.[7] Proposals concerning maternity leave, on the other hand, usually passed without debate in the nineteenth century. Even radical opponents of protective legislation believed that women should receive special protection during the time surrounding childbirth.[8] Norwegian politicians and feminists tended to agree.

Maternity as a Condition in Need of Protection

In an age marked by democratization and modernization, European politicians, feminists, and medical authorities redefined maternity as a condition that required political attention. Previously viewed as a moral issue, maternity took on new meaning as an activity that produced the state's most important product: citizens.[9] With this shift in focus, maternity came to be discussed more as a medical condition than a moral one. Reformers argued that childbirth made women particularly vulnerable, both economically and physically, and expressed concern with how work affected women's reproductive functions.[10]

While all women could potentially encounter difficulties after giving birth, Norwegian activists highlighted unmarried mothers as the group most in need of government protections. Reformers argued that being unmarried exposed new mothers and their babies to a higher amount of risk than other mothers, and that this inequality needed to be addressed for the safety and vitality of the nation. Gaining greater state protections for unmarried women remained controversial, but reformers were assisted in their efforts by a cultural shift in thinking about maternity as a medical issue. The increased medical attention to maternity, coupled with a focus on unwed mothers, helped stimulate the passage of laws in Norway, including the 1892 maternity leave clause, an 1892 revision of child support laws and the 1898 revision of the midwifery law.

As the state become increasingly concerned with promoting maternal health, doctors began to devote more attention to pregnancy and childbirth.[11] In Norway and throughout much of the Western world, doctors attempted to modernize and professionalize medical practice, not least in the fields of obstetrics and gynecology.[12] Midwifery had once been disregarded as uninteresting women's work, but now took on new meaning and importance for doctors. They began to invest resources in the theoretical and empirical study of maternity and tried to cultivate new repute as experts on a matter of great state importance. The Norwegian state recognized doctors' medical expertise and consulted with the Norwegian Medical Association on many proposed laws throughout the late nineteenth century, including maternity policies.

Medical conceptualizations of maternity as a biological state that placed women in significant physical and mental danger informed the types of maternity legislation passed in the 1880s and 1890s. Medical authorities based their modern theories and practices regarding childbirth on established traditions of confinement and beliefs that the mother's life was of primary importance.

In the late nineteenth century, the medical focus remained on caring for the parturient woman and trying to decrease rates of maternal mortality.[13] The (healthy) newborn baby had not yet become an independent subject in need of medical intervention. Medical authorities entrusted the child's mother to decide how often the baby should be fed, where it should sleep, and how it should be dressed. In fact, the little advice doctors had about newborn care barely changed during the entire course of the nineteenth century.[14]

This medical focus on the mother also translated into other areas of social and legal life. European countries had become increasingly interested in infant mortality rates since the 1700s, and Norway was no different.[15] Norwegian statisticians and statesmen worried about increasing rates of infant mortality, especially amongst the working class, and they thought that this situation might be helped by the implementation of a mandatory maternity leave.[16] Yet in debates over the Factory Act's maternity leave clause, legislators presented a parturient woman's need for rest and recovery as the primary reason for the enactment of the proposed legislation. If this also helped reduce infant mortality rates, then this would be an additional benefit, not the primary purpose.

Doctors mainly agreed on what constituted the medically necessary length of time a woman should rest after giving birth by building on older traditions of confinement rooted in Christian doctrine and practice. For much of history, religious teachings required women to retreat from church and community life for a period of six weeks after giving birth. Protestant churches continued to respect this demarcation after the Reformation and often did not allow parturient women to attend church until six weeks had passed. After this period of confinement, the new mother, her midwife, and women from the community would attend a church service where they would sing special hymns and receive blessings. This church service represented the woman's resumed participation in community life after giving birth.[17] In Norway, this practice continued long into the eighteenth century.

Doctors incorporated this tradition of confinement into modern medical practice. They asserted that women no longer needed to rest for six weeks following childbirth for spiritual or "superstitious" reasons, but rather because their physical recovery depended on it.[18] This emphasis on six weeks as the ideal length of recovery time would later form the basis for industrial maternity leave restrictions throughout Europe.

Along with doctors, feminists and cultural elites worked to define unmarried women as vulnerable, deserving of public sympathy and state support. Norwegian authors and artists such as Bjørnstjerne Bjørnson and Christian Krohg helped change perceptions of poor, unmarried women at the end of the nineteenth century. In explosive public debates about sexuality and morality called *sedelighetsdebatten* (the morality debate) the plight of unwed mothers received significant attention. Bjørnson and others advocated that unmarried mothers should no longer be punished as immoral, promiscuous women. Instead, men should be held responsible for acting dishonorably and putting innocent women in difficult positions. At a time where the number of unmarried women and illegitimate births increased, these ideas garnered public attention and political interest.[19]

The main feminist organization in operation at the time, the *Norsk kvinnesaksforening*, or Norwegian Association for Women's Rights (NKF), supported Bjørnson and used the morality debate to gain sympathy for unmarried women who killed their newborn babies.[20] According to the 1874 revision of the Norwegian penal code, a woman who killed her child within one day of birth (neonaticide) could be sentenced to anywhere from six years to a lifetime of hard labor.[21] Feminists argued that in the context of equal standards for men and women, this law was unfair.

For these feminists, parturient women were especially vulnerable after giving birth and it was understandable that if they did not have any support

30   A. M. PETERSON

from the child's father or society that their suffering and despair could drive them to commit such crimes. Their reasoning was that "it takes both a woman and a man to create a human life, but our society acts as if an unmarried woman is all alone in this after she gives birth to a child."[22] The unmarried, pregnant mother should be met with sympathy for even though it must take "an inhuman cruelty to murder a child you yourself have given birth to," despair could have driven a woman to think that she was doing the best for her child.[23]

Feminists argued that unsupportive fathers must also be held accountable for neonaticides. NKF lobbied Parliament to change the penal code so that in cases where a mother killed her child within one day of birth, the child's father would also be punished if he did not offer her any support or assistance. They also wanted the government to strengthen a woman's legal right to financial support from her child's father during pregnancy.[24]

The increased public discussion of the treatment of unmarried mothers led to a series of legislative proposals designed to hold men more financially accountable to their illegitimate children. In 1892, the same year Norway enacted its first maternity leave policy, Parliament also passed a law that strengthened an unmarried woman's right to economic support for herself and her children.[25] Men were required to pay a greater portion of their income to help support their illegitimate children. Parliament also upheld nascent assertions that childbirth left unmarried women particularly vulnerable to economic stress and ordered fathers to pay for any expenses related to childbirth and confinement.[26]

Though Parliament had increased unmarried women's legal access to maternity support, they did little to facilitate the process. It was up to the woman whether she wanted to name the father of her child or not, and if she wanted financial support she was required to initiate the proceedings. Some men escaped ever having to pay this support by moving to a different municipality or even emigrating to America. Unmarried women often had to push bureaucrats to continue trying to locate these men and make them pay child support.[27] Many women never received any money to offset the costs of childbirth or raising their children. Karen Pederstuen, for example, tried desperately to get the state to make her child's father pay her support in 1900. Thirteen years later the situation was still not resolved.[28] Situations like these frustrated many unmarried women and the NKF continued to fight for unmarried mothers' rights throughout the early decades of the twentieth century.

Constructing an image of unmarried mothers as vulnerable and in need of special protections took place alongside political efforts to regulate factory work in Norway and elsewhere. As most women working in industry were unmarried, any proposed policies that targeted women's labor mainly affected unmarried women. As such, policymakers envisioned unmarried women as the primary recipients of the maternity protections proposed in factory legislation. This narrow understanding of who would be affected by maternity leave prohibitions led to the creation of a more restrictive policy.

INDUSTRIALIZATION AND THE NORWEGIAN FACTORY ACT

During the second half of the 1800s, Norway underwent significant political and social upheavals due to the effects of industrialization and urbanization. In this volatile political climate Norwegian statesmen paid close attention to laws passed by countries with longer experiences with industrialization and its effects. Industry had steadily grown in Norway since the 1850s and the number of workers increased from 12,000 in 1850 to over 45,500 in 1875.[29] Most of these people worked in paper mills, distilleries, stoneware, and textile factories.

The first working-class movement developed in Norway in the aftermath of the 1848 revolutions. Inspired by these events, Marcus Thrane led a group of workers in Norway to demand greater economic and social freedoms. This was one of the first political movements in Norway and at its height as many as 30,000 people—mainly small landholders and servants—had joined Thrane's movement.[30] The political elite did not respond favorably to these developments and imprisoned many members of the group, including Thrane himself. The Thrane movement was relatively short-lived, but it had lasting effects on political approaches to the "worker question" in Norway.[31]

The nascent Norwegian working class and its historical ties to the Thrane movement represented more of a symbolic threat to established order than a real one. Up until the 1890s the working class remained economically, politically and organizationally weak.[32] As Norwegian historian Jens Arup Seip so aptly described, the Norwegian working class helped call attention to industrial working conditions "not because they could vote, but merely because they *existed*..."[33] Norwegian fears of workers' revolts and revolutions were also exacerbated by international developments. As Norway was an industrial late-comer it gathered information about the "social question" from other European countries that had

32   A. M. PETERSON

industrialized earlier, such as England, Germany, and Switzerland.[34] From these examples, Norwegian statesmen learned that a disenfranchised working class could cause severe social unrest. They also saw that industrial work could cause worrisome health problems for women and children.

Due to Norway's relatively low level of industrialization, it had still not enacted any comprehensive regulation of industry by the 1880s. It did, however, have laws that set restrictions for certain types of work, including work performed in mines and bakeries. Politicians also passed a public health law in 1860 that aimed to ensure that businesses did not endanger the lives of their employees more than necessary.[35] These laws did little to address the problems that other countries, such as England, had identified as the worst effects of industrialization. Many Norwegian statesmen and employers felt that such legislation was unnecessary in Norway because it was not as industrially developed as other European countries.[36] Yet for a growing number of politicians, Norway's delayed industrial growth meant that Norway could learn from the mistakes of other more industrialized nations. This belief resonated with the liberal *Venstre* party and when a *Venstre*-led government came to power in 1884, Prime Minister Johan Sverdrup quickly set up a Workers' Commission to study the issue.

The stated mandate of the commission to "help the impoverished portion of the population in their struggles to secure their economic positions and improve their quality of life"[37] appealed to powerful agrarian interests that wanted to decrease the working-class reliance on poverty relief and ameliorate social tensions.[38] A similar committee had been formed in Sweden in 1884 and the Swedish king supported a Norwegian Workers' Commission, anticipating that factory legislation should be uniform between the two countries.[39] The Norwegian commission consisted of 11 people, including factory owners, factory workers, a doctor, a demographer, a district governor, and a bureaucrat. Sverdrup expressed the hope that the commission would find "a solution to the worker question."[40]

With this statement, Sverdrup recognized the larger issues at hand in crafting factory legislation. Democratic and nationalistic forces led many statesmen to consider the implications such legislation had for modern conceptualizations of citizenship and individual rights.[41] Workers and women had begun to mobilize around democratic initiatives and while universal male suffrage would not be implemented in Norway until 1898, politicians were already concerned with creating the institutions necessary for a larger democratic society in 1892. During this period, people who received poverty relief lost their right to vote and enter into contracts. If the state wanted more people to participate in political and civil society then it would have to establish some type of "worthy" aid that did not strip recipients of their citizenship rights.[42] Worker protection laws were one way of ensuring that members of the working class were less likely to need poverty relief and thus be eligible for the full benefits of citizenship.

These ideas about individual rights and citizenship came to the forefront in discussing restrictions on women's ability to work. European states were interested in protecting the health of women because of women's reproductive capabilities. Through this protection, the state hoped to increase the number of healthy citizens needed for a modern nation state. Yet ensuring the protection of women's health often involved treating female workers differently than male workers. In the realm of factory legislation, this included bans on women's night work, restricted access to "dangerous" industries like mining, and mandated maternity leaves. These types of protective, or limiting, legislation highlighted women's exclusion from political and social rights and further reified their dependent status in society.[43]

The Workers' Commission and Norway's First Maternity Leave Law

Norwegian politicians' interest in learning from other, more industrialized European countries on matters of industrial regulations and worker protections is particularly evident in the Workers' Commission's discussion of restrictions of pregnant women's industrial work. For the commissioners, the most important reason for including a maternity clause in the government's regulation of industry was out of consideration for the health of the mother and the child. They grounded these arguments in a Swiss physician, Dr. Fridolin Schuler's, claim that infant mortality rates amongst the working class in Switzerland were reduced by 6% after the implementation of a ban on parturient women's industrial labor.

The Norwegian Workers' Commission wanted to reduce infant mortality rates as the Swiss had done, but they thought this goal would be hindered if working-class women were subjected to prolonged unemployment. In their estimation, women would be unable to provide for their newborn babies if they were prevented from earning a living for more than three weeks, and that even the shorter period of three weeks leave would need to be compensated for. They suggested the creation of a worker sickness insurance law, and stated that this sickness insurance should provide necessary medical help to pregnant industrial workers and payment for the three weeks of leave.

A shorter maternity leave would also help with the enforcement problems this type of prohibition posed. The Commission knew from their European counterparts that women who needed to work to survive would not follow the ban on their post-partum employment and instead seek employment at a different factory as a way of getting around the law. Commissioners thought it would be especially difficult to police a prenatal ban on women's work. The Swiss had found that given a choice, women almost never took any leave prior to giving birth unless they had a debilitating illness.[44] These were some of the main reasons the Norwegian Workers' Commission recommended a three-week postpartum maternity leave for industrial workers to be compensated through a national sickness insurance provision.

The Commission presented its report about maternity leave to Parliament in December of 1887, but no law was passed until 1892. In the meantime, Norwegian parliamentarians made changes to the Workers' Commission's proposed law based on domestic and international developments. They gathered opinions from worker's associations and the Norwegian medical community. In addition to this they looked to the international community to help them decide which laws would work best to improve working conditions and prevent strikes and social unrest.

Two years after the publication of the commission's recommendation, in October 1889, 300 women matchstick workers went on strike in Kristiania (Oslo) over wage cuts and poor working conditions. Partially in response to this occurrence, Norway eagerly took part in the first official international worker congress that was held in Berlin in 1890. The Norwegian Parliament also sent an up-and-coming *Venstre* politician, Johan Castberg, to study the factory legislation in place in Austria, Switzerland, and Germany.[45]

When the Norwegian Parliament debated the maternity leave clause proposed in the Norwegian Factory Protection Act in 1892, politicians were unsure of how to balance their desire for a healthier population with women's rights as independent individuals and citizens.[46] The proposed leave recognized new developments in international maternity leave policies and followed a recently passed German example that included a provision to help alleviate the financial burden of a mandated six-week leave: a woman would be allowed to return to industrial work after four weeks of the prescribed six-week leave if a doctor cleared her to do so.[47]

"WHAT NATURE ITSELF DEMANDS:" THE DEVELOPMENT OF MATERNITY... 35

In the debate, Dr. Josef Johnsen's (*Høyre*, Conservative Party) argument that women must not be allowed to work for a *minimum* of six weeks after giving birth, even if she could obtain a medical certificate that stated otherwise, highlighted many of the issues at play in passing such legislation at the end of the nineteenth century. According to Johnsen, working women "would very much like to begin to work again as soon as possible [after giving birth] so that they will not miss out on any profits" and thus they could not be trusted to judiciously evaluate their physical ability to return to work.[48] This distrust of women extended to midwives as Johnsen also worried that midwives, and not doctors, might be the ones to furnish these medical certificates.

Johnsen's critics countered that the proposed wording of the 1892 legislation fell in line with what factory-legislation forerunners Germany and Switzerland had already decided was an adequate amount of time to prohibit women's postpartum work, especially considering that they would not be paid for this mandated time off. Parliamentarians also argued with Johnsen over how long a woman should be kept from working if she was capable of performing the requisite tasks.[49] Parliamentarian Paul Koht (*Venstre*), for example, was unconvinced that a mandatory six-week leave was acceptable, as women "might easily lose their jobs" because of it. Koht's point did not convince Johnsen, and he tried to get the rest of the committee to recognize that his medical background gave him a superior perspective on the matter.

Johnsen was counting on recent developments in the medical field to help solidify his position as a scientific expert on maternity. Parliament had recognized this authority when they asked the Norwegian Medical Association rather than midwives to comment on the maternity leave section of the proposed factory law. As the consulted experts on maternal health, doctors like Johnsen intended to advance their professional position in the crafting of the law. When Johnsen thought that Parliament might give midwives the authority to clear women for work after four weeks, he impressed upon them that this was not "reassuring."[50] He wanted to make sure that Parliament recognized that a midwife's knowledge of maternity was inferior to a doctor's.

The debate over what constituted the optimal length of maternity leave and who had the authority to determine this demonstrated the significant sway medical officials held in policy debates in Norway, as well as the influence international standards had on Norwegian policymaking. Norwegian politicians hoped that by following the examples of larger, more industrialized countries, industrialization would not adversely affect the reproductive health of Norwegian mothers and their children. They believed this protection necessitated the delicate compromise of women workers' rights. While doctors like Johnsen held that women must be kept from industrial work for six weeks after giving birth, European legislative standards allowed for some flexibility. Norwegian statesmen took advantage of these precedents and concluded that while six weeks' mandated leave would be best for women's health, the state should not interfere more than necessary in women's freedom to work. This resulted in the passage of the proposed extension of maternity leave to six weeks with the possibility of a medically approved two-week exemption.[51]

Though Johnsen's demand that a minimum of six weeks be set for industrial maternity leave was not met, his assertion that only medical doctors should have the power to exempt women from part of the mandated leave did convince his fellow parliamentarians. They reworded the maternity leave clause to specify that a woman could return to work after only four weeks of maternity leave if clearance *from a doctor* was given.

When the Workers' Commission furnished its report in 1887 it had called for the creation of a national sickness insurance scheme that would offset the loss of wages women would incur from this mandated maternity leave. By the time the Factory Protection Act passed in 1892 it had been watered down to such an extent that there were no insurance-granting provisions. Instead it regulated the working conditions under which industrial labor could be performed, limited the work of children and women, prohibited new mothers from working, and set up a national factory inspectorate. The Commission's larger goals of establishing a maximum work day, accident insurance, old-age pensions and sickness insurance would have to wait for future parliamentary sessions.

In its completed state, the Factory Act was first-and-foremost a piece of legislation officially designed to protect the health of the Norwegian working class. It targeted the aspects of modern industrial labor that politicians around Europe found the most threatening to a stable and prosperous state: child labor, women's labor, and deplorable working conditions. Norwegian politicians hoped that by following the examples of larger, more industrialized countries Norway could industrialize rapidly without jeopardizing the lives of its current and future generations. As such, the maternity section of the law can be seen as a form of population policy.[52] It aimed to ensure that industrialization would not adversely affect the reproductive health of Norway's mothers or children, and it sought to do so through the restriction of women's rights.

"WHAT NATURE ITSELF DEMANDS:" THE DEVELOPMENT OF MATERNITY... 37

Noticeably absent from late-nineteenth-century debates on maternity leave were the very groups of women who would be instrumental in later revisions of the law. Women's rights activists, midwives, and working women paid little attention to the creation and passage of the first factory law and its maternity clause. These groups of women were more concerned with other issues. Middle-class women's rights activists had only recently formed cohesive movements and were focused on the broader fight for women's rights. As the law did not provide any compensation for medical services, midwives concentrated on their battle with the state over the details of a revision of the midwifery law. Working women were also unconcerned with the creation of maternity leave because the law had little chance of impacting their lives. Women industrial workers were largely unorganized at this time and would have met difficulty in trying to assert any push for maternity compensation. The relatively limited number of Norwegian women who would have been affected by the law could easily avoid its restrictions.

FEMINISTS AND THE FIRST MATERNITY LEAVE LAW

One of the reasons Norway's first maternity leave law was so restrictive was because women were largely uninvolved in its drafting and its passage. It is a customary practice in Norway to get the opinion of relevant organizations on proposed legislative drafts. In the case of the 1892 factory law, politicians asked groups, including the Norwegian Medical Association, the Norwegian Crafts and Industrial Associations and the Polytechnic Association to comment on the proposal. Members of Parliament then took these consultations into consideration when they crafted revisions of the legislative draft. Noticeably absent from the list of consulted groups were women's organizations, especially considering women's associations would be very active in later expansions of the 1892 maternity leave clause.

Women's organizations may not have been consulted in the drafting of the 1892 law because the Norwegian feminist movement had only recently been organized. A leader of the early Norwegian feminist movement, Gina Krog, co-founded the *Norsk kvinnesaksforening* (Norwegian Association for Women's Rights, NKF), with *Venstre* politician Hagbart Berner in 1884.[53] The NKF followed a moderate program meant to attract a wide membership. The association stayed away from pushing for more political rights for women and instead focused on four main areas of reform: women's education, fair wages and more working opportunities for women, women's marital rights,

38   A. M. PETERSON

and for women to be consulted in important societal matters.[54] Though the NKF had officially pledged to improve women's working conditions, it was narrowly focused on jobs for middle-class women. The association discussed the need for equal pay for equal work as early as 1888, but this was mainly in conjunction with teachers.[55]

Krog was an individualist feminist who believed that women must demand full equality with men in all aspects of society.[56] She was heavily influenced by the American and British feminist movements and operated on the radical edge of the women's movement in Norway. Dissatisfied with the fact that the NKF platform did not include a section on women's suffrage, Krog started a parallel organization, *Landskvinnestemmeretts-foreningen*, or National Association for Women's Suffrage, in 1885 to lobby for women's right to vote.[57] She was also involved in forming the Norwegian chapter of the International Council of Women and was editor and publisher for the NKF periodical, *Nylaende*, from 1887 until her death in 1916.

Krog's uncompromising stance on equality for women led her to oppose protective legislation for women, but she only publicly announced this position after the 1892 factory act had been passed. Krog and the NKF would later join forces with other Scandinavian women's rights groups to vehemently oppose any bans on women's night work, but they were surprisingly silent on the issue until the factory law was enacted.[58] Prior to the law's passage, Krog published a short notice in *Nylaende* outlining the portions of the Workers' Commission's proposal that affected women in January 1888. Yet she postponed a thorough discussion of the report.[59] After the factory protection act passed, Krog lamented that "we Norwegian women have the shame to say that we did not open our mouths" in any connection with the law and the effects it could have on issues related to women's work.[60]

When Krog later devoted space in *Nylænde* to review the new factory law, she revealed some of the complexities involved in an individualist feminist approach to maternity leave. Krog argued against special concessions for women in the workplace as she believed this would impede feminist goals of winning equal political, economic and legal rights for women.[61] Though the 1892 law restricted a woman's right to work by mandating a woman take leave of work after giving birth and not compensating her for this leave or protecting her from being fired, Krog thought these restrictions were different from other types of limiting legislation. She even went so far as to say that no one could oppose the maternity clause because "nature has assigned mothers a special position which makes it humane to intervene in these circumstances, and when small children are involved society has a right and a duty to protect them. We do not want to completely deny that there are situations when grouping women and children together makes sense."[62] To Krog, maternity was a condition that warranted differential treatment for women.

Krog's thinking was in line with feminist thought at the time. While special labor protections for women generally divided the feminist movement, feminists of different ideological and political persuasions supported restrictions on parturient women's work.[63] They argued that maternity leave did not regulate a woman's right to work, it regulated a *mother's* right to work. This was an important distinction for Krog and other individualist feminists. A woman should not have her individual rights infringed upon merely because she was a woman, but a mother was different. Mothers had a special role in society and the family. As Krog said, society needed mothers to care for children, especially newborns, and this need gave the state the "right and [the] duty to protect" small children even if this meant hindering a mother's right to earn a living.[64] From this perspective, a woman who became a mother forfeited her right to autonomy, at least for a period of time. This qualified her for special protections (or restrictions) under the law with which even individualist feminists agreed, though they did call for maternity leave to be paid.[65]

Krog and other Norwegian women's rights activists may have agreed that the state had a right to stop new mothers from working, but they were silent on the issue of maternity leave until after the law had been passed. Five years after the 1892 child support and factory laws were enacted, the NKF voiced their discontent with these laws. Feminists thought that the state had not done enough to help poor, pregnant women. Instead, they argued, legislators had passed laws that forbid parturient women from working, which reduced women to begging their children's fathers for money.

NKF feminists supported the idea that the state should facilitate compensation to unmarried women, not provide it. Instead of supporting the creation of national sickness insurance to compensate women for mandated maternity leaves, the NKF called for fathers to support the mothers of their children during this period of time. The NKF agreed that women who had recently given birth should be kept from performing strenuous work, but argued that the factory law had led many women to be fired and left without any chance of earning a living. If the state wanted to keep women from working, then they needed to ensure that fathers offset the loss of wages parturient women experienced. For the NKF, women had a "right not to suffer during pregnancy" and while the 1892 child support law was supposed to ensure this, it had rather caused women to have to beg her child's father for money and threaten him with legal action.[66] Krog suggested that the state act as a mediator between unmarried mothers and fathers. The government should give an unmarried mother the money to which she was legally entitled and seek reimbursement from the father.[67] Until this occurred, Krog argued, unmarried mothers had to experience the "deep shame" of applying for poor relief.[68]

One of the reasons some NKF feminists wanted fathers, rather than the state, to compensate women's maternity leave was to avoid the questionable action of the state financing unmarried mothers' immoral decisions to have sex outside wedlock. Women's rights activist, Thea Ebbell, for example, expressed shock over the fact that working-class wives and unmarried mothers were both covered by the 1892 "protection" of women's postpartum work in an article she wrote for *Nylænde* in 1901. In this piece, Ebbell argued that a better solution would be to force the illegitimate child's father to support the child's mother and that factory managers should be required to fire any woman who had "gotten herself in such a condition." While Ebbell stressed that she felt a good deal of sympathy for the unmarried mother, even one who killed her child shortly after its birth, she made clear that such compassion should not be confused with giving unmarried mothers an equal position in society.[69] Ebbell's critique of granting unwed mothers special dispensations demonstrates that moral discussions of maternity still had a powerful role to play in debates about maternity leave. To what extent unmarried women should be covered by maternity laws would be a question Norwegian feminists would struggle with well into the twentieth century.

Though Ebbell, Krog, and other members of the NKF reacted strongly after the maternity leave law passed in 1892, neither they nor any other women's organization had expressed an official opinion during the policy-making process.[70] The government did not consult them when preparing the law and the women's organizations did not offer any unsolicited advice. The NKF and the National Association for Women's Suffrage rather focused on matters they considered to be of greater and more immediate importance, such as women's political enfranchisement, access to university education and the right to own property. While women's rights activists were concerned with women's economic circumstances, they were mainly interested in securing rights that middle-class women could benefit from, such as equal pay for equal work for teachers. In the future, feminist organizations including the NKF and groups formed after 1900, such as the Norwegian National Women's Council and the Women's Federation of the Norwegian Labor Party, would be very active in shaping debates about women's industrial work and maternity benefits. In the late nineteenth century, NKF's inattention meant that the Factory Protection Act included a maternity leave clause unmarked by feminists.

MIDWIVES AND MATERNITY LEGISLATION

Midwives were also largely absent from discussions concerning the first piece of Norwegian maternity leave legislation. Midwives had long been a group with immense social importance in Norway, and they influenced the types of maternity benefits that were later introduced in the twentieth century. In the 1880s and 1890s, however, Norwegian midwives did not take advantage of the opportunities a maternity leave clause in the Factory Act may have presented for the improvement of their professional and economic status. They were more concerned with issues of undisputed relevance: the 1898 revision of the midwifery law and their struggles to professionalize.

The first Norwegian midwifery law was passed under the joint Dano-Norwegian union in 1810. This law created a framework that would aid in the professionalization of midwives. It outlined the requirements for a midwife's education and defined her responsibilities and working conditions. In Norway the law led to the creation of midwifery districts. Each parish was tasked with appointing a publicly employed midwife to serve the women who lived in that community. The midwife would be paid a small base salary according to a rate set by law and she would also receive free lodging. In exchange for these benefits, a midwife would have to give up her freedom of movement. She was not allowed to travel outside of her district for more than 24 hours without permission, and then only to attend a birth. Midwives were also required to assist all birthing women, regardless of whether or not the woman could pay for midwifery services.[71]

The 1810 midwifery law established a new hierarchy of birthing help in Norway. By the early 1800s medical doctors had replaced church officials as the authorities on matters related to childbirth.[72] Doctors were responsible for educating midwives and supervising their activities. After doctors, the state recognized formally trained midwives, or *jordmødre*, as qualified birthing attendants. The law made it illegal for an uneducated midwife, also called a "helping wife" or *hjelpekone*, to assist a woman in childbirth. Both the uneducated midwife who attended a birth and the birthing woman who sent for a helping wife could be fined. This legislation granted educated midwives a professional monopoly and temporarily resolved some of the challenges helping wives posed to midwives. Unfortunately for midwives, this portion of the law was overturned in 1839. The medical community may have considered helping wives to be backwards and superstitious, but the state no longer restricted their activities and birthing women often preferred to call helping wives to assist them in their time of need.[73]

The unfettered competition between midwives and helping wives was one of the main reasons midwives worked to get a revised midwifery law in the late nineteenth century. The midwives received a salary from the government that was intentionally too small to cover all of a person's costs of living.[74] In order to increase this paltry salary, midwives needed to supplement their salary with payments from birthing women and their families. Midwives complained that they were unable to earn a decent living because too many women still relied on the services of helping wives.[75]

Women often preferred to have helping wives attend their births because most helping wives had deep ties to the local community. Midwives, on the other hand, were trained at midwifery schools in the city and were then hired by local districts. Even though many midwives were farmers' daughters and came from rural areas, they did not have the same local legitimacy as helping wives.[76] Childbirth at the time was an intimate affair filled with danger, and when it came time for birthing women to call someone for assistance they chose someone they knew, someone who had attended other births at their home or in their family. It did not yet matter to these women that the medical community and the state thought that helping wives were an inferior choice of birthing assistant. They were more concerned that they could trust the person who helped them during a time of great physical and emotional trial.[77] Meanwhile, midwives felt that their professional expertise was not appreciated by pregnant women and that this was reflected in their poor pay and working conditions.

Midwives did have some of their demands for better pay and working conditions recognized when the state revised the midwifery law in 1898. The first section of the law reinstated formally trained midwives' monopoly over midwifery assistance. It clearly stated that only women who had received certification from a recognized midwifery school would be allowed to work as a midwife. Though this legislation should have secured educated midwives the economic and professional position they wanted, it still allowed helping wives to assist women if a midwife or a doctor could not attend the birth due to long distances.

In a country with a long coastline, treacherous mountain passes, and a largely rural population spread across vast distances, many midwives and doctors could not be reached in time to attend a birth. The creation of midwifery districts in 1810 was supposed to alleviate many of these issues, but many districts had delayed in hiring formally trained midwives.[78] The 1898 law reiterated the need for midwifery districts, but left it up to the local authorities to divide their provinces into these districts. The establishment of midwifery districts and standing restrictions on publicly employed midwives' movements were supposed to ensure that most, if not all, births would be attended by a midwife. Yet even with these developments, midwives often had to travel extremely long distances with unreliable forms of transportation to serve the women of their district. Midwife Dorothea Efraimsen recalled nights where she had to ski 10 or 20 kilometers to reach a birthing woman, and a harrowing boat trip that threw her and the crew members into the icy waves.[79] Often midwives would overcome these transportation difficulties only to arrive at a home where the birth had already taken place, sometimes successfully and other times with more deadly results.

Midwives frequently recounted the difficulties they faced on an everyday basis to gain sympathy from governmental entities and achieve their wage demands. They referred to midwifery as a higher calling, a job that was both necessary and good. The work that they performed was of enormous social benefit, and they thought that this work deserved greater recognition. Midwives like Mrs. Klavenes argued that midwives had some of the most demanding jobs, because "while others are resting in their warm homes" a midwife could be called out to work at any time of night, any day of the year "no matter if it was raining or snowing." To Mrs. Klavenes, her job was not just any job—she brought life into the world, and if a midwife "were to be of any benefit to her fellow human beings, she must be lifted out of her current position."[80] These appeals were often quite successful and helped midwives garner support from a variety of organizations, including middle-class women's rights associations.

Throughout the end of the nineteenth century midwives fostered a connection with middle-class women's organizations that built on the idea of helping poor, pregnant women. Midwives turned to the NKF and asked them to assist them in their efforts to achieve a more professional status. These appeals worked and the NKF vowed to support midwives.[81] The NKF tied their support for midwives to the need to better the living conditions for working-class mothers. They claimed "if we increase the quality of midwives' lives then we will also improve the conditions pregnant women live under."[82]

According to articles written in *Nylænde*, the best way to improve midwives' lives was to expand their professional arena and solidify their relationship to the state. They argued that midwives' professional arena should be expanded. First, midwives should be the ones to give out free medicine to ill pregnant women.[83] Then, their work should not only encompass the birthing woman, but also the postpartum household. Feminists put forth the idea that midwives should visit a postpartum woman several times after a birth to ensure her health and wellbeing. While midwives had traditionally cared for only the parturient woman, feminists also thought that midwives should provide care for the baby and the household after the birth. Of course, a midwife could not be expected to do this extra work without payment. The government should compensate midwives for this service because of the importance it had for working-class women's health.[84] These ideas did not make it into the 1898 midwifery law, but they did start a discussion about which tasks midwives should perform and the role midwives played in ensuring the health and vitality of poor mothers and children.

Doctors were, on the whole, the ones who defined the professional duties of midwives and trained them in methods to successfully fulfill these duties. Often reserving more "prestigious" forms of gynecological and obstetrical knowledge for members of their own profession, doctors educated midwives in the childbirth-assistance procedures doctors preferred to avoid. Though midwives were to carry out procedures like the laborious undertaking of manually turning a breech fetus, their main role was to support a birthing woman. Doctors wanted to be the ones to perform any operative interventions, especially if it involved new technological tools or drugs. This created a tension between doctors and midwives as midwives struggled to professionalize and gain authority over helping wives.

Midwives had already been assigned the duty of protecting women from outbreaks of disease during confinement. From 1886 to 1890 Norway's average maternal death rate was 5 for every 1000 births.[85] Maternal mortality was a problem that doctors and midwives had been diligently trying to solve for decades. Many of these deaths were attributed to outbreaks of puerperal fever, a condition that midwives and doctors had long been perplexed by. It was not until the 1880s that the majority of Norwegian doctors accepted the theory that the best way to prevent maternal mortality was through aseptic techniques.[86] With this new knowledge, midwives took on the responsibility of making sure that everything that came in the contact with a birthing woman was clean and disinfected. Many midwives complained that this was nearly impossible as they had to work in "dirty, cramped rooms" that were "extremely unappetizing."[87] In spite of these adverse working conditions, midwives' disinfection practices seemed to have helped reduce the rate of maternal mortality to 3 in 1000 by 1896.[88]

Midwives argued that they could save even more lives if they had a broader education in operative procedures, especially the use of forceps. Doctors had withheld midwives the right to be educated in the use of forceps. Instead, a midwife was supposed to call for a doctor if a situation arose during a birth that required the use of forceps. Midwives contended that this was a problem because there were many places in Norway where it was difficult to obtain a doctor's help in time. They recounted stories where waiting for a doctor had cost both the mother and her child their lives. Midwives also claimed that it was inhumane to expect a woman who had been in labor for several hours or even days to wait for a doctor to put an end to her pain.[89] In 1829 Swedish midwives had won the right to use forceps,[90] and Norwegian midwives protested against this incongruity because they thought it would disadvantage Norwegian midwives working along the Swedish/Norwegian border.[91] Of course, midwives wanted to be able to use forceps for more selfish reasons as well.[92] The use of forceps could significantly reduce the amount of time a midwife had to attend a birthing woman. It would have also increased midwives' professional status in relation to both helping wives and doctors.

The 1898 revision of the midwifery law did not solve the conflict between midwives and doctors over the use of forceps. Doctors could not agree amongst themselves over the issue of whether midwives should be trained in the operative use of forceps. Due to the lack of consensus, individual doctors took it upon themselves to educate midwives on the use of forceps.[93] The debate over whether midwives should be allowed to use forceps would be a recurrent feature of midwife-doctor relations throughout the first half of the twentieth century.

In the late-nineteenth century, Norwegian midwives lacked organizational clout and professional status as evidenced in their subordinate relationship to doctors. Though midwives were the ones who had the most direct experience with birthing mothers and physical recovery following childbirth, the government asked doctors at the Norwegian Medical Association for their opinion on the proposed factory law, not midwives.[94]

Another reason Parliament did not consult midwives in the drafting of the factory law may have been because midwives had not yet formed a national organization. Midwives were loosely organized in local associations during the 1800s, but it was not until 1908 that they established the Norwegian Association of Midwives. In the meantime, midwives had trouble exerting any type of formal pressure on the government as a cohesive body. Individual associations did write in to the government to demand higher wages for midwives, but these requests were often based on local conditions.[95] Since 1895, the journal *Tidsskrift for jordmødre*, or *Journal of Midwifery*, had kept midwives throughout the country notified of certain medical and professional issues. Nevertheless, there was no organization that could speak on behalf of all midwives' interests or expertise in the late nineteenth century.

The 1892 factory law also seemed to be of little interest to midwives. They were engaged in a number of issues that had undeniable relevance to their professional and economic lives, but the factory law was not amongst them. Midwives were most concerned with their economic livelihoods in the late nineteenth century, and they did not seem to have any use for a law that regulated industry. The legislation had no compensation mechanism, and this might have been another reason midwives paid it little attention. Had the factory law also included a section on sickness insurance or maternity support, then midwives—albeit through local organizations—might have tried to shape the law to their benefit. As it was, there was no official correspondence between midwives and the government in connection with the proposed factory legislation and midwives did not mention it in their monthly periodical.

Working Mothers and Maternity Laws

Working mothers stood to be the most directly affected by the 1892 prohibition of postpartum work. In the 1880s, women made up 15% of the Norwegian industrial workforce.[96] The majority of industrial women workers were unmarried adults over the age of 18. Most of these women worked in the textile factories, but a significant portion of them also worked in the food and beverage industry.[97] The women who worked in these factories stood to lose up to six weeks of earnings, and potentially their positions, following the birth of a child. In spite of these restrictions on their work, working women would have had a difficult time lobbying against the early findings of the Workers' Commission. Prior to the match worker strike in 1889, women workers were not organized in unions. Even after 1889, there were relatively few women's unions and their membership numbers were quite low.[98] The women workers who were organized mostly focused on getting a reduction in working hours passed.

It is unknown exactly how many women workers were affected by the factory legislation's maternity leave clause. Demographic statistics provide a sense of the scope of those affected. Over 60% of women industrial workers were unmarried, but this did not preclude the possibility that they would have children outside of marriage.[99] In fact, nearly 8.5% of all births were illegitimate in 1900, a number that was comparatively high amongst European nations.[100] Statisticians and lawmakers were alarmed at this number, especially when they found that illegitimate births had increased dramatically in relation to the past.

Statisticians and legislators credited the growth of industry with the high number of illegitimate births. Nicolai Rygg reported that over 74% of illegitimate births in 1897 were to women "workers."[101] Yet he did not separate factory workers from servants. It is very possible that a high number of these children were born to servants, not industrial workers, and servants were not covered under the 1892 law. A 1911 report from Kristiania's Chief Medical Officer did separate housemaids from factory workers. He found that 40% of illegitimate children were born to maids, while 20% of these children had factory workers as mothers.[102]

If we take this number as an indication of how many unmarried factory workers may have given birth in the 1890s, then roughly 1000 unmarried women workers (or 12.5% of all women workers) would have been affected by the law. It is difficult to say with certainty how many women industrial workers gave birth in total each year, but these numbers provide some indication of how many women may have fallen under the restrictions in Norway's first maternity leave law.

A relatively small number of women would have been affected by the maternity leave, and those who were, appear to have successfully evaded its restrictions. To enforce the maternity policy, and all the other industrial regulations, the state set up a factory inspectorate. Determining if a woman had recently given birth, however, was not an easy task for a state inspector from Kristiania. They had little knowledge of local women's personal lives and could rarely tell if a woman had given birth merely by looking at her.[103] Factory inspectors also found it difficult to identify violations of the maternity clause, and other regulations, because there were only two factory inspectors who were responsible for assessing over 4000 industrial enterprises.[104] Even after Norway's first woman factory inspector, Betzy Kjelsberg, was hired, compliance with the maternity leave clause of the Factory Act does not appear to have been prioritized (Fig. 2.1).[105]

Working women did not publicly protest against the prohibition of their postpartum work, but it is likely that they used one of the few resources an industrial worker had—they "voted with their feet." Instead of quitting a job because of unsatisfactory wages or working conditions, pregnant industrial women workers often left a job in order to give birth. Then they would rest as long as they could afford to, perhaps only a few days, and find work at a new factory.[106]

Quitting at one factory and beginning at another soon after giving birth is one of the ways industrial women workers avoided the monetary devastation that prohibitions of their postpartum work entailed. In more established industrial countries, such as Switzerland, policymakers had found that this was often how women responded to unpaid maternity leave. Norwegian legislators were aware of these findings and cited the Swiss case as evidence that mandated maternity leave should not be longer than absolutely medically necessary.[107] The medical community also discussed the difficult choices that a woman had to make when deciding when to return to work after having a child. The Norwegian *Journal of Midwifery* included a report in 1896 from a Hungarian doctor who warned that even though many women resumed their industrial work one or two days after giving birth, they did so only because they had to, not because they were physically ready to work.[108]

Even prior to the implementation of mandatory, unpaid maternity leave, most poor women in Norway, including married, working-class mothers, sought financial assistance from their local poor relief board after giving birth. In fact, up to 80% of people who received poor relief in the 1890s were women and children.[109] Of those who applied for help for the first time, 60% of them received assistance due to an illness.[110] Women who needed assistance because of a pregnancy or childbirth would have had to apply for poverty relief at their local poverty board. These committees were made up of local bureaucrats and pastors. To receive assistance, one had to be found deserving by this committee and many women encountered difficulties in qualifying for support.

Fig. 2.1 Betzy Kjelsberg at a loom with shuttle in hand and wearing an apron (work clothes). In the background there stands the sign "Do not spit on the stairs." 1914. Courtesy of the Norwegian Museum of Science and Technology

Women could be denied poor relief for a variety of reasons, including not fulfilling the ideal image of a "worthy" recipient. The relief boards were holdovers from an earlier time when poor relief was administered by charitable, religious institutions. The boards continued in this tradition

50 A. M. PETERSON

and a woman's reputation could be a deciding factor in whether or not she received assistance. Even if a woman was considered worthy of help, she was eligible for poor relief only if she was an official resident of the community she lived in.[111] Many women who moved to Kristiania to find work, were denied poverty relief because they had moved outside of their home municipality. Lina Larsen, for example, was desperate for child support from her illegitimate child's father because she had recently moved to Kristiania and she was not eligible for any poor relief. She was not even able to get the poverty board to pay for medicine for her child.[112]

Municipal assistance may have allowed some women to help pay for the extra costs associated with childbirth and confinement, but recipients had to be prepared to sacrifice a lot in their dealings with the relief board. Recipients of poor relief lost their citizenship rights. They were no longer allowed to vote in local or national elections and they could not enter legal contracts. Beyond this loss of legal rights, women also experienced a loss of privacy. Poverty boards could investigate the intimate details of a woman's life, including her sexual experiences, in order to evaluate her worthiness as a candidate for assistance. These investigations were often very personal and exposed women to ridicule and ostracization from members of her local community. Yet poor mothers did not have many other options. Many endured this scrutiny in the hope that they would receive the money they needed to survive.[113]

The economic constraints that unmarried mothers lived within led many of them to place their children in rural homes so that they could return to work as soon as possible after giving birth. Sometimes this involved sending their children to live with relatives, but working-class women also paid non-relatives to care for and raise their children so that they could continue to work. After the working woman married, or the child reached an age where he or she could attend school, the child would often move back in with his or her mother. Until then most working-class, unmarried mothers lived separately from their young children. This prevented unwed working-class women from breastfeeding their children for any substantial length of time. Many of the children who were placed in foster homes died because of inadequate access to safe nutrition and proper childcare. People began to refer to foster mothers as *englemakere*, or angel-makers, because of the high number of children who died in their care.[114] The practice of working-class mothers living separately from their young children so they could continue to work alarmed lawmakers and led to important developments in maternity legislation during the first decades of the twentieth century.

Most unmarried mothers defied the restrictions placed on them by the 1892 maternity leave law and continued to place their children in foster care soon after giving birth so that they could continue to work. Had the law included a compensatory mechanism for the mandated leave, women may have been able to rest and recover after birth without relying on the goodwill of the poor relief board. The 1892 law had no such mechanism and was solely a restriction placed on women's ability to work, not a benefit women could use to their advantage. Women who needed to work to survive could not afford to go without any wages for six, or even four, weeks. As such, most women returned to work as soon as they were able after giving birth, regardless of whether the mandated six weeks had passed. Their responses to the restrictive nature of the policy would have important ramifications for later discussions of the law's revision.

Conclusion

One of the most important developments in the history of Norwegian maternity legislation was the creation of the first maternity leave law in 1892. For this law, Norway followed the example of other European countries and included a maternity leave policy in the passage of its first factory law. Legislators prohibited women from partaking in industrial work for the first six weeks following childbirth, with exceptions for women who received a doctor's permission to work after four weeks. Women were largely absent from the development of this factory legislation. Instead, feminists, midwives, and working women had only recently organized and were focused on other issues.

Women did, however, take part in redefining maternity as a site of state intervention in the 1880s and 1890s. They fought to revise standing child support provisions and midwifery statutes. In many cases, unmarried working mothers became the image feminists and midwives used to illustrate the need for maternity protections. They painted a picture of a "slave" who worked 16 hour days, endured "unimaginable tribulations dealing with children, pregnancies, and births," and tried to make the best out of a home that was "neither particularly healthy nor comfortable."[115] Doctors and legislators also used this idea of the poor, pregnant woman when they emphasized women's need for postpartum rest from industrial labor and support from their children's fathers.

In later years, children themselves would become more instrumental to rhetorical justifications for maternity legislation, but poor women's maternal mortality rates and maternal health were at the heart of maternity legislation in the 1880s and 1890s. Norwegians had yet to systematically address infant mortality as a problem. As a result, there was scarce a mention of breastfeeding in discussions about the need for more protections for pregnant women. Instead, legislators, feminists, and midwives claimed that both mother and child would be helped if poor, pregnant women received more support during childbirth.

In the name of protection, the government set up a legal framework to try to mitigate some of the worst effects a pregnancy could have on poor women's lives. In 1892 industrial women workers (predominantly unmarried women) were prohibited from working six weeks after giving birth and fathers were held more financially accountable for their illegitimate children. In 1898 the state strengthened its regulation of midwifery, partially in order to make sure that they were providing help to women who could not afford to pay for their services.[116] The state did not yet want to get involved in providing services directly to unmarried mothers, especially those that might be considered benefits. Instead Norwegian politicians extended their regulatory arm into some of the more private aspects of women's lives. Childbirth was no longer solely an intimate event experienced by an individual woman, but in the case of poor and working-class women, an act that warranted state intervention.

Women seemed to have benefitted little from nineteenth-century maternity legislation. Many tried to use the new child support law to access the economic support that was rightfully theirs, but they most often failed in getting fathers to pay child support. The state was not of much help to them in these efforts either and left it up to the women to initiate and follow up with the legal proceedings. When it came to the maternity leave clause, working women often avoided many of the prohibitions and returned to work when they needed to, not according to the state's schedule. The revision of the midwifery law further solidified a poor woman's right to receive birth assistance even if she could not pay. Yet many poor women still preferred to use helping wives instead of midwives. On the whole, poor, working-class women resisted the medical emphasis placed on maternity through midwifery and factory legislation.

In the decades to come, feminists, midwives, and working women would work to expand maternity protections to their benefit. They would be influential in redefining maternity as a condition that warranted not only regulation, but also compensation. Their efforts to tie maternity legislation to a rhetoric of benefits would incorporate a greater number of women under the umbrella of the emerging welfare state. As a result, the 1892 maternity leave clause would become a relic of the past—a marker of an antiquated way of thinking about maternity and social protections as punitive and restrictive limitations placed on women's lives.

NOTES

1. The title reference is from: Stortingsforhandlinger, Forhandlinger i Odelstinget. nr. 66, "Ang. lov om tilsyn med arbeide i fabriker," 7 juni, 1892.
2. Stortingsforhandlinger 1914, Odelstinget, Ot. prp 32, "Sykeforsikringsloven §16," vol. 3, 250.
3. The term "social question" was first introduced in Germany as "die soziale Frage" and was subsequently translated into many other languages in countries where industrial developments had—or had threatened to— take hold. In Norway it was referred to as "det sociale spørgsmaal" or "arbeidersagen" (the worker issue).
4. Ann Taylor Allen, *Feminism and Motherhood in Western Europe, 1890–1970: The Maternal Dilemma* (New York: Palgrave Macmillan, 2005), 71; *The History of the European Family: Family Life in the Long Nineteenth Century, 1789–1913*, edited by David I. Kertzer and Marzio Barbagli, vol. 2 (London: Yale University Press, 2002), 184.
5. Frida Ros Valdimarsdottir, *Nordic Experiences with Parental Leave and Its Impact on Equality Between Women and Men* (Copenhagen: Nordic Council of Ministers, 2006), 11.
6. Karen Offen, *European Feminisms, 1700–1950: A Political History* (Stanford: Stanford University Press, 2000), 163.
7. Norway's reluctance to impose a ban on women's night work continued into the twentieth century and has been the subject of several articles. See Gro Hagemann, "Protection or Equality? Debates on Protective Legislation in Norway," in *Protecting Women: Labor Legislation in Europe, the United States, and Australia, 1880–1920* (Urbana: University of Illinois Press, 1995); Ida Blom, "A Double Responsibility: Women, Men, and Socialism in Norway," in *Women and Socialism, Socialism and Women: Europe Between the Two World Wars* (New York: Berghahn Books, 1998).
8. Ulla Wikander, "'Some Kept the Flags of Feminist Demands Waving': Debates at International Congresses on Protecting Women Workers," in *Protecting Women: Labor Legislation in Europe, the United States, and Australia, 1880–1920* (Urbana: University of Illinois Press, 1995), 37.
9. Taylor Allen, *Feminism and Motherhood*, 66.
10. Kathleen Canning examines this in the German case in: *Languages of Labor and Gender: Female Factory Work in Germany, 1850–1914* (Ann Arbor: University of Michigan, 2002), 170–200.

54 A. M. PETERSON

11. In Norway, this focus on maternal health was a part of a larger public health project that the state had been involved in since the 1860s. For a discussion of the development of a public health agenda see Aina Schiøtz, *Det offentlige helsevesen i Norge – Folkets helse – landets styrke 1850–2003* (Oslo: Universitetsforlaget, 2003).

12. Charlotte Borst, *Catching Babies: The Professionalization of Childbirth, 1870–1920* (Cambridge, MA: Harvard University Press, 1995). For the Norwegian context see: Kristina Kjærheim, *Mellom kloke koner og kvitkledde menn: Jordmorvesenet på 1800-tallet* (Oslo: Det Norske Samlaget, 1987), 93–102; Ida Blom, *"Den haarde dyst" Fødsler og fødselshjelp gjennom 150 år* (Oslo: Cappelen, 1988), 183–191.

13. Midwifery textbooks emphasized that while midwives should try to ensure the health and survival of the child, the baby was always second to the mother. For example, doctors educated midwives in how to support the birthing woman and assist her during labor and delivery, but little attention was paid to how to care for the child once it was born. See Edvard Schønberg, *Lærebog for jordmødre* (Kristiania: Aschehoug, 1897).

14. Blom, *"Den haarde dyst,"* 60.

15. Sølvi Sogner, ed., *I gode og vonde dagar: Familieliv i Noreg frå reformasjonen til vår tid* (Oslo: Det Norske Samlaget, 2003), 179; Anne Løkke, *Døden i barndommen: Spædbørnsdødlighed og moderniseringsprocesser i Danmark, 1800–1920* (Copenhagen: Gyldendal, 1998), 31; Margunn Skjei Knudtsen, "Fra frelse til helse': spedbarnsdødelighet og omsorgssyn i Norge ca. 1700–1830 med særlig vekt på forholdene i Vår Frue sokn, Trondheim" (PhD diss., Norges teknisk-nat.vit. Univ., 1997), 210.

16. Infant mortality rates did increase from 14.5% in rural areas and 24.3% in cities in 1876 to 16.1% and 28.3%, respectively, by 1900. See Nicolai Rygg, "Om børn, fødte udenfor ægteskab," Norges officielle statistik nr. 37 (Kristiania: Aschehoug, 1907), 41.

17. Daniel E. Thiery, *Polluting the Sacred: Violence, Faith and the 'Civilizing' of Parishioners in Late Medieval England* (Boston: Brill, 2009), 71; Beth Kreitzer, *Reforming Mary: Changing Images of the Virgin Mary in Lutheran Sermons of the Sixteenth Century* (Oxford: Oxford University Press, 2004), 67–68.

18. Dr. R. Temesvery, "Omsorg av fattige Barselkvinner," *Tidsskrift for Jordmødre*, August 1, 1896, 96–97.

19. Gro Hagemann, "De stummes leir? 1800–1900," in *Med kjønnsperspektiv på norsk historie: fra vikingtid til 2000-årsskiftet*, eds. Ida Blom og Sølvi Sogner (Oslo: Cappelen Akademisk Forlag, 1999), 170–171; Harald Beyer and Edvard Beyer, *Norsk litteraturhistorie* (Oslo: Aschehoug, 1978), 241–242.

"WHAT NATURE ITSELF DEMANDS:" THE DEVELOPMENT OF MATERNITY... 55

20. Novelists also turned the public's attention to the issue of women who committed neonaticide. Henrik Wergeland published *Barnemordersken* (*The Child Murderess*) in 1835, Ragnhild Jølsen wrote *Rikka Gan* in 1904 and Knut Hamsun's *Markens Grøde* (*The Growth of the Soil*) won the Nobel Prize in Literature in 1920.

21. Den norske straffelov, 3. Juni 1874, kapittel 14, §16.

22. "Foredrag holdt i Kvindesagsforeningen i Trondhjem den 27de. Marts," *Nylænde*, May 1, 1890, 134.

23. "Foredrag holdt i Kvindesagsforeningen i Trondhjem den 27de. Marts," *Nylænde*, May 1, 1890, 135.

24. *Nylænde*, June 15, 1890, 186–187.

25. Norwegian fathers had been obliged to pay child support for their illegitimate children since 1763, but it was fairly easy for a man to avoid these regulations.

26. Anna Caspari Agerholt, *Den norske kvinnebevegelsens historie* (Oslo: Gyldendal, 1973), 117–118.

27. Statsarkivet i Oslo, Underfogden i Christiania, dokumenter til saksjournalene nr. 44 (510–661) 1900–1915.

28. Letter from Karen Pederstuen to Lensmann, September 25, 1900. Statsarkivet i Oslo, Underfogden i Christiania, dokumenter til saksjournalene nr. 44 (510–661) 1900–1915.

29. This is out of a population of around 1.5 million in 1855 and 1.8 million in 1875. Sentral statitisk byrå, Folketelling 1900. Also in Bernt Hertel-Aas, *Den sosiale og politiske bakgrunn for Norges første fabriktilsynslov, loven av 1892* (Oslo: Nasjonal Samlings Rikstrykkeri, 1944), 12.

30. Edvard Bull, *Arbeiderklassen i Norsk historie, annen utgave* (Oslo: Tiden Norsk Forlag, 1948), 60–82.

31. Eivind Falkum, "Makt og opposisjon i norsk arbeidsliv" (PhD diss., University of Oslo, 2008), 176.

32. Øyvind Bjørnson and Inger Elisabeth Haavet, *Langsomt ble landet et velferdssamfunn: Trygdens historie, 1894–1994* (Oslo: Ad Notam Gyldendal, 1994), 18.

33. Jens Arup Seip, *Utsikt over Norges historie* (Oslo: Gyldendal Forlag, 1981), 126.

34. England was the first Western European country to industrialize and the first to enact restrictions on children's work in the textile industry in 1802. This initial law was expanded to encompass more people and industries in 1833, 1844, 1867 and 1878.

35. Lov angaaende Bergværksdriften, 14 juli 1842; Lov om Indskrænkning af Arbeidstiden i Bagerier, 17 juni 1885; Lov om Sundhedscommissioner og om Foranstaltninger i Anledning af epidemiske og smittsomme Sygdomme, 16 mai 1860.

56 A. M. PETERSON

36. Stein Evju, "Arbeidsrettshistoriske notater: om fabrikktilsysnslovene av 1892 og 1909 og arbeiderbeskyttelsesloven av 1915 – særlig om helsevernreglene," *Stensilserie*, no. 31 (Oslo: Institutt for offentlig rett, University of Oslo, 1979), 2–3.
37. St. prp. Nr. 82, 1885, 1.
38. The agrarian elite were interested in decreasing poverty relief because this was paid through local land taxes. When people migrated from rural areas to the city, many of those who endured economic hardship were still entitled to poverty relief from their home municipality. This meant that large landowners were significantly burdened economically by problems wrought by mass urbanization and industrialization. Agrarian interests were also involved in development of early Danish welfare policies for this same reason. See: Peter Baldwin, *The Politics of Social Solidarity: Class Bases of the European Welfare States, 1875–1975* (Cambridge: Cambridge University Press, 1990).
39. Hertel-Aas, *Den sosiale og politiske bakgrunn for Norges første fabriktilsynslov*, 69.
40. Quoted in Halvdan Koht, *Johan Sverdrup*, vol. III (Kristiania: Aschehoug & Co., 1925), 170.
41. This also led many politicians to think strategically about future voting constituencies.
42. Øyvind Bjørnson and Inger Elisabeth Haavet, *Langsomt ble landet et velferdssamfunn*, 29.
43. Alice Kessler-Harris, *In Pursuit of Equity: Women, Men, and the Quest for Economic Citizenship in 20th Century America* (Oxford: Oxford University Press, 2001), 34.
44. Arbeiderkomissionens Indstilling I 1888, 31–32.
45. Castberg had an active role in a radical wing of *Venstre* called *Arbeidersamfund* or *Arbeiderdemokratene*. While not socialist, *Arbeiderdemokratene* represented the interests of workers and small landholders.
46. Politicians around Europe had similar difficulties reconciling their eagerness to decrease infant mortality with the deprivation of women's rights. For a discussion of the English context, see Carolyn Malone, *Women's Bodies and Dangerous Trades in England, 1880–1914* (Woodbridge, Suffolk: Boydell Press, 2003).
47. Stortingsforhandlinger 1892, Odelstinget, ot. prp 26, "Utfærdigelse af en lov om tilsyn med arbeide i fabriker §21," vol. 3b, 6.
48. Stortingsforhandlinger 1892, Forhandlinger i Odelstinget, nr. 66, "Ang. lov om tilsyn med arbeide i fabriker §21," vol. 8, 549.
49. Stortingsforhandlinger 1892, Forhandlinger i Odelstinget, nr. 66, 549–550.

"WHAT NATURE ITSELF DEMANDS:" THE DEVELOPMENT OF MATERNITY... 57

50. Stortingsforhandlinger 1892, Forhandlinger i Odelstinget, nr. 66, "Ang. lov om tilsyn med arbeide i fabriker §21," vol. 8, 549.
51. The final vote in Parliament passed with 14 votes for the section as written.
52. Ida Blom, "Barselkvinnen mellom befolkningspolitikk, sosialpolitikk og kvinnepolitikk fra 1880-årene til 1940," *Historisk tidsskrift* 2 (1982), 150.
53. Prior to this date Norwegian women had been very active in philanthropic and temperance societies, but 1884 marked the creation of the first women's organization devoted to achieving women's economic, social and political rights. See Birgitta Jordansson and Tinne Vammen, eds., *Charitable women: Philanthropic welfare 1780–1930: A Nordic and Interdisciplinary Anthology* (Odense: Odense University Press, 1998).
54. Ida Blom, "Modernity and the Norwegian Women's Movement from the 1880s to 1914: Changes and Continuities," in *Women's Emancipation Movements in the Nineteenth Century: A European Perspective*, eds. Sylvia Paletschek and Bianka Pietrow-Ennker (Stanford: Stanford University Press, 2004), 130.
55. "Samme arbeide, samme lønn," *Nylænde* March 1, 1888.
56. For a discussion of the different uses of the term feminism and efforts to clarify types of feminism, see Karen Offen, "Defining Feminism: A Comparative Historical Approach," *Signs: Journal of Women in Culture and Society* 14, no. 1 (1988): 119–157; Karen Offen, *European Feminism, 1700–1950: A Political History* (Stanford, CA: Stanford University Press, 2000); Gisela Bock and Susan James, eds., *Beyond Equality and Difference: Citizenship, Feminist Politics, Female Subjectivity* (London: Routledge, 1992).
57. Gina Krog remained an active member of the NKF even after she started the National Association for Women's Suffrage.
58. Gro Hagemann, "Protection or Equality?," 273.
59. "Forskjelligt," *Nylænde*, January 15, 1888, 27.
60. "Børn og kvinder," *Nylænde*, July 15, 1892, 183.
61. "Særskilt arbeidslovgivning for kvinder," *Nylænde*, June 1, 1899.
62. "Børn og kvinder," *Nylænde*, 184.
63. Offen, *European Feminisms*, 235.
64. "Børn og kvinder," *Nylænde*, 183.
65. Equal rights feminists did not oppose maternity leave legislation, but over time they did start to advocate for its compensation. This is something we will come back to in later chapters.
66. "Om underholdningsbidrag under svangerskabet," *Nylænde*, October 1, 1897, 257.
67. "De uægte barn og vor lovgivning," *Nylænde*, May 15, 1902, 151.

58 A. M. PETERSON

68. "Om underholdningsbidrag under svangerskabet," *Nylænde*, October 1, 1897, 257.
69. Thea Ebbell, "Ugifte mødre," *Nylænde*, July 1, 1901, 200–201.
70. Ida Blom also came to similar conclusions in her survey of women's involvement in maternity legislation in "Barselkvinnen mellom befolkningspolitikk, sosialpolitikk og kvinnepolitikk," 153.
71. Reglement for Gjordemodervæsenet, Indretning og Bestyrelse i begge Riger, 1810.
72. Now the emphasis was on a woman and her child's physical wellbeing instead of their spiritual health. See: Tora Korsvold, *Sykehusfødselen tar form: med en nærstudie av E.C. Dahls stiftelse* (Oslo: Abstrakt Forlag, 2001), 33.
73. It is not known exactly why this portion of the law was revised, but some scholars think it may have to do with liberalization of other laws that took place around the same time. Korsvold, *Sykehusfødselen tar form*, 36.
74. Part of the reasoning behind this was that midwives should be married women with a husband to support them. The reality was that many midwives were widows or unmarried women.
75. Ingeborg Holthe, "Letter to the editor," *Tidsskrift for jordmødre*, February 1, 1898, 96.
76. Kristina Kjærheim, *Mellom kloke koner og kvitkledde menn*, 33.
77. Ida Blom, "*Den haarde dyst*," 44–45.
78. Part of this was due to a dearth of educated midwives in the beginning, but economic concerns were also at play here. In 1898 the state only covered 2/5ths of the costs of publicly-employed midwives' salary. The rest was left to local authorities. Of course, even if a district did try to hire a midwife many midwives did not want to move to remote areas. Northern Norway remained especially in need of educated midwives throughout the 1800s.
79. Dorthea Efraimsen, "En Jordmoders Tilbageblik ved Utrædelsen af sit Kald," *Tidsskrift for jordmødre*, April 1, 1896, 40.
80. Fru Klaveness, "Lidt om Jordmødrenes økonomiske Kaar og sociale Stilling," *Tidsskrift for jordmødre*, February 1, 1896, 17.
81. "Atter om jordmødrenes kaar," *Nylænde*, April 15, 1898, 120.
82. "Et kvinde-og arbeiderspørsmål," *Nylænde*, March 1, 1897, 59.
83. Ibid.
84. "Et kvinde-og arbeiderspørsmål," *Nylænde*, February 1, 1897; "Et kvinde-og arbeiderspørsmål," *Nylænde*, March 1, 1897, 59; "I anledning artikkelen et kvinde-og arbeiderspørsmål," *Nylænde*, March 1, 1897, 65.
85. This number steadily decreased and just after World War Two it was 1 for every 1000 births. Blom, "*Den haarde dyst*," 216.

"WHAT NATURE ITSELF DEMANDS:" THE DEVELOPMENT OF MATERNITY...   59

86. Siv Frøydis Berg, *Den unge Karl Evang og utvidelsen av helsebegrepet. En idehistorisk fortelling om sosialmedisinens fremvekst i nork mellomkrigstid* (Oslo: Solum Forlag, 2002), 32.

87. Fru Klaveness, "Lidt om Jordmødrenes økonomiske Kaar og sociale Stilling," *Tidsskrift for jordmødre*, February 1, 1896, 19.

88. Blom, "*Den haarde dyst,*" 216.

89. Blom, "*Den haarde dyst,*" 69.

90. It is worth noting that Sweden had an even fewer number of doctors per inhabitant than Norway. In 1900 Sweden had half the ratio of doctors to inhabitants that Norway had. Ida Blom, "*Den haarde dyst,*" 68.

91. "Fra et grænsedistrikt," *Tidsskrift for jordmødre*, May 1, 1899, 59.

92. In fact, a delivery by forceps was still a very risky procedure. From 1881 to 1890 the average mortality for mothers was 3 per 100 births with the use of forceps and 13 per 100 for babies. Blom, "*Den haarde dyst,*" 223.

93. Bergen was one of the few places that doctors taught midwives how to deliver a baby through the use of forceps in the nineteenth century.

94. In 1902 (the first year we have comprehensive data) midwives attended 78% of all births in Norway. P.M. Drejer, "Om dødeligheden paa barselseng i Norge," *Norsk Magasin for Lægevidenskaben* (1907): 600.

95. Kjærheim, *Mellom kloke koner og kvitkledde menn*, 67–68.

96. The Worker Commission reported in 1888 that out of the 51,617 industrial workers 8079 of them were women.

97. Arbeiderkommissionens Indstilling I, 1888, Table II, 14.

98. By 1907 there were 14 women's labor unions with 700 members. Kirsten Hofseth, "Fra stemmerettskrav til kvinneregjering: et historisk studiehefte" (Oslo: Det norske arbeiderpartiet, 1988), 5.

99. Ida Blom and Sølvi Sogner, *Med kjønnsperspektiv på norsk historie: Fra vikingtid til 2000-årsskiftet* (Oslo: Cappelen Akademisk Forlag, 1999), 391.

100. Det Statistiske Centralbureau, "Om uægte fødte børn," *Statistiske Meddelelser* 1889, 199.

101. Nicolai Rygg, "Om børn, fødte udenfor ægteskab," Norges officielle statistik nr. 37 (Kristiania: Aschehoug, 1907), 24.

102. Stortingsforhandlinger 1914, Ot prp. nr. 5, "Om utfærdigelse av lover om barn, født utenfor ekteskap," Bilag, Forskjelliger statistiske oplysninger om barn født utenfor ekteskap, 139.

103. Enforcement difficulties had been acknowledged in the parliamentary discussion of the maternity clause. This is one of the reasons they voted for a reduction in the amount of time a woman should refrain from work as long as a doctor gave her medical clearance.

104. Arbeiderkommissionens Indstilling I, 1888, Table II, 14.

105. Betzy Kjelsberg was hired in 1909 as Norway's first woman factory inspector. There are no numbers for these early years but in 1910 and

60 A. M. PETERSON

1911 factory inspectors found 3 women in violation of the maternity prohibition. This represented 0.02% of all cited infractions. It is unlikely that this was because no women continued to work after giving birth. As we will see in later chapters, legislators and doctors continued to mourn the fact that so many women refused to follow the legal guidelines for postpartum work.

106. Unfortunately I have been unable to find statistics for this early time period of maternity legislation. Yet even after maternity leave was compensated through the national health insurance and other significant policies for poor mothers were implemented, many mothers returned to work soon after giving birth. In 1919 for example, nearly 40% of unmarried mothers in Kristiania resumed waged labor within six weeks of giving birth. Oslo helseråd årsberetning 1919, Oslo byarkiv.

107. Stortingsforhandlinger 1892, Forhandlinger i Odelstinget, nr. 66, 549–550.

108. Dr. R. Temesvery, "Omsorg av fattige Barselkvinner," *Tidsskrift for jordmødre*, August 1, 1896, 96–97.

109. Anne-Lise Seip, *Sosialhjelpstaten blir til: Norsk sosialpolitikk 1740–1920* (Oslo: Gyldendal Norsk Forlag, 1994), 140.

110. Although no more information is given, it is reasonable to assume that pregnancy and childbirth would have been included under the category of "illness:" Seip, *Sosialhjelpstaten blir til*, 142.

111. As poverty relief was now mainly paid for through taxes, municipalities wanted to avoid giving any support to non-residents. Seip, *Sosialhjelpstaten blir til*, 148–150.

112. Lina Larsen to Lensmann, July 25 1900, in Underfogden i Christiania, dokumenter til saksjournalene nr. 44 (Oslo: Statsarkivet, 1900–1915), 510–661.

113. Statsarkivet i Oslo, Underfogden i Christiania, dokumenter til saksjournalene nr. 44 (510–661) 1900–1915.

114. Inger Elisabeth Haavet, "Milk, Mothers, Marriage: Family Policy Formation in Norway and its Neighbouring Countries in the Twentieth Century," in *The Nordic Model of Welfare: A Historical Reappraisal*, eds. Neils Finn Christiansen, Klaus Petersen, Nils Edling, and Per Haave (Copenhagen: Museum Tusculanum Press, 2005), 193.

115. "Et kvinde-og arbeiderspørsmål," *Nylænde*, February 1, 1897, 29.

116. There continued to be fights between midwives and local poverty boards over this issue. When a woman couldn't afford to pay for childbirth assistance then the poverty board was supposed to reimburse midwives for their services. Often midwives had trouble recovering the money. For example, in 1899 midwives in Kristiania threatened to stop giving help to poor women unless the poverty board raised the rate of reimbursement. *Tidsskrift for jordmødre*, June 14, 1899.

CHAPTER 3

"For the Health of the People:" Public Health and the Compensation of Maternity Leave in the 1910s

Anne Marie Ellingsdatter Høidal was jailed just two days after giving birth under suspicion of having killed her newborn baby in August 1919.[1] The chaplain at the jail, Peder Christensen, published her account in the Bergen newspaper in order to garner political attention to what he believed was an unjust practice.[2] He strongly objected to jailing a woman who had just given birth because "everyone knows that a parturient woman needs care, antiseptic, clean medical attention, a midwife, rest, and good nutrition." Christensen then asked women's rights activists, more generally, and M.P. Johan Castberg, specifically, to lobby for penal reform so that no woman could be jailed until she was "healed" from giving birth.[3]

His appeal worked and just two years later the revised penal code precluded any woman from being jailed during the last six weeks of her pregnancy and the first six weeks after giving birth. In addition, a breastfeeding mother was not supposed to be arrested before nine months had passed since the child's birth.[4] These revisions to the Norwegian penal code demonstrate how politically effective it had become to draw connections between maternity and public health. By 1919 maternity leave had become accepted as an elemental part of "civilized" society, necessary to the health and vitality of a nation. Statesmen were willing to pass legislation that expanded the concept of maternity leave far beyond the boundaries of sickness insurance and factory laws. Now even women suspected of breaking

© The Author(s) 2018

A. M. Peterson, *Maternity Policy and the Making of the Norwegian Welfare State, 1880–1940*, https://doi.org/10.1007/978-3-319-75481-9_3

the law could benefit from parturiency, not monetarily, but by being able to delay the start of their jail sentences. In some cases, a woman who had recently given birth could avoid jail for up to nine months after committing a crime.

The success of the 1921 penal reform built on the work Johan Castberg and his sister-in-law, Katti Anker Møller, had completed six years prior. In 1915, under the leadership of Møller, social reformers pushed through a comprehensive addition to the Sickness Insurance Law that provided paid maternity leave and birthing assistance to working-class women and expanded the Factory Act. In these proposals Møller and Castberg used a different tactic than they would for the other laws they helped pass in 1915, the laws on children born outside of marriage. As will be discussed in the next chapter, for the laws on children born outside of marriage, Møller and Castberg emphasized the benefit the laws would have on children. In comparison, for the revisions to the Sickness Insurance Laws, Møller and Castberg utilized developments in the medical management of maternity and the public health movement to demand greater maternity benefits for women. They argued that maternity benefits would not only increase children's wellbeing, but also improve women's health, ultimately securing the health of the nation.

Katti Anker Møller has often been described in the historiography as "the champion of mothers."[5] A maternalist feminist, Møller would come to dedicate her life to the improvement of the lives of mothers as she saw it. Born in 1868 to prominent parents who emphasized the importance of leading an open and active life, Møller grew up in an environment devoted to radical liberalism, women's rights and public education.[6] Her interest in the conditions of motherhood developed at an early age. Møller's own mother birthed ten children and died at the age of fifty. Her mother's death, along with traveling to France as a young woman, deeply affected Møller.[7] She would become intensely involved in many of the movements related to motherhood at the time, including hygienic initiatives and the women's rights movement. A woman of the upper class with extensive political connections, Møller may have been a radical, but her ideas were deeply rooted in classed expectations of women. She believed that mothers should be rewarded by the state for their services, but that these benefits should be contingent on mothers fulfilling rigorous standards of child rearing and household cleanliness (Fig. 3.1).

Fig. 3.1 Portrait of Katti Anker Møller by Eivind Enger, 1916. Courtesy of the Norwegian Museum of Science and Technology

Møller's sister had married Johan Castberg, and he and Møller's shared political interests along with their close family connection brought the two of them together during the early twentieth century to push for greater rights for mothers and children. Johan Castberg had important political connections and held a number of high ranking political positions in the course of his career. Educated as a lawyer, Castberg would come to serve the court as a barrister, district magistrate, and eventually Supreme Court Justice during his life time. He was also very active in politics and the leader of *Arbeiderdemokratene* (The Radical People's Party).[8] In 1900 Castberg was elected to parliament as a representative for this party and spent most of the rest of his life as an M.P. Castberg's passion for social

Fig. 3.2 Portrait of Johan Castberg by Ernest Rude, 1921. Courtesy of the Oslo Museum

issues also led to his appointment as Norway's first Minister of Social Affairs in 1913. In addition, he served as Minister of Justice from 1908 to 1910.[9] Due to Castberg's powerful political positions and connections, he was able to place many of the issues he and Møller cared about, such as maternity benefits and illegitimate children's rights, on the political agenda (Fig. 3.2).

In 1915, Castberg and Møller successfully took the punitive maternity leave mandated in the 1892 Factory Act and transformed it into a paid, broadly defined issue of national importance. This work aided in the positioning of maternity leave compensation as a benefit rather than assistance. It placed maternity leave within the realm of the developing welfare state, which focused on the rights of citizens rather than the old welfare model of public assistance, which emphasized charity and worthiness. As such, 1915 was a pivotal year in the development of Norwegian maternity legislation. By 1916, maternity leave in Norway was compensated, had expanded in length, and included paid birthing assistance available to both working women and working-class housewives.

Due to the implications this legislation had for the improvement of women's economic rights, Castberg and Møller were also able to gain more support from women's rights activists and midwives. Feminists and midwives contributed to Castberg and Møller's efforts to classify pregnancy and childbirth as an illness and frame greater maternity benefits for women as a public health matter. As a result, the concept of maternity leave became germane to social issues far beyond their original conceptualization in the 1892 Factory Protection Act. While the results of this are most evident in the inclusion of comprehensive maternity benefits in the 1915 Sickness Insurance Law, they are also reflected in Peder Christensen's 1919 belief that even accused women "required" maternity leave from serving jail time.

The development of paid maternity leave in Norway followed a general Western European trend of compensating women for wages lost during the period of time surrounding childbirth. While most Western European countries began compensating maternity in the years leading up to the First World War, who was eligible for the benefit, the types of benefits available, and how the benefit was funded varied from country to country. Germany was the first country to introduce maternity support for mandated maternity leave through a contributory workers' insurance system in 1883. This provision included medical assistance as well as financial compensation for maternity leave for insured women workers. Both unmarried and married workers were eligible so long as they fulfilled the insurance membership requirements.[10] Starting in 1911 Britain granted a lump sum maternity benefit through the National Health Insurance Act to both directly insured women and the wives of insured men. The amount given was supposed to cover the medical costs of childbirth as doctor, nurse, or midwifery assistance was not included separately. Unmarried British women were excluded from eligibility for the first seven years of their employment.[11] Due in part to heightened population concerns, France had the most comprehensive and extensive maternity benefits of all European countries in 1913.[12] French family allowances and maternity assistance was available for both married and unmarried mothers and was paid through tax revenues rather than contributory insurance systems.

The maternity insurance created in Norway during the 1910s was not particularly innovative or original compared to its Western European counterparts, but it was more comprehensive than the British and German contributory forms of maternity insurance. This is perhaps surprising given the fact that the often-cited reasons for maternity compensation during this period were absent in Norway. Norway did not participate in World War One nor did it have a particularly strong population policy movement.[13] Instead, Norway's recent status as a newly independent nation allowed reformers to successfully tie the need for maternity provisions to a burgeoning public health movement. Passed a few years after British and German maternity insurance, in 1915, the Norwegian variant combined elements from British and German models. Norwegian insurance provided free midwifery assistance and maternity compensation to both unmarried and married, directly-insured women and the wives of members.

The maternity insurance passed in 1915, though more comprehensive than other European countries, was not particularly innovative. When seen in conjunction with the maternity assistance granted under the Castbergian Children's Laws, however, Norway was offering something different than other European countries by 1915. There were two pathways to accessing Norwegian maternity benefits: maternity assistance funded through tax revenues and contributory workers' maternity insurance. Other countries would not follow suit with similar approaches until the 1930s.[14] In Norway it was the work of women, including Katti Anker Møller, but also midwives, working women and feminist organizations, that contributed to the broader conceptualization and legislation of maternity benefits.

PUBLIC HEALTH AND THE MEDICAL MANAGEMENT OF MATERNITY

In their work to create comprehensive maternity insurance, Norwegian women and other reformers framed maternity leave as something medically necessary and imperative to the health of the nation. This rhetorical framing had its roots in the Norwegian public health movement. The discovery of bacteria and medical practitioners' acceptance of germ theory in the 1880s fueled this movement and reformers promised that new methods would both prevent illness and save lives.[15] Their ideas influenced the development of nascent government healthcare programs and promised that preventative measures would lead to a healthier population.[16] Civil servants, including doctors, often took the lead in these efforts. Already in 1860 the government had set up municipal health councils in an effort to educate the masses about new hygienic measures. Doctors led these councils and used them to spread medical knowledge and prevent outbreaks of disease.[17]

Antepartum care was a vital component of public health initiatives across Europe and the United States during the first few decades of the twentieth century. Reformers promised that if the state provided women with the resources necessary to birth their children in clean and sanitary environments, breastfeed for as long as possible, and properly attend to and care for infants and young children, then child health and welfare would be secured.

This was welcome news to Norwegian statesmen and capitalists. Politicians at the time were concerned with creating a strong and healthy nation that could gain independence from Sweden and thrive. Industrial capitalists needed workers that could withstand the rigorous and often dangerous demands of factory work. As a result, politicians looked upon the ability to decrease the presence and severity of disease, especially ones that affected mothers and children, with great interest.

The public health movement was closely tied to the work of social scientists. Statisticians and demographers catalogued birth and death rates and detailed the prevalence of illnesses across different population groups. Often the statistics they presented instilled fear in prominent members of society, bolstering the work of public health reformers.

When it came to mother and child welfare, studies of infant mortality rates were particularly salient. In 1907 social scientist and future director of the Central Statistical Agency, Nicolai Rygg, published a report on infant mortality rates that concluded illegitimate children were twice as likely to die within the first year of life as children born to married parents.[18] While illegitimate children may have had a higher rate of infant mortality than children born in wedlock, Norway's combined infant mortality rate for illegitimate and legitimate children was significantly lower than most other European countries. Still, Rygg's findings alarmed Norwegian politicians who were concerned with building a new nation state.[19]

Rygg's report led to increased political focus on mothers and their children and further strengthened the idea that parturient women's health was of the utmost importance to the health of infants. He connected high infant mortality rates to the rate at which women placed their children in care outside the home. He also stressed the importance of hygienic living conditions for pregnant and postpartum women as directly correlated to infant health.

These claims reflected and reinforced the growing importance doctors, statisticians, and politicians had started placing on women's pregnant and postpartum bodies. Between 1880 and 1920 there was a dramatic increase in the medicalization of pregnancy and childbirth. Previously, pregnant women had been told that they could live their lives as usual and that women knew best how to care for their children. This reflected the belief that pregnancy and childbirth were natural phenomenon and that women themselves were authorities on these subjects.[20] The establishment of medical specialties like gynecology and obstetrics changed attitudes toward pregnancy, childbirth, and what were often referred to as "women's illnesses."[21] The theoretical and clinical scrutiny of women's reproductive processes led medical men to conclude that pregnancy and childbirth were not natural, but rather medical conditions that warranted medical supervision.[22]

By the 1910s the idea that pregnancy was pathological was largely accepted by medical practitioners. This shift in thinking about pregnancy and childbirth is reflected in the director of the maternity hospital, Dr. Professor Kristian Brandt's, textbook on midwifery published in 1913. While Brandt still asserted that pregnancy and childbirth were "natural" he warned that women who were pregnant or had recently given birth "hover[ed] between health and illness."[23]

To alleviate the threat posed by pregnancy and childbirth, doctors advocated the use of scientific management concepts and implemented hygienic approaches to pregnancy, childbirth and infant care.[24] These medical dictates and recommended care regimens often focused on maintaining rigorous cleanliness standards and routines that few working-class women would have been able to follow because of poor working-class housing conditions and the time demands of industrial work life.[25]

While doctors were mainly concerned with the effect pregnancy had on women's health, they also started to pay more attention to infant care and wellbeing in the early twentieth century. As a result, breastfeeding gained new importance.[26] Previously, doctors had had a much more relaxed approach to breastfeeding that largely left it up to women to decide how to best feed their babies. For example, prior to 1900, Norwegian doctors had emphasized that breast milk was the best nutrition for infants, but had also provided instructions on safe alternatives. Medical instructions included advice on how to choose suitable wet nurses and the best methods for sanitizing cow's milk and preparing bottles. These instructions largely left the subject of how often or how much breast milk an infant should receive up to the mother.

When Brandt wrote his midwifery textbook in 1913 the belief that women knew how to best feed their babies had changed. Brandt asserted that breast milk was the only suitable form of nutrition for a child and that this breast milk should not come from a wet nurse, but rather needed to come from the child's own mother. To Brandt, a child had a right to his/her mother's milk. Brandt also recommended strict rules for breastfeeding, including feeding the child on a schedule of every three hours for a period of nine months.[27] This regimen was to protect the health and character of the infant to make sure it was not only well-fed but also disciplined.

The medicalization of maternity and infant care was partially fueled by the state's growing interests in women's reproductive health and child welfare. As pregnant women and infants gained more political significance, doctors' knowledge of pregnancy, childbirth and infant care became even more valuable. Doctors became the recognized experts on parturient women and were seen as allies in the fight to decrease infant mortality and improve the overall health of the population. Midwifery also became more politically significant during the first decades of the twentieth century. Even though midwives did not possess the same theoretical and clinical understanding of maternity, they were often the only trained medical representatives in isolated areas of the country and were most often the ones who attended birthing women. The state needed midwives to embrace modern hygienic practices and ensure that parturient women and their children remained healthy. With these increased demands, midwives hoped a commitment to improve midwives' salaries and working conditions would also follow.

FEMINISTS AND THE FIGHT FOR GREATER MATERNITY PROVISIONS IN THE NATIONAL SICKNESS INSURANCE LAW

A national Sickness Insurance Law promised to help alleviate many pressing public health issues, including maternal and child welfare. As early as 1887 the Workers' Commission had recommended that a national health insurance scheme be created alongside the Factory Act. While parliament put any serious discussion of such a law on hold until 1907, activists and reformers continued to push for a national Sickness Insurance Law that included a compensatory mechanism for maternity leave. In 1896 a parliamentary committee noted that much of the distress a parturient woman faced would be alleviated with the passage of a law on health insurance for workers.[28]

In spite of these calls for action, lawmakers continued to drag their feet on the issue and feminist organizations like the *Norsk kvinnesaksforening*, or Norwegian Association for Women's Rights (NKF), worked to influence discussions of health insurance and ensure maternity benefits were included in any proposed legislation. As a liberal political organization focused on equal rights for women, the NKF was particularly concerned with women's legal and economic rights. Not surprisingly then, in 1903 activists in the NKF protested that the Factory Protection Act's maternity clause infringed on a woman's freedom to earn a living and pushed for a woman's right to compensation during the six weeks she was prohibited from working.[29] The NKF argued that the best way to solve the issue of compensation for parturient women workers was through the creation of obligatory health insurance funds.

In their work to include maternity leave compensation in a sickness insurance law, the NKF recognized the political utility of having pregnancy and childbirth classified as an illness. They stressed in their writings on the subject that maternity was an illness and as such should be covered under any health insurance legislation passed.[30] One of Norway's first women doctors, Dagny Bang, helped shape these discussions about maternity leave and health insurance in several articles she wrote for the NKF's publication, *Nylænde*. In 1908 Bang wrote a piece supporting mandated maternity leave as a "matter of course" even while vehemently opposing all other special protections for women such as prohibitions on night work. Bang argued that the content of the maternity leave clause in the Factory Act was something she "completely agree[d] with" but that the entire paragraph would be better placed in a sickness insurance law.[31] Bang believed that maternity leave was less about protections in the workplace and more about the safeguarding of women's and children's health. This assertion reinforced the association between maternity and sickness.

In this way, members of the NKF contributed to debates about the national Sickness Insurance Law and ensured maternity leave was a part of these discussions. When parliament considered a national health insurance proposal in 1907, Castberg spoke in favor of the inclusion of maternity in the drafted law. He argued that support for parturient working women was perhaps a small piece of the entire legislative initiative, but it was nevertheless an important one. In his speech to Parliament he stressed that it was imperative that health insurance cover maternity leave because "the law itself forbids mothers to work during the time surrounding their confinements."[32] This line of reasoning echoed much of what the NKF had demanded in 1903. Parliament did not pass a Sickness Insurance Law in 1907, but thanks in part to the work of the NKF and Castberg, lawmakers viewed maternity leave as a natural part of proposals for the Sickness Insurance Law moving forward.

When parliament passed the first national Sickness Insurance Law in 1909, provisions for women who were unable to work because of the mandated maternity leave were included. Every insured working woman, regardless of whether she was married or unmarried, could receive six weeks of compensation at 60% of her average daily wage. The benefits were set at the same rate as other illnesses, which kept maternity compensation from being characterized as less important than other types of medical conditions. Additionally, if complications arose because of the delivery, women could receive free assistance from a doctor[33] and if illness occurred after the birth the maternity leave would be considered sick leave, and the woman would be eligible for all of the associated economic and medical benefits.

These benefits did not completely cover the loss of wages a woman suffered because of maternity leave, but they did offset some of the economic burden involved in taking the mandated time off from work after giving birth. More problematic than the gap between lost and covered wages was the stipulation that a woman had to have been a member of the health insurance for an uninterrupted period of ten months prior to having a child in order to receive the benefit. Many women were unable to fulfill this requirement due to the temporary nature of their work and were rendered ineligible to receive the maternity benefit.

The ten-month membership requirement did not go undebated in 1909. Lawmakers had included this requirement to prevent women from purposefully getting pregnant in order to reap financial rewards from the health insurance, a problem they foresaw especially with the voluntary option of health insurance available to some workers. Lars Olsen Sæbø (*Arbeiderparti*, Labor Party) disagreed with this notion and stated that the thought that women would abuse the law by getting pregnant in order to receive the maternity benefit was "ridiculous." He proposed setting the membership requirement at six months, instead of ten, an idea that the rest of Parliament voted down.[34] Parliamentarians clearly wanted safeguards in place to prevent women from unduly benefitting from the insurance.

The other part of the legislative proposal that incurred debate was the fact that unmarried as well as married women could receive compensatory maternity leave so long as they were insured. Lawmakers briefly considered changing this aspect of the law and excluding unmarried women from eligibility for paid maternity leave.[35] Though no one specifically stated the reasoning behind this, it is reasonable to assume that this was for moral reasons. Many other countries, such as the Netherlands, had difficulty passing legislation that could be seen as encouraging or even rewarding women who had sex outside of marriage.[36] In Norway, however, society had begun to view unmarried mothers as victims in need of sympathy and governmental support in the late nineteenth century, and parliamentarians ultimately decided that unmarried women should also be eligible for maternity benefits under the Sickness Insurance Law. In 1909, they came to this conclusion mainly for "the good of the child."[37] This reasoning represented a slight shift of emphasis in thinking about maternity legislation. Instead of women being the primary beneficiary, children were now equally—if not more—important, especially when considering children born outside of marriage. As will be discussed in the next chapter, emphasizing children when considering unmarried women's eligibility for maternity benefits would be instrumental to discussions of assistance for mothers included in the Castbergian Children's Laws.

No other changes were put forth, which suggests that the maternity benefit was not a controversial part of the Sickness Insurance Law by 1909. In particular, parliamentarians agreed with the established idea that maternity qualified as an illness. They referenced recommendations from Surgeon General Michael Holmboe and specialist in gynecology and obstetrics Dr. Kristian Brandt, and pediatrician, Dr. Axel Johannessen, as supporting the need for women to receive compensation for a six-week maternity leave.[38] These medical opinions added legitimacy to this aspect of the proposal and further solidified maternity's classification as an illness.

The political acceptance of a clearly medically defined maternity leave is also reflected in changes proposed to the Factory Act in 1909. The passage of the Sickness Insurance Law allowed a woman to receive six weeks of maternity leave, something that was at odds with the flexible length of maternity leave set in the factory law. As the Factory Act was up for revision in 1909, a minority group suggested that the part of the law that allowed women to return to work four weeks after giving birth with a doctor's approval should be removed. These members referenced the medical community's findings that parturient women needed a minimum of six weeks of rest following childbirth to support this proposed change. Additionally, parliamentarians such as Olav Andreas Eftestøl

(*Arbeiderdemokratene*, Radical People's Party) argued that lawmakers should not allow a woman to cut her maternity leave too short because of the negative effect this could have on her infant's health as well as her own. Eftestøl stressed that high infant mortality rates might be remedied if the law required women to take the medically dictated length of maternity leave.[39]

Eftestøl and his supporters reasoned that the recently passed Sickness Insurance Law would protect women from suffering any undue economic effects caused by a mandated six-week maternity leave. The only voice of dissent came from *Venstre* (Liberal) politician Andreas Hansson. In Hansson's opinion women should not be forbidden from working any longer than an individual doctor determined, because of the fact that women who worked in factories needed to work to survive. The minority group was not swayed by these arguments and reiterated the positive effect a longer maternity leave would have on public health. In the words of Lars Kristian Abrahemsen, parliamentarians needed to establish a six-week minimum maternity leave because "of the significance it held for coming generations."[40]

Ultimately, the majority of the social committee was swayed by the minority group's arguments and altered the factory protection law to include a mandated six-week maternity leave, regardless of whether or not a doctor certified that a woman was physically able to return to work after only four weeks. This was partly due to the fact that the Sickness Insurance Law removed some of the economic burden previously placed on women who followed the compulsory maternity leave. Yet to these politicians of even greater importance than infringing on a woman's ability to earn a living was the effect a longer maternity leave could have on the health of the Norwegian people.

Foremost in their minds was Rygg's report on infant mortality rates and the idea that maternity leave could decrease these rates and strengthen the Norwegian population. As Ludvig Larsen Kragtorp (*Venstre*, Liberal Party) concluded right before the proposal was put to a vote: "We are unfortunately plagued in this country with a disproportionately high infant mortality and one should participate in everything that can be done to change this, [especially] when this can occur with a measure that does not have harsher repercussions than this."[41] Kragtorp was exaggerating. As Rygg detailed in his report, Norway's combined infant mortality rate for illegitimate and legitimate children was, in fact, substantially lower than most other European countries.[42] The politicians had these statistics available, yet they did not use them to argue that Norway's comparatively low rate of infant mortality meant that there was no need for this type of legislation. Instead, politicians argued that even if Norway had a lower rate of infant mortality than other countries, this rate was still too high. Even though the women who qualified for the sickness insurance maternity coverage would receive only 60% of their normal wages and could be fired during their absence, politicians believed that this cost was outweighed by the potential benefits such a law promised for the health of the nation.

Parliament also revised the Factory Act in 1909 to read that any governmental assistance given to parturient women during the mandated maternity leave should not be considered poor relief. This change to the law meant that women who received economic support from local poor relief boards would not be stripped of their right to vote or enter contracts, something that would hold increased importance once women won the vote in Norway in 1913. Parliament passed this portion of the law with little debate, further strengthening women's economic rights as mothers in hopes of bolstering public health.[43]

In 1911 the Sickness Insurance Law was implemented, representing the first time parturient women were eligible to receive compensation for the mandated maternity leave that had been passed nearly twenty years earlier. As a result, maternity leave in principle went from the restriction of a working woman's ability to receive wages to paid time off from industrial labor and domestic service.[44] Women could now take six weeks off of work after giving birth without suffering dire economic consequences. This paid leave enabled women to rest and recover for a period of time after childbirth, during which they could breastfeed and care for their infants. As a result, the insurance legislation promised to accomplish what parliamentarians had hoped, namely, to decrease rates of infant mortality and safeguard parturient women's health.

The Sickness Insurance Law did not achieve the anticipated results. In 1913, the director of Kristiania's health insurance fund, Marius Ormestad, reported that only 481 women had received maternity compensation.[45] This represented little more than 1.5% of the Kristiania (Oslo) health insurance's entire yearly budget.[46] Ormestad credited this with the fact that most working women did not meet the ten-month membership requirement needed to receive the benefit. Many of the women covered by the health insurance worked in seasonal, temporary jobs. Many women also could not, or did not want to, continue to work up until the day of delivery and were either fired or had to quit a few weeks prior to giving birth. This meant that while the Sickness Insurance Law had helped improve the lives of some women, it did not have nearly the impact that legislators had hoped. Most working women continued to endure economic hardships during their confinements and this often meant that they placed their children in foster care and returned to work earlier than the mandated six weeks.

KATTI ANKER MØLLER'S EFFORTS TO EXPAND MATERNITY LEAVE

Feminists were dissatisfied with the underuse of the maternity provisions outlined in the Sickness Insurance Law and used this as an opportunity to try and significantly expand the maternity benefits included in the health insurance and factory protection laws. Katti Anker Møller, in particular, worked to get feminist organizations like the NKF and the Norwegian National Council of Women to adopt her ideas for what she called "mothers' insurance." Møller gave a series of speeches about the Sickness Insurance Law to these women's organizations and engaged the help of Castberg to craft a new proposal on maternity insurance for parliamentary review.

In her speeches, Møller highlighted the effect an expanded maternity insurance could have on the health of the Norwegian people. She related examples from her work at the White Ribbon maternity home to illustrate how poor women often had to resume working soon after giving birth and how their children were not able to receive "natural nutrition." While she credited the six weeks of compensation allowed for under the 1909 Sickness Insurance Law with helping to alleviate some of these issues, she stressed that the leave needed to be extended to two weeks prior to giving birth. She based this on a medical study that found that women who worked up until the day of delivery had babies who weighed less than women who rested for several weeks before giving birth.[47] In addition, Møller emphasized that increasing the length of maternity leave would further decrease infant mortality rates.

Midwives were an essential part of Katti Anker Møller's plan for expanded maternity legislation. As a maternal feminist, Møller thought that motherhood was a way for women to achieve greater social and economic rights and that midwives should be rewarded for the essential role they played in childbirth. This is one of the reasons she tried to further incorporate midwives into maternity legislation. Møller believed that by emphasizing the need for birth to take place in hygienic conditions and under the supervision of a medical expert she could bolster midwives' position in society.

According to Møller, free midwifery should be included in a revised maternity insurance law because midwives would ensure that working-class women gave birth in the best conditions possible. Møller highlighted the medical and social experience a midwife had with her "emphasis on cleanliness and disinfection and her serious attention to the social significance of her work" to tie the need for free midwifery to public health issues. She also argued that midwives could use their training to assess and supervise the parturient woman's home, as she believed working-class women were largely ignorant of issues surrounding childbirth, care, cleanliness and hygiene. Møller wanted midwives to serve the role of public health officials in these households and to educate their inhabitants on the latest sanitation standards. Møller did not believe that this would be easy because, in her estimation, more working-class women resisted the latest teachings on public health and preferred untrained "helping wives" over midwives. It was for exactly this reason that Møller stressed that women must lobby to get free midwifery included in the health insurance, because this would put a stop to the use of helping wives and bolster public health initiatives in poor, working-class homes.[48]

Møller also included maternity homes in her call for a revision to the Sickness Insurance Law. Again, she tied the need for the creation of these homes to the concern for maternal and infant health. Møller claimed that even if midwives delivered working-class women's babies, there would still be situations that not even a midwife's training could solve. Homes where women gave birth in the same room as their other family members and rural cottages were of particular concern to Møller. She asserted that in those cases the health insurance should cover a stay at a maternity home. Midwives could staff these maternity homes and guarantee that all working-class women gave birth in hygienic conditions. As Møller so adamantly put it to women's organizations: "If even one woman has to give birth in unhygienic circumstances then this is a shame for us all."[49]

Møller had connections to the leaders of the *Norske kvinners nasjonalråd*, or Norwegian National Women's Council (NKN), and after listening to her speeches the NKN decided to allow Møller to craft a proposal for these legislative changes on their behalf.[50] The Norwegian Parliament was going to debate revisions to the Sickness Insurance Law in 1912 and the NKN hoped that they could send this recommendation in time for it to be included in the proposal. However, many members of the NKN, which had branches throughout the country, did not immediately agree with Møller's ideas and this delayed the NKN's adoption of Møller's text until 1913.

In the meantime, Møller turned to her brother-in-law, parliamentary representative, and soon-to-be Minister of Social Affairs, Johan Castberg. Møller was already working closely with Castberg on the series of laws that would grant illegitimate children the same rights as legitimate children, and she involved him in her work for expanded maternity provisions as well.[51] Møller was able to use her close relationship with Castberg to gain a parliamentarian's perspective and garner support for her maternity insurance proposal.

Castberg took an active role in assisting Møller's efforts to increase maternity leave provisions. He tried to get Møller to include a section in her proposal that would reduce a woman's reliance on the ten-month membership requirement to receive the insurance benefits. Castberg urged Møller to include a suggestion in her proposal that this requirement be changed to ten months out of the last one and a half years prior to giving birth.[52] Another of Castberg's main recommendations was for Møller to get the support of Drs. Brandt and Johannessen. He believed that their status as experts on maternity and childbirth could bolster Møller's credibility and provide her with statistical evidence for her claims.[53] Doing so would also firmly ground the proposal for maternity insurance in the realm of medicine and public health, in addition to its social implications.

Castberg's work on the drafted legislation ultimately led him to feel quite possessive of the proposal and at one point he stressed to Møller that she must not allow the leader of the NKF, Gina Krog, to commandeer the issue.[54] As leader of the Radical People's Party, it is also likely that Castberg was the one to include "expanded maternity insurance and protection of infants" on their 1912 party platform.[55]

Møller took Castberg's ideas under consideration when she wrote the recommendation that the NKN would finally approve and send to Parliament in February 1913. The NKN recommendation for revision of the Sickness Insurance Law included four main parts: maternity benefits for six weeks following and two weeks prior to a woman giving birth, free midwifery, the creation of maternity homes and extending the benefit to male members' wives.[56] Also mentioned was the need for midwives to examine pregnant women prior to labor and delivery and for working-class women to receive assistance in running their households during confinement. These recommendations were quite comprehensive and represented a substantial increase in the benefits covered by the 1909 Sickness Insurance Law.

In order to justify the amount of changes requested, Møller framed them in terms of the effect they would have on the health of women and children. She claimed that it did not do any good to compensate women for a six-week postpartum maternity leave if they had to work up until the very day they gave birth. This would result in working-class women's children coming "into the world weakened and defenseless." Instead, according to Møller, women who rested for two weeks prior to giving birth would deliver healthier children. Møller also argued that if ensuring the birth of healthy children was the goal, then free midwifery and the creation of maternity homes were also needed. Møller reasoned that just as the "factory laws state that work has to be performed in adequate and hygienic conditions" so too should the Sickness Insurance Laws make certain that other forms of labor also took place in the best conditions possible.[57]

THE RECEPTION OF KATTI ANKER MØLLER'S IDEAS

The Ministry of Social Affairs, with Castberg at its head, reviewed the NKN's proposal in 1913. The Ministry had received the NKN's recommendation and supporting letters from nine other women's organizations.[58] The Ministry of Social Affairs, along with the Ministry of Justice,[59] supported the NKN's recommendations on all counts.[60] These governmental entities were particularly interested in extending the maternity insurance to cover married women through their husbands' health insurance membership. According to them, this part of the proposal held the "greatest social significance, namely, that to give the family and marriage the best possible economic foundations with an eye towards population growth and public health."[61] However, such legislation would precipitate an enormous expansion of the health insurance funds both financially and administratively.

The directors of the national health insurance were quite skeptical of the type of comprehensive maternity legislation the NKN, Ministry of Social Affairs and Ministry of Justice proposed. National sickness insurance had only recently been implemented in 1911 and the leaders of the insurance funds were worried that such legislation would cripple the fund's legitimacy, threaten its economic solvency and burden an already overworked staff.

One of the first things the health insurance funds did was to try and determine exactly how much extra the proposed expansion of maternity insurance would cost and whether this would necessitate raising member premiums. The cost of member premiums were especially important as the majority of the health insurance expenses were member-financed with over half of the funding coming directly from members.[62] Director of the Kristiania fund, Marius Ormestad, took the lead in collecting this data and determined that certain restrictions would have to be put in place so that the expanded benefits would not place undue burdens on the fund and its members. In his estimation, some of the more costly services should be restricted to the directly insured members. For example, Ormestad recommended that stays in maternity homes would cost more money than paying out the maternity leave benefit and should accordingly be offered only to directly insured members, not members' wives.[63]

The cost of free midwifery was another of Ormestad's main concerns. He was worried that midwives would attempt to use the vague language of "free midwifery" to earn as much money as possible. Therefore, he initially thought it best that the funds set a rate for midwifery services that included attendance at the labor and delivery and a predetermined amount of pre- and postpartum visits. This would prevent "misuse" and the "temptation to visit too many times" in order to increase the total midwifery payment.[64]

To help determine the economic impact of free midwifery, Ormestad tried to find out if the implementation of the health insurance in 1911 had led to more doctor-attended births. Under the 1909 Sickness Insurance Law, directly insured women and members' wives had the right to free doctor assistance at a birth if there was necessary medical cause. Ormestad asked four of the doctors in Kristiania who had provided the most birthing assistance to insurance members a series of questions designed to assess whether birthing women had abused their right to medical care once it became free. The doctors' overwhelming responses were that while the insurance had led more women and their families to utilize a doctor's help during childbirth, this was done only in cases where a doctor's surgical training or expertise was needed.[65] In other words, these doctors reported that the health insurance did exactly as it was meant to: it provided necessary medical assistance to people who might not otherwise have been able to afford it. This did not allay Ormestad's fears, however, and he continued to investigate the effect maternity insurance would have on health insurance costs.

Ormestad and other fund managers were not only concerned with the economic costs of the proposed maternity expansions, but also the possible threat to the fund's legitimacy among workers. They were especially concerned that maternity insurance would further anger workers who felt that the obligatory nature of the health insurance, and the premiums it included, were unjust. To many of these men, maternity benefits had no place in the Sickness Insurance Law because they defied the basic principles of insurance. The Sickness Insurance Law had been passed as a way to mitigate the risks a certain group of people, mainly industrial workers, faced. Maternity was not a common risk that all working-class people faced. Only women risked becoming pregnant and suffering the physical consequences of childbirth.

Additionally, many people believed sickness was something erratic and unknown, whilst pregnancy was something inevitable in marriage. As someone quipped in the March 1914 issue of *Sykeforsikringsbladet* (The Health Insurance Magazine), maternity insurance would be like having "theatre insurance to go to the theatre once a year."[66] This had not been as much of an issue with the 1909 insurance law because so few women were eligible members of the health insurance. The proposed inclusion of members' wives, however, threatened to significantly expand maternity benefits and put the entire legitimacy of the Sickness Insurance Law in question.

Møller's inclusion of members' wives in the proposed maternity insurance promised to make the legislation more redistributive than extant types of state-funded insurance schemes and consequently, the National Association of Sickness Insurance Funds thought it should be a separate law. In essence, critics argued that working men's premiums would unfairly benefit working-class women who became pregnant and gave birth. Working men who were either too young or too old to have wives had no chance of reaping any of the rewards of maternity insurance even if their premiums increased as a result. Many leaders of the insurance funds concluded "mothers' insurance was not insurance" and recommended that the government pass a law on mother's insurance that was separate from the Sickness Insurance Law.[67]

The *Arbeiderpartiets kvindeforbund*, or the Women's Federation of the Norwegian Labor Party (AKF), agreed with this idea, but for a very different reason. These representatives of working-class women wanted a separate law outside of the health insurance that provided maternity benefits for all women, not only working-class women. In doing so, they argued against what medical authorities and feminists had so firmly asserted, namely, that parturiency was an illness. They wanted maternity to be seen as a natural condition that all women faced. Due to this fact, they argued that society as a whole should be responsible for the health of mothers and children. To them, maternity insurance was a class insurance that targeted working-class women and forced them to finance their own maternity leave. The AKF wanted the government to take over all of the costs of the maternity benefit, and they believed this would be best accomplished outside the Sickness Insurance Law.[68]

Even if she agreed with the AKF in principle, Møller did not want mothers' insurance to face the political difficulties of being put up as a separate law and fought hard to keep it within the confines of the already-established Sickness Insurance Law. It would have been much more radical to lobby for the passage of a piece of maternity legislation that could perhaps have been expanded to be a universal benefit that all mothers could receive. As much as this would have fit with Møller's larger goals, she knew that it would be much easier to get Parliament to expand the existing maternity clause in the Sickness Insurance Law than for them to create a new legislation that would benefit only mothers.[69]

With this in mind, Møller continued to cultivate support for her proposal from medical experts. She took Castberg's advice and contacted Drs. Kristian Brandt and Axel Johannessen and asked for their endorsements. In the course of their correspondence, Brandt warned Møller that she should "make sure [her efforts to improve the position of midwives did] not lead to midwives' arrogance."[70] Brandt's brash response led Castberg to recommend to Møller that they stop working with him.[71] In contrast to Brandt, Johannessen did not want to get publicly engaged in the issue, but he did speak to the Minister of Justice, Fredrik Stang, about the maternity insurance proposal on Møller's behalf in 1912. He also promised to continue to quietly exert his political influence in 1913.[72]

Brandt's concern about midwives was related to the fact that midwives were central to Møller's vision for maternity insurance and she involved them in the legislative process. Midwives were eager to have the law passed because it promised to improve their professional status and incomes. The Norwegian *Journal of Midwifery* contains many articles and letters to the editor in 1913 and 1914 that discussed the proposed maternity insurance and debated as to how midwives should collectively respond. As one midwife wrote, mothers' insurance and free midwifery would certain help women, particularly those living in cities, but midwives needed to determine how "midwives can benefit

82   A. M. PETERSON

from it."[73] Midwives were particularly concerned about how much money they would receive from the insurance funds, if the law would lead to more work for midwives, and how they could use the legislation to lessen the competition from helping wives.

Through meetings with Castberg and Møller, *Den norske jordmorforening*, or the Norwegian Association of Midwives (DNJ) attempted to shape the debates about the proposed midwifery services. In particular, DNJ impressed upon Castberg the importance of having the insurance funds hire midwives in permanent positions, instead of having privately employed midwives negotiate terms with the health insurance. This would give them greater economic security.[74]

In addition to direct dealings with Castberg and Møller, DNJ also sent a letter of support for the maternity insurance proposal to Parliament in which they emphasized the important impact free midwifery could have "during the critical period of time that childbirth represents, especially for families with few resources."[75] DNJ did not present any specific demands about free midwifery in its recommendation to parliament, and rather trusted Castberg and Møller to champion the issues they had privately discussed.

While Castberg and Møller had their own reasons for including midwives in their health insurance proposal, when it came to the Sickness Insurance Law, Møller and Castberg largely agreed with midwives' demands and incorporated them into their legislative proposals. As Minister of Social Affairs, Castberg had proposed that each district health insurance fund should employ a set midwife to work with its members. He argued that this would help the midwife build relationships with the women in her district. It would also fulfill public health goals, because the midwife would live near insurance members and be able to visit their homes more frequently to ensure that the home met basic sanitation requirements.[76] In this way, Castberg incorporated DNJ's requests into the maternity insurance proposal without having to specifically mention that it was the midwives' association that wanted these changes. Ultimately, the parliamentary committee on social affairs did not agree with this part of the proposal and changed the bill so that a parturient woman could use the midwife of her choice.[77]

In order to detail the need for free midwifery and elicit greater sympathy for midwifery, the Ministry of Social Affairs, under Castberg's direction, also included a letter from a district midwife in Bergen in its legislative proposal. In this letter, Nicoline Falck Ellertsen described the conditions in working-class homes and recommended changes to the law based on her twenty-three years of midwifery experience. Ellertsen painted a desperate picture of working-class life where not a crumb of bread could be found and women gave birth on the floor in the same room as their husbands, children, and dogs. She stated that the need for adequate compensation was great during women's confinements so that women could receive necessary rest and recovery time instead of having to get up the day after giving birth and take care of the household.

To help solve this problem, Ellertsen thought that the maternity insurance should provide expert and comprehensive assistance for fourteen days after giving birth instead of six weeks. This would involve providing household help to the parturient woman and her family in addition to economic support and midwifery services. She also believed that the best way to prevent midwives from misusing the insurance would be to set a rate for midwifery services that included a certain number of visits prior to and following the birth. This, coupled with the additional money for household help, would stop midwives who were only interested in "getting the most amount of money possible out of poor wretches."[78]

Ellertsen and others argued that free midwifery would help many of the families who lived in poverty and did not have the ability to pay for medical services during their confinements. The Ministry of Health found that nearly 8500 women gave birth in 1911 without the assistance of a midwife. This represented nearly 14 percent of all Norwegian births for that year.[79] Many of those women were probably attended by untrained helping wives, a fact that alarmed medical experts and statesmen who had come to believe that professional medical experts were the only ones who could ensure a safe and hygienic birth. By incorporating Ellertsen's voice and the opinion of other medical authorities, Møller hoped to persuade Parliament that mothers' insurance was imperative if public health was to be secured (Fig. 3.3).

Møller also tried to involve the masses in her lobbying for an expanded maternity insurance. She went on a lecture tour and presented the issue to various women's organizations throughout Norway. This work allowed her to reach audiences that might not otherwise have heard of these legislative reform efforts, including small groups of women workers. In addition to these public lectures, Møller also wrote short editorials on the topic for several newspapers, including *Dagbladet*, *Aftenposten*, *Morgenbladet* and *Nylænde*. By presenting the proposal to large groups of people, Møller expanded the debate on maternity legislation beyond the walls of Parliament and solicited popular support for the bill.

Fig. 3.3 Photograph of Midwife with a newborn baby, by Martin Evensen, 1920. Courtesy of Domekirkeodden Museum

Debating the Proposed Expansions to Maternity Leave

When parliamentarians sat down in June 1914 to discuss revisions to the Sickness Insurance Law, they framed most of the debates about the proposed expansions to the maternity insurance in terms of public health. Castberg opened the debate by stating that the issue of maternity insurance was one of protecting mothers, children and the family, and as such was "one of the largest tasks that lies before ... all civilized nations now and in the future."[80]

He characterized the proposal in such strong terms because of the effect he believed this legislation could have on a parturient woman's health, and thus impact the health of coming generations. Under the existing legislation, Castberg argued that "in many cases these women do not receive the nutrition, the care, [nor] the rest required. They do not receive the peace of mind [necessary to] stop working in time and avoid resuming their work too early, but instead they get worn out before their time and their children are weakened."[81] In Castberg's estimation, the expansion of maternity coverage and compensation and inclusion of free

"FOR THE HEALTH OF THE PEOPLE:" PUBLIC HEALTH...   85

midwifery would lead to a "future with fewer worn out and crippled mothers in our country, fewer weak and marked-for-death children, a little more strength among women and children and therefore also better conditions for ... coming generations."[82]

Castberg's claims were supported by the recommendations sent in by Brandt and the Ministry of Health. Dr. Brandt emphasized in his letter to Parliament that the proposed legislation would have a significant impact on women's and children's health, and in turn the overall health of the Norwegian population. By ensuring that a woman rested prior to and immediately following childbirth, parliament would be able to guarantee the birth of a healthier child. Plus, Brandt asserted that over 70% of all illnesses women had in their lives could be attributed to problems that occurred during pregnancy and childbirth.[83] For that reason, he argued that if the state provided free midwifery and bolstered a parturient woman's economic position, many of women's health problems would be resolved. This would allow women to lead more productive lives. The Ministry of Health concurred with Dr. Brandt and supported the implementation of free midwifery because of the impact it would have on women's health. In particular, the Ministry noted the potential it had to reduce maternal mortality rates.[84] The fact that medical authorities voiced support for the bill helped strengthen Castberg's dramatic assertions that if women's ability to care for and feed their children was weakened then "the people are doomed."[85]

Nearly all of Castberg's fellow parliamentarians agreed with his claims about maternity insurance's ability to bolster public health, even if they did not agree with the content of the bill. Representatives like Kristian Friis Petersen (*Venstre*, Liberal Party) voiced hearty support for the proposed maternity insurance because they were convinced by the recommendations from the medical authorities.[86] Others, such as Meyer Nilsen Foshaug (*Arbeiderparti*, Labor Party), echoed Castberg's opinion that "this is one of the most important questions now facing our society, [namely,] that of getting support for birthing mothers" even though he wanted this objective to be achieved in a different way.[87] Even the most vocal opponent of the legislation, Henrik Ameln (*Høyre*, Conservative Party), admitted that the issue was "worthy of discussion" because of the potential effects it could have on people's health.[88] This widespread political support may have been because the public, as reflected in newspaper articles, also supported the maternity insurance because of the "significance it ha[d] in terms of public health and for future generations."[89]

While population politics were ubiquitous throughout Europe and particularly in France, in Norway they were largely absent from these discussions though parliamentarians did at times relate the belief that maternity insurance could improve the health of the Norwegian people to concerns about the falling birth rate. When the Ministry of Social Affairs proposed the bill and it was sent to the parliamentary committee on social affairs in 1914, they emphasized how the law could counteract declining birth rates. First they argued that the law could strengthen the family, which "represents to the highest degree the next generation, on which the spiritual, moral and physical development of the country's future rests."[90] The Ministry then included a list of European birth rates, on which Norway ranked second to last.[91] They used this comparison to highlight the need to improve the conditions in which women gave birth. In their estimation, this would help regulate the decrease in births.

Norwegian parliamentarians did not, however, argue very strongly for the implementation of maternity insurance because it might lead to an increase in births. For some, like Ameln, this type of legislation was not means to increase birth rates.[92] For others, such as Guttorm Fløistad (*Arbeiderparti*), the law should be careful not to encourage the horrifying "breeding habits of the working class."[93] Parliamentarians were wary of using the legislation to try and get women to have more children.

Not even the outbreak of World War One caused parliamentarians to justify the passage of the maternity insurance with the need to increase the birth rate. Elsewhere in Europe, maternity provisions were bolstered by the war and the attention it brought to the need for a large population of healthy men able to serve as soldiers.[94] In June 1914 Kragtorp had presented the need for maternity insurance as instrumental in "determining how many men we have under the banners ... as recruits."[95] Yet when debates about the law continued after fighting had broken out on the continent in August 1914, parliamentarians did not once mention a desire to use the insurance to help stimulate births because of the war. In fact, the war was only ever mentioned as a reason *not* to pass the proposed legislation. Norway was neutral during the war, but parliamentarians were concerned about the negative effects the war might have on the Norwegian economy though Castberg reminded them that the war had actually benefitted Norway economically.[96] The idea that bolstering the health of mothers and children would ensure a better military defense of Norway was never brought up in Parliament after the war had begun.

Due in part to the war, one of the main concerns parliamentarians had with the maternity insurance was its expense. The inclusion of free midwifery for insured members and members' wives particularly worried lawmakers. The addition of free midwifery services promised to benefit midwives and birthing women and fulfill the state's desire to increase the medical supervision of working-class mothers. Free midwifery for working-class women was, however, a major addition to the health insurance legislation and threatened to cost a great deal of money. Under the existing law, working-class women could receive medical attention during labor and delivery only if a medical complication occurred. The proposed bill would have allowed any working-class woman to be attended by a midwife for free as long as she or her husband fulfilled the insurance requirements.

A faction of parliamentarians maintained that free midwifery was not necessary and merely had been included in the proposal as a way to increase midwives' social positions. At the very beginning of the debates Ameln stated that he did not "think it [was] good politics to use the funds in this way. Even if midwives are in a bad situation then that should be solved by giving them a better wage not connecting them to health insurance."[97] Later in the debate, Ameln expanded on this claim when he said: "A mistake is being made here, that one wants to use health insurance as a universal medicine for all types of social evils."[98] In these statements, Ameln (quite accurately) accused Castberg of using the Sickness Insurance Law to push through other social reforms.

As was common in Norwegian politics, tension between local and national governmental control drove much of the debate about the inclusion of free midwifery in the Sickness Insurance Law. Both conservatives and liberals did not want to grant the central government too much power in dictating provisions that did not consider Norway's varied local conditions. Ameln and other representatives believed that local health insurance funds should be allowed to decide whether or not to offer their members free midwifery. According to Ameln, this was a matter of choice and when a family was faced with the question of: "Do you want to buy food or do you want to get yourselves a midwife?" the government should not decide for the family that, "No, you must first get yourselves a midwife."[99] Liberal representatives supported Ameln's sentiments that local governments should decide what types of birthing assistance to provide. Lasse Torkelson Trædal, a *Venstre* representative from a small region on the west coast,[100] highlighted these differences when he argued that most rural places in Norway did not need free midwifery because they had their own birthing traditions. He claimed that these local traditions would go extinct if such legislation was put into place, though he recognized that industrialized regions might have more use for free midwifery and thus agreed with Ameln that local funds should have the power to decide whether or not to implement free midwifery.[101]

Parliamentarians were also concerned with how much covering midwives' transportation would cost, especially in large districts with difficult terrain. Lawmakers worried that midwives who lived in parts of the country where they had to travel long distances over land and sea to attend birthing women would saddle the health insurance funds with astronomical transportation fees. Even when Castberg assured them that transportation costs were not included in the proposed legislation, many of his colleagues were not persuaded by free midwifery and attempted to get it removed from the proposed legislation.[102]

Castberg countered these arguments in favor of leaving decisions up to local funds by bringing up women's recently acquired voting power. On this issue, Castberg went tit-for-tat with Ameln. Castberg tried to discount Ameln's proposal to grant local funds more discretionary power by mentioning that in Germany the decision to leave these issues up to individual funds made German women very upset. He reminded his colleagues that women in Norway had the same political rights as men and as such their interests needed to be protected. Ameln was not persuaded by this information and instead used Castberg's mention of Germany to argue that the German example demonstrated that the country with the longest experience with social insurance chose to leave decisions up to local statutes. Castberg retorted that Norwegian women had the right to expect that their interests would be better protected than in a country where not a single woman had the right to vote. Ameln brushed this assertion off by stating that he didn't think one should listen too much to the women in Norway who reminded him of the English suffragettes, and reiterated that Parliament did not need to heed the wishes of "the hysterical portion of women in Norway." Ending the conversation, Castberg snapped: "it is completely incomprehensible to me what [Ameln's] last comment has to do with the issue at hand."[103]

These arguments against free midwifery did not dissuade the majority of voting parliamentarians who believed that free midwifery was of such importance that it must be nationally legislated. For many representatives, however, it was not women's voting power that made free midwifery imperative to pass. Parliamentarians instead used class-based arguments and emphasized the effect free midwifery would have on public health to argue for the passage of free midwifery assistance. For many, it was important to pass free midwifery for the sake of the "poor wretches."[104] As Kragtorp so eloquently put it: "The process of birth itself ... concerns that of life and death, success or doom for mother and child in a short period of time and expert help at this time can make it so that the family rises in power, economically and socially while the lack of [help] can destroy the family, tear it apart and often scatter the children to the winds."[105] Arguments like these, along with the fact that lawmakers included a clause that explicitly left it up to the local funds to decide whether or not transportation was included, led parliamentarians to vote in favor of free midwifery.[106]

Another point of debate amongst Members of Parliament was the issue of extending maternity benefits to wives of insured members. Along with free midwifery this expansion threatened to cost the most. Lawmakers agreed that members' wives should receive some type of maternity benefit, but debated how much this should be. They were especially concerned with how the benefit for members' wives compared to the benefit for directly insured working women. As in 1909, some members were concerned that unmarried women should not be "rewarded" for having a child outside of wedlock.[107] As most of the directly insured women were unmarried, this meant these politicians wanted the wives of members to receive a higher benefit.

Most of the parliamentarians argued the opposite. They thought that since working women paid their own insurance premiums they deserved a greater maternity benefit than the wives of insured men. Additionally, they argued that married women had more economic protections than unmarried women, especially during the time surrounding giving birth and therefore they needed less of a benefit. Castberg had asked for a lump sum payment of 48 kroner for the wives of insured members and due to this debate, the amount settled on by parliament was 40 kroner plus free midwifery assistance when the law was debated in 1914. When discussions of the law were taken up again in 1915 the lump sum further decreased to 30 kroner. The minimum rate of payment for directly insured women was set at 1 kroner per day for 8 weeks, effectively guaranteeing that directly insured women received more maternity compensation than the wives of members.

The only other major point of debate amongst parliamentarians over maternity insurance was whether or not maternity benefits should be a separate law. Just as the AKF had argued, some Members of Parliament believed that maternity benefits were of such importance that all women should receive them regardless of class and occupation and that the cost of this should be paid for through taxes. Many of the members of parliament who spoke in favor of this were social democrats who wanted to see universal welfare benefits created. The social democrats also had the support of representatives from rural districts who wanted to see benefits applied to more people than just industrial wage earners and conservatives who believed maternity benefits had no place in the Sickness Insurance Law.[108] To those Members of Parliament who thought this would be too costly, they referenced increases in the defense budget and claimed that this was just as important as they were talking about saving "a little child that enters the world in poverty from looking death in the eyes right after it is born..."[109] M.P. Foshaug and David Olsen Bakke (*Venstre*, Liberal Party) even put forth a proposal for a separate law that would provide all women with a benefit of 12 kroner per birth. Though Castberg liked the proposal, he urged Parliament to vote now in favor of maternity insurance and revisit the idea of a separate law in the future.

In July 1915 the maternity insurance gained legislative approval. Over a year had passed since Parliament first debated the proposal for maternity insurance and in the meantime a world war had broken out. The war caused renewed and amplified concern for the cost of the maternity insurance, and in some cases, such as the money provided to the wives of insured members, the benefits it included had decreased in size. Yet the scope of the legislation remained intact and while some Members of Parliament wanted to further delay its passage, the maternity insurance passed in 1915 largely out of recognition of its "vital importance for public health."[110]

The legislation that passed was shaped by Møller, and many of Møller and Castberg's suggestions were incorporated into the law. Considering the fierce debates, free midwifery was perhaps one of their greatest triumphs. While transportation costs were not included and midwives would have to negotiate set rates with local health insurance funds, this portion of the law was thought to be the most costly of all the proposed changes.

The health insurance revisions also included a minimum rate of maternity compensation for directly insured members—that they were entitled to receive for the entire period of maternity leave, now determined to be a total of eight weeks, two prior to the birth and six after. To receive this benefit, members would still have to fulfill a ten-month membership requirement, but this could include shorter interruptions of up to two weeks. While this was not exactly what Møller and Castberg had proposed, it did represent a loosening of the restrictions. The wives of members were also eligible to receive a lump sum and free midwifery assistance, representing a huge increase in the number of women covered by the national health insurance's maternity provisions. The law included a clause on maternity homes as well. The local insurance fund could determine whether or not a woman had to give birth in a maternity home in order to receive the confinement benefits.[111] Parliament had designed all of these benefits to best ensure children were born in hygienic circumstances, bolstering the health of women, infants, and the nation as a whole.

CONCLUSION

In all, the maternity insurance passed in 1915 represented a substantial increase in maternity services and compensation for working-class women. Between 1900 and 1920 women worked to expand the maternity leave first legislated in the 1892 Factory Act. Against the backdrop of a strong public health movement and increased medicalization of maternity, feminists like Møller used these ideas to push for greater maternity benefits for women. Møller drew upon her connections to parliamentarians such as Castberg and recognized medical experts Drs. Brandt and Johannessen to gain support for her ideas. She, along with other feminists, also engaged the general public in innovative ways, to involve them in their efforts to achieve expanded maternity provisions.

Midwives were also interested in allying themselves with these feminist initiatives because of the potential they held to advance midwives' professional and economic positions. They met with Castberg and Møller and tried to shape the content of the proposed maternity legislation to fit their needs. Some individual midwives, such as Nicoline Falck Ellertsen, became directly involved in the parliamentary debates about maternity by detailing the work of midwives and recommending which actions should be taken to help working-class mothers. Many of these recommendations were based on the premise that hygiene was paramount to the health of mothers, infants and children. In all of these cases, midwives hoped that any expansion of maternity provisions would also benefit them professionally.

The strategies that feminists and midwives employed, especially in relation to public health, were largely successful because they resonated with the concerns of the time. During the 1910s Norway witnessed its largest expansion of maternity legislation to date, which ranged from the creation of maternity insurance to the protection of parturient women from serving jail time. The inclusion of maternity in the 1909 Sickness Insurance Law represented the first time working-class women would receive financial assistance during the maternity leave they were required to take. This was an important step in thinking about maternity leave in terms of a benefit as opposed to a restriction. Perhaps even more impressively, women were some of the primary actors involved in getting Parliament to pass a massive expansion of this initial insurance law. In 1915 parliament not only extended the length of time of maternity leave, but also increased the number of benefits women could receive and the number of beneficiaries eligible to receive them. Both directly insured women and the wives of insured men were entitled to maternity compensation and the assistance of a midwife during and after the birth.

Despite these efforts and successes, many women never received maternity benefits under the Sickness Insurance Law; however, because the fragile nature of working-class jobs compromised their ability to fulfill the ten-month membership eligibility requirement. As such, many women turned to another law championed by Møller and Castberg in 1915, the Castbergian Children's Laws, which included maternity provisions for single mothers. This law will be the focus of the following chapter.

NOTES

1. Høidal was later convicted of the crime of clandestine birth and sentenced to 15 months of jail time. She served most of this time at the National Women's Prison in Kristiania. Gulating lagmannsretts dombok, October 22, 1919, Statsarkivet i Bergen; Dom 8293, Fangeprotokoller, rekke 4 Dagbøker over innkomne fanger 1913–1923, Landsfengselet for kvinner, Riksarkivet.
2. No fewer than eleven responses were written to Christensen's article and published in both Bergen newspapers and national newspapers. "Ansvar," *Bergens Aftenblad*, August 15, 1919; Dagny Tyvold, "Arrestationen. Svar til Pastor Christensen," *Bergens Aftenblad*, n.d.; Georg Madsen, "Til Pastor Christensens Artikel," *Bergens Aftenblad*, n.d.; Peder Christensen, "Misbrugt sin stilling som sjælesørger," *Bergens Aftenblad*, August 16,

1919; Peder Christensen, "Den Fængslede Kvinde: Frøken Læge Tyvold!" *Bergens Aftenblad*, n.d.; L. Andree Winciansen, "Til Dagny Tyvold," *Bergens Aftenblad*, n.d.; Cand. Jur. Conrad Falsen, "Fængslede Barnemødre," *Bergens Aftenblad*, n.d.; "Anmeldt," *Bergens Aftenblad*, August 18, 1919; En mor, "Arrestationen," *Bergens Aftenblad* August 19, 1919; "Barselkvinden i fængslet: En artikel av srenskriver Sitje," *Bergens Tidende*, August 16, 1919; "Barselkvinden I fængslet," *Bergens Tidende*, August 22, 1919. Many of these articles were reprinted in the national newspaper, *Tidens Tegn*.

3. Peder Christensen, "Politiforhold som trænger Reformation: En Arrestation," *Bergens Aftenblad*, August 13, 1919.

4. *Norsk lovtidene*, "Revision of straffesaker," 1921, 317; "Fængsling av barselkvinder," *Nylænde*, 1921, 323.

5. Inger Elisabeth Haavet, ed., *Katti Anker Møller: mødrenes forkjemper 125 år* (Bergen: Senter for humanistisk kvinneforskning, 1994).

6. In fact, Møller's parents Herman Anker and Marie Elisabeth Bojsen ran Norway's first folk high school at Sagatun near Hamar.

7. Møller developed close connections to women who worked for mothers' rights in other European countries, especially France and England. Ida Blom, "Voluntary Motherhood 1900–1930: Theories and Politics of a Norwegian Feminist in an International Perspective," in *Maternity and Gender Policies: Women and the Rise of the European Welfare States, 1880s–1950s*, eds. Gisela Bock and Pat Thane (London: Routledge, 1991), 28–33.

8. The Radical People's Party was not socialist, but a leftist party concerned with workers' and small landholders' rights.

9. Øivind Bjørnson, "Johan Castberg: jurist og politiker," Norsk biografisk leksikon, Foreningen SNL, March 18, 2015, accessed March 10, 2013, http://snl.no/.nbl_biografi/Johan_Castberg/utdypning.

10. The length and services granted to insured women expanded throughout the 1910s. For a comparison of the development of German and Swedish maternity policies, see: Teresa Kulawik, "An den Grenzen des Maternalismus. Der Kampf um eine Mutterschaftsverischerun in Schweden und Deutschland," *Feministische Studien* 18, no. 1 (2000): 99–103.

11. Seth Koven and Sonja Michel, "Womanly Duties: Maternalist Politics and the Origins of Welfare States in France, Germany, Great Britain, and the United States, 1880–1920," *American Historical Review* 95, no. 4 (1990): 1706–1109; Jane Lewis, "Dealing with Dependency: State Practices and Social Realities 1870–1945," in *Women's Welfare: Women's Rights*, ed. Jane Lewis (London: Croom Helm, 1983), 31–32.

94   A. M. PETERSON

12. Karen Offen, "Body Politics: Women, Work and the Politics of Motherhood in France, 1920–1950," in *Maternity and Gender Policies*, eds. Gisela Bock and Pat Thane (London: Routledge, 1991), 138–160; Susan Pedersen, *Family Dependence, and the Origins of the Welfare State: Britain and France, 1914–1945* (Cambridge: Cambridge University Press, 1993), 17–18.

13. In contrast, Marian van der Klein credits the absence of these two factors as "allowing the Dutch state to remain uninvolved in maternity issues." Marian van der Klein, "Risks of Labour: Maternity Insurance and Economic Citizenship in Pre-1940 Europe," in *Reciprocity and Redistribution: Work and Welfare Reconsidered*, ed. Gro Hagemann (Pisa, Italy: Pisa University Press, 2007), 98.

14. van der Klein, "Risks of Labour," 102.

15. One of the ways they tried to achieve this was through encouraging women to implement hygienic measures in their homes. This was especially important to middle-class women and a clean and sterile home became a marker of social status. More information on the Norwegian case can be found in: Karin Ericson, "'Renslig med sin Person og i sit Arbeide': Hygenisering av kvinner 1888–1910" (master's thesis, NTNU, 2007).

16. Aina Schiøtz, *Folkets helse – landets styrke: 1850–2003* (Oslo: Universitetsforlaget, 2003), 51.

17. Schiøtz, *Folkets helse*, 44.

18. Nicolai Rygg, "Om børn, fødte udenfor ægteskab," Norges officielle statistik nr. 37 (Kristiania: Aschehoug, 1907), 32.

19. Norway's combined infant mortality rate for illegitimate and legitimate children born between 1896 and 1900 was 266 for every 1000 live births. In comparison, France had a rate of 404 out of 1000 and Finland 325 out of 1000 births. Rygg, "Om børn, fødte udenfor ægteskab," 32.

20. Blom, *"Den haarde dyst": fødsler og fødselshjelp gjennom 150 år* (Oslo: Capplen, 1988), 49.

21. Charlotte Borst, *Catching Babies: The Professionalization of Childbirth, 1870–1920* (Cambridge, MA: Harvard University Press, 1995).

22. Of particular concern were medical findings that pregnancy and childbirth allegedly could alter a woman's psychological state. In 1902 the Norwegian *Journal of Midwifery* reported on the findings of an English doctor who discovered that 7.5% of insane women had become that way because of pregnancy or breastfeeding. He advised that these women should be kept in asylums for six weeks, at which point the women would return to a normal state. Brandt also mentioned that parturient women were in danger of suffering psychologically from giving birth.

23. Kristian Brandt, *Lærebok for jordmødre* (Oslo: Aschehoug, 1913), 1, 191.

24. Judith Leavitt, *Brought to Bed: Childbearing in America, 1750–1950* (Oxford: Oxford University Press, 1986).
25. Tora Korsvold, Sykehusfødselen tar form: med en nærstudie av E.C. Dahls stiftelse (Oslo: Abstrakt Forlag, 2001), 98.
26. Some of this is related to the statistics gathered by Nicolai Rygg.
27. Blom, "Den haarde dyst," 107.
28. Indstilling S. No. 171, (1896).
29. MS 4 2416:III Morstrygd 2, "Om sykeforsikringsloven" Norwegian National Library, Katti Anker Møller's archive.
30. Norsk kvinnesaksforening, Aarsberetning, November 30, 1903; *Nylænde*, February 1, 1909, 37.
31. Dagny Bang, "Fabriktilsynsloven: Saerlove for kvinder," *Nylænde*, March 15, 1909, 83.
32. Stortingsforhandlinger 1907, Odelstingstinget, 6. mai 1907.
33. Lars Olsen Sæbø (*Arbeiderparti*) mentioned that he would also like midwives included but understood that this would be impossible to pass in 1909. Forhandlinger i Odelstinget, August 20, 1909, 1365.
34. Forhandlinger i Odelstinget, August 20, 1909, 1365.
35. Stortingsforhandlinger, Indstilling O. IX, (1909). "Forslag til lov om sykeforsikring av sykeforsikringskomite, 1907," 39.
36. Marian van der Klein, "The State, the Women's Movement and Maternity Insurance, 1900–1930: A Dutch Maternalism?" in *Maternalism Reconsidered: Motherhood, Welfare and Social Policy in the Twentieth Century*, eds. Marian van der Klein, Rebecca Jo Plant, Nichole Sanders, and Lori R. Weintrob (New York: Berghahn Books, 2012), 54; van der Klein, "Risks of Labour," 98.
37. Stortingsforhandlinger, Indstilling O. IX, (1909). "Forslag til lov om sykeforsikring av sykeforsikringskomite, 1907," 39.
38. Ot. Prp. nr. 19, 1909, 27.
39. Stortingsforhandlinger 1909, Forhandlinger i Odelstinget (nr. 80), "Fabriktilsynsloven, §28," 632–634.
40. Stortingsforhandlinger 1909, "Fabriktilsynsloven," 633.
41. Stortingsforhandlinger 1909, Forhandlinger i Odelstinget, "Fabriktilsynsloven," 634.
42. Rygg, "Om børn, fødte udenfor ægteskab," 32.
43. Stortingsforhandlinger 1909, Forhandlinger i Odelstinget, August 20, 1909, 1365.
44. At this time the national health insurance largely only affected women employed in factories and domestic service. Other industries would slowly be covered by this legislation during the 1930s.

96 A. M. PETERSON

45. The vast majority of these women came from the two middle income classes covered through the obligatory insurance, making between 300 and 900 kroner a year. Marius Ormestad, "Kristiania Health Insurance Fund Report on 'Mother Insurance," August 29, 1913, Forhandlinger med legene 1915/1916, Oslo Trygdekontor, Statsarkivet i Oslo.

46. "Utgifter per medlem og procentvis i 1916, 1915, 1914, 1913," Oversikt over kassens stilling, Oslo Trygdekontor, Statsarkivet i Oslo.

47. Katti Anker Møller, "Om sykeforsikringsloven," MS 4 2416:III Morstrygd 2, Håndskriftsamlingen, Nasjonalbiblioteket.

48. Katti Anker Møller, "Om sykeforsikringsloven (Utvidet sykeforsikring, fri jordmorhjelp)," MS 4 2416:III, Håndskriftsamlingen, Nasjonalbiblioteket.

49. Katti Anker Møller, "Om sykeforsikringsloven," MS 4 2416:III Morstrygd 2, Håndskriftsamlingen, Nasjonalbiblioteket.

50. Norske kvinners nasjonalråd to Katti Anker Møller, September 10, 1913, Katti Anker Møllers archive, MS 4 2416: III, Mødreforsikring, Morstrygd 3, "Udkast til lovbestemmelser om m;dreforsikring," Håndskriftsamlingen, Nasjonalbibliotekt.

51. Johan Castberg to Katti Anker Møller, February 15, 1912. "Om sykeforsikringsloven," MS 4 2416:III Morstrygd 2, Håndskriftsamlingen, Nasjonalbiblioteket.

52. Johan Castberg to Katti Anker Møller, February, 1912 and February 15, 1912, "Om sykeforsikringsloven," MS 4 2416:III Morstrygd 2, Håndskriftsamlingen, Nasjonalbiblioteket.

53. Johan Castberg to Katti Anker Møller, February 15, 1912, June 13, 1913 "Om sykeforsikringsloven," MS 4 2416:III Morstrygd 2, Håndskriftsamlingen, Nasjonalbiblioteket.

54. Johan Castberg to Katti Anker Møller, February 15, 1912.

55. "Arbeiderdemokratenes program: Sociale opgaver," *Partidokumentarkivet*, 1912, From Norsk sammfunnsvitenskapelig datatjeneste, http://www. nsd.uib.no/polsys/data/parti/partidokumentarkivet/?q=Arbeiderdemo kratenes%20program%20&rows=100&fq=&sortresult=aarstallstigende, accessed February 12, 2013.

56. Ot. Prp. Nr 35 1913, additions to the health insurance law of 1909 with additional law of April 1911, 24.

57. Katti Anker Møller, "Mødreforsikring," MS 4 2416:III, Mødreforsikring, Morstrygd 2, Håndskriftsamlingen, Nasjonalbiblioteket.

58. Forslag om Moderskapsforsikring 1913, Syketrygd: lover, Handels og industridepartement, Sosialkontoret D, Riksarkivet.

59. This may have been arranged by Dr. Axel Johannessen who spoke to the Minister of Justice, Fredrik Stang, about the maternity insurance on Møller's behalf in 1912. Axel Johannessen to Katti Anker Møller, 1912,

MS 4 2416:III, Mødreforsikring, Morstrygd 3, Håndskriftsamlingen, Nasjonalbiblioteket.

60. Ot. Prp. Nr 35 1913, additions to the health insurance law of 1909 with additional law of April 1911, 24.

61. Ot. Prp. Nr 35 1913, 24.

62. According to the 1909 law, premiums were paid 6/10 by the mandatory member, 1/10 by the employer, 1/10 municipality and 2/10 by the state. For voluntary members: 7/10 by the voluntary member, 1/10 municipality, 2/10 state.

63. Ormestad, "Moderforsikring," September 11, 1913, Forhandlinger med legene 1915/1916, Oslo Tygdekontor, bidrag til mødrehygienekontorets drift 1931–1932, Statsarkivet i Oslo.

64. Ibid.

65. Letter to Medicinaldirektøren, October 2, 1913, Mødreforsikring 143, folder 4, 1913, Oslo Trygdekontor, S1913/143 Mødreforsikring, Statsarkivet i Oslo.

66. "Om sykeforsikringsloven," *Sykeforsikringsbladet*, March 1914, 38.

67. *Morgenbladet* nr 127 quote from Dr. Lund: "Mødreforsikring er ingen forsikringer" in "Om sykeforsikringsloven" *Sykeforsikringsbladet*, March 1914, 38. At the national meeting this proposal was accepted with a vote of 37 to 3. "Beretning fra Kredssykekassernes landsforenings 2. landsmøte," Statsarkivet i Oslo, 7.

68. "Mødreforsikringen," *Kvinden*, August 1, 1915.

69. She noted that such was the case in other countries, such as Germany, that had already passed maternity legislation. Katti Anker Møller, "Om sykeforsikringsloven," (undated speech) MS 4 2416:III Morstrygd 2.

70. Kristian Brandt to Katti Anker Møller, July 10, 1913, "Om sykeforsikringsloven," MS 4 2416:III Morstrygd 2.

71. Johan Castberg to Katti Anker Møller, July 16, 1913, "Om sykeforsikringsloven," MS 4 2416:III Morstrygd 2.

72. Axel Johannessen to Katti Anker Møller, March 1, 1913, MS 4 2416: III, Mødreforsikring, Morstrygd 3, Håndskriftsamlingen, Nasjonalbiblioteket.

73. "Romdals amts jordmorforening," *Tidsskrift for jordmødre*, November 1, 1913, 132.

74. Castberg to Møller, July 16, 1913 and August 28, 1913, MS 4 2416: III, Mødreforsikring, Morstrygd 3, "Udkast til lovbestemmelser om mødreforsikring."

75. Ot. Prp. Nr. 1, changes to the health insurance law 1914, 6.

76. Ibid., 25.

77. Stortingsforhandlinger 1914, indstillinger og beslutninger B. Inst. O III, 48.

78. Ot. Prp. Nr. 1, Appendix 5, "Skrivelse til Socialdepartementet av 5te september 1913 fra distriktsjormoren I Aarstad pr. Bergen," 69.

98   A. M. PETERSON

79. Ot. Prp. Nr. 1, changes to the health insurance law 1914, 9.
80. Forhandlinger i Odelstinget, nr. 28, "Sykeforsikringsloven §16," 1914, 216.
81. Ibid., 216–217.
82. Ibid., 220.
83. Ot. Prp. Nr. 1, changes to the health insurance law 1914, 12–13.
84. Ibid., 9.
85. Forhandlinger i Odelstinget, nr. 28, "Sykeforsikringsloven §16," 1914, 220.
86. Ibid., 236.
87. As a social democrat, Foshaug wanted maternity insurance to encompass all birthing women, not just those in the lowest social classes. Forhandlinger i Odelstinget, nr. 28, "Sykeforsikringsloven §16," 1914, 220.
88. Ibid., 221.
89. "Mødreforsikringen," *Dagbladet*, October 16, 1913.
90. Stortingsforhandlinger 1914, indstillinger og beslutninger B. Inst. O III, 42.
91. The list started was topped by Russia (45 births per 1000 inhabitants), while Norway was listed as having just over 26 births per 1000 inhabitants.
92. Forhandlinger i Odelstinget, nr. 28, "Sykeforsikringsloven §16," 1914, 222, 244.
93. Forhandlinger i Odelstinget, nr. 166, "Sykeforsikringsloven §16," 1915, 1321–1322.
94. Harry Hendrick, *Child Welfare: Historical Dimensions, Contemporary Debates* (Bristol: The Policy Press, 2003), 64. For a detailed discussion of the British and French cases, see also: Susan R. Grayzel, *Women's Identities at War: Gender, Motherhood, and Politics in Britain and France During the First World War* (Chapel Hill, NC: University of North Carolina Press, 1999).
95. Forhandlinger i Odelstinget, nr. 28, "Sykeforsikringsloven §16," 1914, 249.
96. Forhandlinger i Odelstinget, nr. 166, "Sykeforsikringsloven §16," 1915, 1319.
97. Forhandlinger i Odelstinget, nr. 28, "Sykeforsikringsloven §16," 1914, 223.
98. Forhandlinger i Odelstinget 1914, 245.
99. Ibid., 244.
100. He was a representative for Ytre Sogn, which is north of Bergen.
101. Forhandlinger i Odelstinget 1914, 227–228.
102. Forhandlinger i Odelstinget, nr. 28, "Sykeforsikringsloven §16," 1914, 216–240.

"FOR THE HEALTH OF THE PEOPLE:" PUBLIC HEALTH... 99

103. Forhandlinger i Odelstinget 1914, 269–270.
104. Ibid., 242–243.
105. Ibid., 249–250.
106. The measure passed overwhelmingly in Odelstinget with 71 to 18 votes in June 1914, but the legislative debate was further delayed and only barely passed again in July 1915 with 45 to 40 votes. This discrepancy was most likely caused because WWI broke out in between the voting and parliamentarians were concerned about the effects WWI might have on the Norwegian economy.
107. Forhandlinger i Odelstinget 1914, 274.
108. Ibid., 231.
109. Forhandlinger i Odelstinget 1915, Lov om sykeforsikring, 1326.
110. Ibid., 1317.
111. This restrictive aspect of the law was not debated in parliament. "Lov om sykeforsikring," *Norsk lovtidende* 1915, 643–645.

CHAPTER 4

"Protecting Mothers and Children:" The Castbergian Children's Laws and Maternity Assistance for Single Mothers in the 1910s

On the night of October 9, 1912 Othilie Pettersen, a twenty-four-year-old servant, gave birth to a baby boy in her employers' rural farmhouse near Lillestrøm. She lay with the baby in her bed for several hours before placing her hands around his neck and strangling him until he no longer struggled to breathe. At around four in the morning she ran his lifeless body outside and hid it near the outhouse. Yet she did not try to rid the evidence of the birth from her sheets and it was this oversight that soon had the local police knocking at the door.

Pettersen was arrested and stood trial for neonaticide, or the act of murdering her own child within the first twenty-four hours of the child's life. She pled guilty and expert medical witnesses corroborated her story of how the birth and murder took place. The jury, however, found her innocent and she was set free.[1]

Following this court decision, a storm of media attention focused on Pettersen's trial, and while the outcome was contested many expressed sympathy for Pettersen and her situation.[2] The jury and the public generally agreed that rather than placing the blame on Pettersen, society should take responsibility for the circumstances that led Pettersen to kill her child and institute reforms to prevent neonaticides from occurring in the future.[3]

The debate over who was to blame in the Othilie Pettersen case took place within the context of larger discussions concerning the needs of

© The Author(s) 2018

101

A. M. Peterson, *Maternity Policy and the Making of the Norwegian Welfare State, 1880–1940*, https://doi.org/10.1007/978-3-319-75481-9_4

unwed mothers and their children and the responsibilities of fathers and the state. Just three years later in 1915, the Norwegian government passed a series of laws commonly referred to as the the Castbergian Children's Laws (CCL), which secured illegitimate[4] children greater legal and economic rights. When passed in 1915 the Laws consisted of six distinct pieces of legislation that guaranteed equal naming and inheritance rights to children, altered certain marriage and divorce regulations, defined parental rights and responsibilities, and provided public assistance for the children of single mothers. While the most radical and internationally known aspects of the Castberg Laws were the passage of equal naming and inheritance rights for children, the legislation also included significant maternity and postpartum assistance for single mothers as a part of the Child Welfare Act.

At the very same time Katti Anker Møller and Johan Castberg were working to include more comprehensive maternity benefits in the Sickness Insurance Law, they were also fighting to pass the CCL. Although both passed in 1915, these two laws differed in numerous other ways. In contrast to the maternity insurance, the CCL were not only expensive, but controversial as well. In order to garner support for this polemical proposal, Møller and Castberg consistently identified children, not mothers, as the primary intended beneficiaries of the laws.

Even more than the maternity insurance, the CCL maternity provisions had the potential to bolster substantially the autonomy of poor women by providing them with access to financial assistance during an economically precarious time in their lives. The CCL included monetary benefits that lasted longer and were more comprehensive than those provided under the maternity insurance. They also promised to help women who were not eligible for insurance benefits, because of either the type, or lack, of employment they had, or because of their inability to meet the 10-month membership requirement.

The maternity support included in the CCL also had international significance. The Laws represented an early departure from established European approaches to supporting mothers and infants. Outside of maternity insurance, the state counted on philanthropic organizations, charities, poor relief, and self-funded working-class schemes to provide monetary assistance for mothers and infants in most European countries. The CCL recognized the state's obligation to support mothers and children, particularly through the Child Welfare Act. This state remuneration of motherhood not tied to employment started Norway down the path toward other publicly funded welfare policies, such as mother's pensions and child allowances. In most other European countries, it was not until after World War One that discussions of the "endowment of motherhood," or paying women for their reproductive labors, took hold.[5] Even then, much of these discussions were not translated into law until after World War Two.

The maternity support in the CCL may have been an early outlier in European developments toward the public compensation of women's reproductive labors, but they conformed to other contemporary European ideas regarding the supervision and surveillance of recipients of social welfare. In particular, lawmakers in Norway followed the lead of Møller and Castberg and designed the legislation to prioritize the protection of children's health over women's greater economic equality and individual autonomy. This protection required women to submit to state supervision and conform to rigorous standards of work, breastfeeding, household management, and childcare in order to receive assistance. As a result, the potential the CCL had to benefit recipients and bolster their economic and social positions was hindered by these forms of means-testing.

Ultimately, when compared to other pieces of Norwegian maternity legislation passed in the 1910s, the emphasis on children's rights contributed to the maternity provisions included in the CCL becoming some of the most means-tested and restrictive. These restrictions affected poor women's ability to exercise control over their own bodies and practices of motherhood. The Laws characterized women who received maternity support as dependent and in need of proving their worthiness of assistance, which not only affected people's perceptions of the law, but also the self.[6]

In comparison, Castberg and Møller framed other maternity assistance to women, including the free midwifery and maternity leave compensation included in the 1915 Sickness Insurance Law, as a right to which women were entitled.[7] Castberg and Møller did not label the maternity support included in the Castberg Laws as a right, but rather a form of state protection of its most vulnerable citizens: children. While the difference between this rhetorical emphasis may seem subtle, it was extremely influential. Due to the emphasis on children's health needs, legislators included supervisory mechanisms in the law to encourage poor mothers to do what the state believed was best for their children. Lawmakers acknowledged at the time that some of these policies were coercive for women, but justified these restrictions in terms of the benefits children would receive. This resulted in the Castberg Laws placing the most restrictions on the lives of women who received assistance. The framing of the maternity provisions as primarily for children's benefit helps explain this disparity in outcomes.[8]

The Background for Reform

As the driving forces behind the passage of the CCL, Castberg and Møller carefully framed maternity support for unwed mothers in terms of the state's need to protect women and, even more importantly, children. In doing so, they connected their demands for increased assistance for poor mothers and children to extant state interests in creating and maintaining a healthy population. Illegitimate children's natural and unnatural deaths became important ammunition in their fight for expanded provisions for unmarried mothers and their children. Just as with the 1915 passage of the maternity insurance, Castberg and Møller used recent reports on infant mortality rates as evidence for the need of state involvement in this issue. Castberg and Møller also used tales of unwed mothers who murdered their newborns, such as in the Othilie Pettersen case, to highlight the particular risks illegitimate children faced compared to children born inside of marriage. If the state wanted to lower illegitimate children's risks of natural and unnatural death, Castberg and Møller argued, then it needed to guarantee unmarried mothers access to financial support and lessen the legal and economic consequences, as well as the social stigma, a pregnancy outside of wedlock represented.

Møller and Castberg took advantage of the increased concern for illegitimate children and their mothers that grew out of the greater sociopolitical context present in Norway at the turn of the twentieth century. It was within this context of an increased focus on the health and wellbeing of mothers and children that Castberg worked alongside Møller to put the issue of illegitimate children's rights on the political agenda. In many ways, the origins of both Castberg's and Møller's life-long commitments to the improvement of mothers' and children's lives started with the CCL. By 1901, Castberg and Møller had crafted a proposal that included legal equality for children born in and outside of marriage, the compensation of pregnancy, childbirth, and childrearing for unwed mothers and state responsibility for defining and determining paternity.[9]

Castberg and Møller's call for the passage of a law that benefitted illegitimate children and unwed mothers encountered significant resistance in Parliament—due mainly to the inclusion of equal naming and inheritance rights for children born outside of marriage. Members of the bourgeoisie saw these ideas as threatening to both the institution of marriage and class structures. The legislative process continuously stalled on the issue of illegitimate children's rights throughout the first decade of the twentieth century due to these highly contested sections on naming and inheritance rights.[10]

In an effort to garner support for their proposal, Castberg and Møller used the latest social science research to prove that illegitimate children were a vulnerable group that encountered greater health risk than other populations and were in need of special protections. Social reformers, including Castberg and Møller, had long purported that an infant was adversely affected by her mother's unmarried status, especially because many single mothers had to work outside the home. Until Nicolai Rygg published his report in 1907, however, there was little statistical evidence available to support this belief. This changed with Rygg's staggering finding that children born outside of marriage were twice as likely to die within the first year of life as children born in wedlock.[11]

Rygg's report led to increased political attention to the health risks children born to unmarried mothers faced. According to Rygg, infants born outside of wedlock lived in "unhygienic, poor living conditions" and were "treated with little care" by their mothers.[12] Yet Rygg emphasized that those children were better off when compared to the majority of illegitimate children whose mothers placed them in foster care soon after giving birth so that they could return to paid employment. It was this practice of placing children in foster care that Rygg cited as the main reason children born outside of marriage faced a disproportionally high rate of infant mortality. Rygg believed that it was not foster care in general that caused this to occur, but rather the fact that most illegitimate children were not breastfed and instead received what he deemed dangerous substitutes, including coffee and salted herring.[13]

Rygg's assertion fell in line with the new medical emphasis on maternal breastfeeding as one of the most important factors for infant and child health. Surgeon General Michael Holmboe and Drs. Axel Johannessen and Kristian Brandt agreed that the best way to decrease the high rate of infant mortality amongst illegitimate children was to ensure that mothers breastfed their children.[14] These experts admonished women who returned to work soon after giving birth and placed their children in foster care, stating: "depriving an infant of natural nutrition, a home, and care commits a sin against the child."[15]

Møller and Castberg used these statistical findings and medical assertions to make a case for a comprehensive piece of children's rights legislation to members of the general public and to the men who sat in Parliament. They presented Rygg's conclusions that children born to unmarried parents had a much higher rate of mortality than children born inside of marriage to demonstrate class inequality and to gain sympathy for these

106   A. M. PETERSON

children. Additionally, Møller and Castberg made the medical connections between infant mortality and breastfeeding the basis of much of the maternity provisions they included in their legislative proposal. The statistics and medical opinions lent credibility and authenticity to Castberg and Møller's calls for legislative reform for illegitimate children.

MAKING THE CASE FOR REFORM

Møller incorporated some of these nascent ideas about the important role mothers played in ensuring the health and wellbeing of their children when she introduced the legislative proposal on illegitimate children's rights to women's rights activists. In 1901 Møller wrote two articles for the *Norsk kvinnesaksforenings* (Norwegian Association for Women's Rights, NKF) journal, *Nylænde*, and outlined how the protection of children could benefit society. She did not bring up the more controversial elements of inheritance and naming rights in these articles. Rather, Møller focused on the aspects of the proposal that affected unmarried mothers and their children, a strategy Møller and Castberg would employ throughout the legislative process.

Møller argued in *Nylænde* that maternity support for unwed mothers, both prior to and following labor and delivery, would positively affect the whole of Norwegian society. She emphasized that the legislation would significantly bolster children's health because the financial assistance would afford women the opportunity to live with and breastfeed their young children. According to Møller, this would not only increase children's wellbeing but also spur the creation of better citizens because women would form motherly bonds with their children, benefitting mother, child and society. In fact, she claimed that the fostering of motherly bonds would ultimately lead to a decrease in the number of people in "jail and correctional facilities, which burden society with considerable taxes."[16] This claim highlighted the broad range of positive effects the economic protection of unmarried mothers would have on Norwegian society and suggested that this investment could actually lead to an overall decrease in government spending on social issues.

Møller also suggested that the proposed legislation would reduce the number of instances where unmarried women, such as Othilie Pettersen, resorted to neonaticide. To illustrate this point Møller emphasized the despair many unmarried mothers felt towards the prospect of having a child outside of marriage and how this often led a woman to "plan to kill her child."[17] She asserted that "if society wants to protect children, it must step in and create just laws..."[18] Møller believed that it was essential for the state to actively engage in this issue because fathers could not be counted on to voluntarily provide for the children they fathered outside of wedlock (Fig. 4.1).

In these articles, Møller consistently highlighted the effects the laws could have on the health and wellbeing of children through policies that provided financial assistance to unwed mothers. While Møller also mentioned the potential the legislation had to improve women's lives, this was not emphasized as the primary purpose of the law. If women were to benefit from the laws, it was only in relation to the betterment of their children's position.

These sentiments fit with the general thinking at the time regarding help for unwed mothers. In the late-nineteenth century many philanthropic moral reform organizations had supported the creation of maternity homes for unwed mothers as a part of their criticism of the sexual double standard. These were some of the organizations Møller collaborated with when she helped establish *Den hvide baand* (The White Ribbon)[19] maternity home for unwed mothers in the capital, Kristiania (Oslo) in 1902.

Fig. 4.1 Sick mother with 7 children, 1910. Courtesy of the Norwegian Museum of Science and Technology

In their attempts to establish homes for poor, unmarried mothers, reformers had encountered significant resistance from members of the general public. Nineteenth-century attitudes toward unwed mothers held that women who had children outside of marriage deserved to bear the physical, social, economic and legal burdens of this decision. Many people accused unmarried mothers of being "wild, animalistic, immoral" and unworthy of help.[20] When working to establish forms of assistance for unwed mothers, reformers also encountered people who believed that any support for these women could be seen as a reward for depravity and perhaps even encourage immoral women to have more children outside of wedlock, stimulating the rate of illegitimate births. It is noteworthy that though Parliament debated the merits of unmarried women's eligibility for maternity insurance, ultimately they supported the inclusion of unmarried women in this benefit. Insurance differed from assistance in that parliament perceived unmarried women as entitled to maternity insurance due to the premiums they paid. In comparison, unmarried women did not have a right to public assistance and charity.

To effectively counter these assertions, women reformers had been careful to portray unwed mothers as innocent and sympathetic and stress the impact the assistance had on the health and wellbeing of children. Such was the case when Didrik Konow wrote in *Nylænde* in 1897 that many believed an unmarried mother "should bear the consequences of her own actions, but out of *concern for the fetus*" the unwed mother needed access to financial assistance during pregnancy.[21] Konow made the argument that in order to protect the health of the child, people would need to overcome their prejudices toward unwed mothers.

The presence of these attitudes toward unwed mothers made many reformers reluctant to get involved in the controversial issue of rights for children born outside of marriage. Many of the conservative women's groups that had been actively involved in establishing maternity homes for poor, unmarried women were interested in a law that increased assistance for these women and held men more accountable for their children. As such, they supported Møller's efforts to strengthen the economic protection of unmarried mothers and illegitimate children, but did not agree with the more radical parts of the proposal. The women Møller had worked with in founding the *Hvide baand* maternity home, for example, knew that providing assistance to unwed mothers was controversial enough and worried that inheritance rights for illegitimate children would put the "little sympathy [people] have for unmarried mothers" at risk.[22] When it became clear that Møller wanted to go far beyond assisting wayward women and helping them reform their ways, many of Møller's more conservative allies distanced themselves from her ideas and withheld their support for the legislative proposal.[23]

Møller also struggled to get her ideas supported by many bourgeois feminist organizations. Møller had been active in the *Norske kvinners nasjonalråd*, or Norwegian National Women's Council (NKN) since its creation in 1903, but the types of proposals she brought forth, including illegitimate children's rights and access to contraceptive knowledge were not accepted in this fairly conservative women's organization.[24] Members of *Norsk kvinnesaksforening*, or Norwegian Association for Women's Rights (NKF), were also resistant to proposals for illegitimate children's inheritance and naming rights because they worried that supporting the illegitimate children's rights laws would weaken their ability to achieve greater rights for married women. In particular, the NKF wanted marriage reform and women's economic rights in marriage secured prior to fighting for the rights for illegitimate children.[25]

That said, the head of the NKF, Gina Krog, did write a few articles in support of the illegitimate children's laws, highlighting aspects of the proposal that resonated with the goals of the NKF, such as equal rights for all people.[26] As editor, Krog also published many articles in *Nylænde* written both in support of and in opposition to Castberg and Møller's legislative proposal. The majority of these articles voiced support for the sections of the law that provided maternity support to unwed mothers and increased fathers' legal responsibility for their illegitimate children, but the issue of inheritance and naming rights was highly contested.[27]

Legislating Support for Single Mothers

By 1912, some people may have continued to be critical toward assistance for unwed mothers, but the idea that the state needed to protect mothers and children had become widely accepted amongst politicians due in part to the believed effect this would have on public health. This acceptance is evidenced by the legislative proposal Minister of Justice Fredrik Stang (*Høyre*, Conservative Party) put forth in 1912. While Møller and Castberg were still trying to gather support for their legislative proposal, Stang sponsored an opposing bill. Stang's proposal was nearly identical to the one Castberg had encouraged Parliament to pass in 1909 except it removed the controversial sections on equal naming and inheritance rights for illegitimate children.

The fact that *Høyre* proposed a law that would significantly strengthen public assistance for unmarried mothers and their children demonstrates that these ideas were not considered especially radical or controversial. Instead, they were perceived as being legitimate social welfare measures within the realm of state responsibility.

Parliament did not have sufficient time to debate Stang's proposal in 1912, and when Castberg presented a new version of his legislative proposal to Parliament in 1914, he made sure to highlight the positive impact the laws would have on children's health and wellbeing. This was a rhetorical strategy he and Møller had used to garner public support for the laws, which Castberg now used to cultivate support in Parliament. People recognized the importance of using the resources Norway had in order to build a stronger, independent country, and he used this consensus to argue that children were the most precious natural resource Norway had. Castberg introduced the proposal by stating that "the hygienic, social, and economic conditions in which a human being is born into and raised during his first years of life is crucial for his later development. They determine to a significant degree whether or not the child will become a healthy individual and a useful member of society."[28] He went on to say that as the child could not protect its own interests during this crucial period of time, the state must. According to Castberg, this was especially needed in the case of children born to unmarried parents and was the primary purpose of the law on illegitimate children's rights.[29]

Given this statement, it is not surprising that maternity provisions formed an integral component of the proposal Castberg presented. They were included in two separate sections of the law, which newly defined paternal and state responsibility for supporting women's reproductive work. In the main law on illegitimate children an entire subsection was devoted to outlining a man's financial duty to compensate the unmarried mother of his child/ren during pregnancy, confinement, and several months after the birth. For those men who could not be made to comply, and for married women who had been abandoned or were separated from their spouses, the government offered women financial assistance to help them care for their newborns in a separate law on municipal support for single mothers.

If passed, the public assistance outlined in the proposal would make Norway one of the first countries to grant assistance to mothers and children outside of the context of poor relief. The CCL has often been upheld as innovative due to the inclusion and extension of rights to unmarried mothers and their children, but in most European countries not even married mothers and infants were eligible to receive state-sponsored support outside of the insurance laws. The proposal for the CCL deviated from the European norm then, in multiple and significant ways.

Proposal for State-Mandated Paternal Support

The section of the law that mandated paternal support was not necessarily innovative—Norwegian men had been required to pay child support for children they fathered outside of marriage since 1763—but it did represent a significant expansion of men's financial responsibilities toward the children they fathered and their children's mothers, and increased the state's role in facilitating this support.[30] In order for this law to be of the most benefit to mothers and children the proposal obliged men to compensate women for wages lost due to pregnancy or confinement.

The proposed law included a clause that called for a father's financial support of a pregnant woman during the four months prior to the birth of her child and state regulation of a minimum rate for this support. The Ministry of Social Affairs, with Castberg as Minister, introduced the bill and emphasized that it was "during this exact period of time that she could feel unhappy and abandoned ... and confusing and dark thoughts could tempt her to kill her child" implying that a father's lack of support would not only negatively affect the mother's wellbeing but also lead her to contemplate neonaticide.[31] Following the birth, the Ministry proposed that the father should also provide the mother with financial support for nine months, but only if the child was born alive. In the case of a stillborn birth, a mother was to receive one month of financial support to allow for physical recovery.

These sections of the law were designed to bolster infant health by financially enabling unmarried women to keep their children in their care after giving birth. Politicians and medical experts agreed that the best way to improve infant health and decrease the high rate of infant mortality amongst illegitimate children was to make sure mothers stayed at home with their infants, mainly to facilitate breastfeeding. Contrary to contemporary gender ideals, many unmarried women had to work for wages regardless of the fact that they were mothers. State actors saw this as undesirable especially because of the negative effect they thought women's work had on children's health. Therefore, the state wanted to expand men's financial responsibility to encompass the children they fathered outside of wedlock and these children's mothers. Doing so would enable

112   A. M. PETERSON

women to refrain from waged labor at the end of their pregnancies to care for and feed their children for what was thought to be a crucial period of time after giving birth. This reasoning was behind the Ministry of Social Affair's recommendation that fathers pay financial support to unmarried mothers of their children for a period of nine months after giving birth.

PROPOSAL FOR STATE SUPPORT FOR SINGLE MOTHERS

The Ministry believed breastfeeding to be of such importance that it recommended the state go beyond holding fathers accountable and become a direct provider of assistance for mothers. As a result, the proposed law on children born outside of marriage included a section on public assistance for single mothers and their children, called the Child Welfare Act of 1915. In cases where fathers either could not afford or be made to pay support for the care of their illegitimate children, the state would provide women with the money necessary to keep her infant child in her care. This included municipally funded financial assistance for six weeks prior to the birth and three months afterwards.[32]

Originally, Castberg had wanted to make this public assistance available to all poor women regardless of their civil status, but he was not able to gain political support for this. The outbreak of World War One caused difficulties for Castberg on this issue, similar to the ones he encountered in getting certain aspects of the maternity insurance passed. Because of the economic uncertainty caused by the war, Castberg had to cede his position. The legislative proposal introduced to Parliament in 1914 included only unmarried women and specific groups of married women, namely those whose husbands were dead, had abandoned them, or were separated from their spouses for some special circumstances. This political compromise deeply disappointed Castberg.[33]

Castberg's disappointment aside, the proposed legislation substantially expanded traditional forms of welfare by including public assistance for single mothers in addition to holding fathers responsible for their illegitimate children. This represented a major financial commitment on behalf of the government, which politicians likely wanted to lessen by only including certain groups of women. The fact that a major war was developing on the continent, the scope and duration of which were yet unknown, probably exacerbated these financial concerns.

By limiting the public assistance to cases where women did not have men to support them, the state was also upholding and reinforcing extant gender norms. Reformers may have believed that the state had a duty to step in and protect vulnerable groups, such as unmarried women or widows, but this did not extend to married women already covered by the protection of her husband, who was supposed to provide for her and their children. As such, it would have been easier to convince politicians (and their constituents) that women without a male "breadwinner" in their households needed special assistance. It was politically defensible to limit the assistance to married women who did not have husbands that provided for them and their children.

The Cost of Public Assistance for Single Mothers

The proposed Child Welfare Act not only limited the scope of public assistance for single mothers to women who did not have a male breadwinner, it also included supervisory mechanisms that aimed to cultivate and enforce certain standards of motherhood amongst welfare recipients. The rhetoric that had been used to justify the passage of the Castberg Laws emphasized protection and highlighted the benefits these policies would have on children. The state wanted to be sure that its interests in the protection of children were secured. As a result, the Castberg Laws included some elements that legislated and monitored poor mothers' behavior.

The law on public assistance for mothers and infants was set to be administered at the municipal level and local health councils were to oversee the implementation of the law and ensure that women used maternity support in the way politicians intended. According to the law, the local health councils had the power to approve or reject women's applications for support. The health councils also had the task of making sure that the women who received public assistance used it in the best interest of the child, loosely defined.[34] This meant that women often had to meet rigid standards of childcare and hygiene in order to receive maternity support under the Castberg Laws.

In order to secure the state's interests in protecting the health of children, this legislation sought to influence the way women mothered their children starting with where they gave birth. Recent developments in medical theory and practice upheld sterile, aseptic environments as ideal birthing conditions. Midwives, who delivered the vast majority of Norwegian babies, described working-class and poor women's homes as "dirty, crowded ... [and] highly unappetizing."[35] Midwives and reformers characterized these homes as unable to meet the medical guidelines for a safe birth and linked unhygienic birthing conditions to the high rates of infant mortality amongst illegitimate children.[36] Correspondingly, politicians wanted poor women to practice modern hygienic measures and strove to ensure that childbirth took place in sanitary conditions and under state-sanctioned medical supervision. This reasoning was behind Møller's similar push to get maternity home stays included in the maternity insurance.

The Child Welfare Act of 1915 also included a provision in the law that gave local health councils the power to require a woman give birth in a government-run institution in order to receive assistance.[37] This inclusion represented the state's embrace of medical ideas about maternity and encouraged the professionalization and institutionalization of childbirth. The intent was to protect the health of infants and their mothers by limiting women's ability to make decisions about where and how they gave birth.

While both the maternity insurance and the Child Welfare Act of 1915 included compulsory mechanisms for maternity home stays, only the public assistance for single mothers also made women's eligibility contingent on adhering to the most recent standards of childcare. First and foremost a woman who received support had to live together with her child.[38] Placing the child in foster or family care would render a woman immediately barred from receiving assistance. Beyond this, the law allowed the municipal health councils significant leeway in supervising poor women's mothering. For example, local health councils could, but did not necessarily have to, require women to have a separate bed for the child to sleep in and present a clean and tidy house to the people who came by to inspect the home.[39]

Often in countries with similar pieces of legislation the criteria to receive support included women breastfeeding their children for a certain length of time. Norwegian politicians hoped that the public assistance for single mothers would enable women to breastfeed their children, but they did not make the aid contingent on breastfeeding. Other states more concerned with population politics—most notably France—often withheld monetary benefits if a woman could not prove that she was breastfeeding her child.[40] These ideas were less prevalent in Norway, where population concerns were less acute and reformers concentrated on improving the population rather than increasing it.

While Norwegian politicians did not find it necessary, or feasible, to make maternity benefits contingent on breastfeeding, it did warrant discussion. In the 1914 legislative proposal, the Ministry of Social Affairs noted different models of public assistance for mothers, including the French model, and decided that compulsory breastfeeding should not be a part of the Norwegian law.[41] The Ministry believed that in most cases requiring the mother to live with her child would be enough to encourage mothers to breastfeed. Even so, politicians noted that findings from the Central Statistical Agency indicated around ten percent of women did not breastfeed even when given the opportunity to do so.[42] As we will see in the next chapter, perhaps it was these cases that led some local health councils to require women to breastfeed for a certain length of time in order to receive public assistance after the law was implemented, even though the law itself did not end up making breastfeeding compulsory for recipients.

The Proposed Laws Under Debate

When the law on public assistance for single mothers, or the Child Welfare Act, was put before Parliament, the restrictive aspects of the proposed law concerned the parliamentarians who debated the law, in particular, the measures they feared would inhibit the state's ability to realize its goal of protecting children's health. The requirements that limited women's agency—but did so in order to secure children's health and wellbeing—either did not warrant debate or were able to sustain parliamentary scrutiny. As a result, the majority of the clauses in the proposed law that regulated women's lives survived debate and became incorporated into Norwegian law.

Similar to the maternity insurance debate, urban/rural divides and tensions between women's rights and children's needs punctuated the discussions. When the Child Welfare Act was debated in Odelstinget in 1915, politicians worried that some of the restrictive aspects of the proposed law would negatively affect child welfare. Of particular worry was a section of the law that required a woman to report her illegitimate pregnancy to the authorities prior to giving birth in order to receive public assistance. Guttorm Fløistad (*Arbeiderparti*, Labor Party) called the proposed requirement "barbaric" and Birger Stuevold-Hansen (*Venstre*, Liberal Party) argued that the requirement directly contradicted the entire point of the law, which was to "protect the continuation of the race."[43] These arguments were largely persuasive because parliamentarians believed children's health would be adversely affected by such an inclusion. The members of Odelstinget subsequently voted unanimously to remove this requirement from the law.[44]

116   A. M. PETERSON

The portions of the legislation that required the woman to submit to the supervision of local health councils were not debated nor described as unreasonable or "barbaric," most likely because they bolstered the law's main goal of protecting children's health. When it came time to discuss the sections of the law that concerned its administration by local authorities, parliamentarians were more worried about the logistics of implementation rather than the restrictions it might place on women.

The section that allowed local authorities to require a woman to give birth in an institution instead of at home was one of the few that parliamentarians debated in terms of its effect on limiting women's choices. Some parliamentarians from rural areas wanted to know if a woman could be made to give birth in any government-run institution, including old-age homes and poor houses. Ivar Petterson Tveiten (*Venstre*) thought it was particularly important to clarify this because there were no maternity homes or hospitals in most rural areas, and in lieu of these medical institutions it might be advantageous to have poor women give birth in other governmental facilities.[45]

In response to this, Castberg urged his fellow parliamentarians to "remember that [the legislation] involved a type of coercion."[46] He believed Parliament should not make this even more apparent by forcing women give birth in old-age homes or poor houses. Instead, Castberg stated that the health councils should only be able to require women to give birth in "exceptional" places so that women did not consider the stipulation onerous and coercive, but enjoy their time at the institution. Other parliamentarians such as Otto Bahr Halvorsen (*Høyre*) thought that requiring women to give birth in poor houses would counteract the law's main goals of preventing women from being tainted by the act of receiving poor relief.[47] Ultimately, Odelstinget did not change the wording of this section of the law and left it open for health councils to be able to require women to give birth in any kind of governmental "care facility."[48]

The debates over what types of facilities authorities could require women to give birth in reflected tensions within Parliament over urban/rural divides that were common in Norwegian politics, such as we saw in the previous chapter. Ivar Petterson Tveiten's concern over the lack of maternity homes in rural districts and his suggestions for suitable replacements demonstrated some of the problems inherent in creating national social policies built on the model of Kristiania. In contrast to Kristiania, many rural areas in Norway did not have modern medical facilities, and it would have been impossible to require women who lived in these districts to give birth at such a place. Parliamentarians such as Tveiten brought this to the attention of other Members of Parliament in an effort to not only prevent unattainable requirements from being included in the law, but also to elicit a larger discussion about crafting legislation that could apply to both rural and urban areas. This was a common point of contention for parliamentarians who represented rural districts and ultimately their points were seen as valid. It was important that policies were adaptable to the diverse conditions present in Norway in the early-twentieth century, and this is likely the reason Parliament decided to leave "care facility" open to interpretation at the local level.

The debate over the requirement that women give birth in government-run institutions also reflected politicians' beliefs about social policies and women's rights. For instance, parliamentarians' concern that the law could be implemented at the local level outweighed Castberg's worry that women would experience these requirements as coercive. While the rights of women were certainly a topic of political discussion—especially as women had only recently won the right to vote and the impact this would have on politics was yet unknown—parliamentarians were not persuaded by Castberg's arguments. To many of these politicians it was not unusual for welfare measures to include certain criteria for eligibility and this was not in conflict with women's rights as citizens. Women's voting power and citizenship rights were not brought up during the debates as they had been during the discussion of women's rights and maternity insurance.

There were many reasons to defend the inclusion of a requirement that women give birth in an institution: the state had an interest in ensuring public monies were used for the purposes intended by lawmakers and even more importantly, the primary goal of the legislation demanded that children's health be protected. If the only way to ensure children's health was protected was to require women to give birth at an institution where government employees could monitor the conditions women gave birth in, then it did not matter if this institution was a hospital or a poor house; politicians believed the state was justified in legislating this. In this case the state's interest in protecting children's health superseded any desire women might have to decide where they gave birth.

CONCLUSION

Castberg and Møller's efforts to ensure greater economic protections for illegitimate children and single mothers were actualized in 1915. The passage of the Castberg Laws was a major triumph for Castberg and Møller and represented a substantial increase in the economic protection of poor mothers and children. When passed, the Laws promised to benefit a significant number of poor Norwegian mothers and their children. Women were guaranteed financial help during a particularly precarious time in their lives—at the end of pregnancy and for a crucial amount of time following their children's births. This support would have likely helped keep poor mothers off poor relief rolls and allow them to maintain their citizenship rights, something which held increased importance after the implementation of women's suffrage in 1913.

The state first sought to hold men financially accountable to the women with whom they had children. If those men could not, or would not, provide the legislated compensation to unwed mothers then the state offered a program of assistance. This assistance was comprehensive and innovative for the time, but because its primary goal was to protect children's health—rather than achieve greater equality for women—it included measures that aimed to ensure children were born and raised in a safe and healthy manner, which often came at the expense of poor women's autonomy. In order to receive assistance, poor, single mothers had to negotiate state interference in their private lives.

The maternity support included in the Castberg Laws illustrates the simultaneously progressive and restrictive nature of early Norwegian welfare policies that targeted poor women. First of all, the Laws represented a real financial benefit to poor mothers. The comprehensive nature of the Laws and their extension to previously neglected segments of the population represented a significant expansion of the nascent Norwegian welfare state.

The maternity provisions contained in the CCL were also much more progressive than similar laws in existence in other European and North American countries. In many places, including the Netherlands and the United States, it was extremely difficult to pass legislation that benefited unmarried mothers because of intense moral and religious debates.[49] Due to the strength of these moral arguments in certain political contexts, "worthy" widows were often the only women who were able to receive maternity benefits. In France where the perceived *crise de natalité* allowed for the passage of legislation that targeted unwed mothers, these same depopulation anxieties emphasized the importance the policies had for children's, rather than women's, health and wellbeing. As such, French maternity policies included the close supervision of women who received assistance to make sure they complied with the fairly stringent breastfeeding and other care requirements.[50]

The 1915 passage of maternity insurance and the maternity assistance provided under the Castberg Laws represented a monumental expansion of maternity benefits and services available to Norwegian women. There were two pathways to benefits, including both the contributory insurance system and publicly funded maternity assistance. The Child Welfare Act signaled Norway's early steps toward paying mothers for the work they performed for the state. The "endowment of motherhood" in other European countries did not gain political traction until after World War One. In Norway, a neutral country, this political recognition of mothers and the central role they played in the protection of the state's most vulnerable citizens started in 1915 with the passage of the CCL. The CCL offered public funds to single mothers, many of whom did not qualify for the health insurance's maternity benefits. In an effort to enable mothers to care for their children and breastfeed as long as possible, this assistance could last up to six months. There were certainly coercive aspects to this design, but the law also included the economic acknowledgement of the reproductive labors women performed in caring for young children. Feminists, midwives, and working women would build on this facet of the law in their work for mothers' pensions and child allowances in the interwar period.

When compared to other contemporary instances of state-driven maternity care across Europe, the expansive and progressive aspects of the Castberg Laws' maternity provisions are clear. Comparing the Castberg Laws to other Norwegian maternity policies, especially the maternity insurance also passed in 1915, throws the Laws' limitations into relief. The Castberg Laws placed the most restrictions on the lives of women who received assistance. This may have to do with their incorporation into a set of laws that contained more radical and controversial features such as equal naming and inheritance rights, which necessitated a heightened focus on children's rights. By focusing on children's wellbeing and presenting the law as something that would primarily benefit children, the Castberg Laws subsumed the interests of women under the interests of children.

In spite of their limitations, feminists, midwives, and single mothers stood to benefit from the maternity laws passed in 1915. The next chapter will examine the varied effects maternity insurance and the CCL's maternity assistance had on women's lives. It will also demonstrate the ways in which women's responses to these effects influenced the interpretation and revision of maternity legislation at the local and national levels.

NOTES

1. Retsbok, Case nr. 4, 1912 Akershus court. Adjudicated December 10, 1912, Oslo Lagdømme, Rettergang, Statsarkivet i Oslo.
2. Not everyone thought that mothers who murdered their newborn babies should be free from punishment. Knut Hamsun, for example, vehemently opposed the expression of sympathy for these women and wanted the death penalty reinstituted as punishment for these crimes.
3. Johan Evje, "Barnedrapet," *Dagbladet*, December 16, 1912.
4. For the sake of simplicity, I will use the contemporary term "illegitimate" throughout this chapter to refer to children who were born to unmarried parents.
5. The notable exception is France where subsidies to poor families with multiple children were paid starting in 1913.
6. Eva Feder Kittay and Ellen K. Feder, eds., *The Subject of Care: Feminist Perspectives on Dependency* (Lanham, MD: Rowman and Littlefield, 2002); Nancy Fraser and Linda Gordon, "A Genealogy of Dependency: Tracing a Keyword of the U.S. Welfare State," *Signs* 19, no. 2 (1994): 309–336.
7. Anna M. Peterson, "The Birth of a Welfare State: Feminists, Midwives, Working Women and the Fight for Norwegian Maternity Leave, 1880–1940," (PhD diss., The Ohio State University, 2013).
8. It is worth noting that the two laws under discussion in this article are the two that deal the most with financial exchanges, assistance and support, or what many would consider to be forms of welfare. The other laws are mainly concerned with codifying and regulating legal responsibilities and relationships between parties. The law on inheritance obviously contains financial aspects but for a very different reason. For these reasons, the conclusions I have drawn about these two laws and the particular sections of these laws that concern maternity are not readily applied to the other laws.
9. Bjarne Markussen, *Rettshistorier: Foreldre og barn i litteratur, film og lovgivning* (Oslo: Unipub, 2008), 126.
10. Odelstingstidende 1904/1905, 350.
11. Nicolai Rygg, "Om børn, fødte udenfor ægteskab," Norges officielle statistik nr. 37 (Kristiania: Aschehoug, 1907), 34.
12. Ibid., 34–35.
13. Ibid., 34.
14. Ot. Prp. Nr. 5 1914, "Om utfærdigelse av lover om barn født utenfor egteskap," 19–20.
15. "Hjemløse mødre og spædbarn," *Nylænde*, February 1, 1908, 40.
16. Katti Anker Møller, "Ugifte mødre," *Nylænde*, May 15, 1901, 151.
17. Katti Anker Møller, "Ugifte mødre," *Nylænde*, April 15, 1901, 116.
18. Ibid., 117.

"PROTECTING MOTHERS AND CHILDREN:" THE CASTBERGIAN... 121

19. The White Ribbon was a symbol of the temperance movement and this maternity home was operated in cooperation with the Norwegian chapter of the Women's Christian Temperance Union.
20. "Ugifte mødre," *Nylænde*, January 15, 1903, 29.
21. Italics added for emphasis. Didrik Konow, "Om underholdningsbidrag under svangerskabet," *Nylænde*, October 1, 1897, 258.
22. Hvidebaands Hjem to Katti Anker Møller, April 28, 1904, MS 2416:I, Håndskriftsamlingen, Nasjonalbiblioteket.
23. Ibid.
24. Norske kvinners nasjonalråd to Katti Anker Møller, May 3, 1913, Gina Krog, Håndskriftsamlingen, Nasjonalbiblioteket.
25. Beretning om Norsk Kvindesagsforenings 25 aarige virksomhet June 28, 1884–June 28, 1909 utarbeidet av Alette Ottesen, 13. "Norske Kvinneforening 1904–1915," Randi Blehr, Riksarkivet.
26. Gina Krog, "De 'uaegte' barn og vor lovigning," *Nylænde*, May 1, 1902.
27. Lise Rosenberg, "Hagar og Ismael I Saras Telt? Holdninger til familie og ekteskap i debatten om de Castbergske barnelovene, belyst gjennom studiet av sentrale kvinnetidsskrifter," (Hovedfagsoppgave i historie, Universitetet i Bergen, 1981).
28. Ot. Prp. Nr. 5 1914, "Om utfærdigelse av lover om barn født utenfor egteskap, egtebarn m.m," 1.
29. Ibid.
30. Inger Elisabeth Haavet, "Milk, Mothers and Marriage: Family Policy Formation in Norway and its Neighbouring Countries in the Twentieth Century," in *The Nordic Model of Welfare – A Historical Reappraisal*, ed. Niels Finn Christiansen, et al. (Copenhagen: Museum Tusculanum Press, 2006), 193.
31. Ot. Prp. Nr. 5 1914, "Om utfærdigelse av lover om barn født utenfor egteskap," 47.
32. Ibid., 130.
33. Johan Castberg to Katti Anker Møller, n.d., MS 2416, Håndskriftsamlingen, Nasjonalbiblioteket.
34. Ot. Prp. Nr. 5 1914, "Om utfærdigelse av lover om barn født utenfor egteskap," 130.
35. Fru Klaveness, "Lidt om Jordmødrenes økonomiske Kaar og sociale Stilling," *Tidsskrift for jordmødre*, February 1, 1896, 19.
36. Rygg, "Om børn, fødte udenfor ægteskab," 34–35.
37. Ot. Prp. Nr. 5 1914, "Om utfærdigelse av lover om barn født utenfor egteskap," 130.
38. Ibid., 88–103.
39. Ibid., 130.

122   A. M. PETERSON

40. Ann Taylor Allen, *Feminism and Motherhood in Western Europe, 1890–1970: The Maternal Dilemma* (New York: Palgrave Macmillan, 2005), 82.
41. Ot. Prp. Nr. 5 1914, "Om utfærdigelse av lover om barn født utenfor egteskap," 88–103.
42. Ibid., 94.
43. Stortingsforhandlinger 1915, Forhandlinger i Odelstinget, "Lov om forsorg for barn," 228.
44. Ibid., 232.
45. Ibid., 239–240.
46. Ibid., 240.
47. Ibid., 241.
48. Ibid., 243.
49. For the United States case, see: Molly Ladd-Taylor, *Mother-Work: Women, Child Welfare, and the State, 1890–1930* (Urbana, IL: The University of Illinois Press, 1994); For a discussion of the Dutch case, see: Marian van der Klein, "The State, the women's movement and maternity insurance, 1900–1930: a Dutch maternalism?" in *Maternalism Reconsidered: Motherhood, Welfare and Social Policy in the Twentieth Century*, eds. Marian van der Klein, Rebecca Jo Plant, Nichole Sanders, and Lori R. Weintrob (New York: Berghahn Books, 2012).
50. Mary Lynn Stewart, *Women, Work and the French State: Labour, Protection and Social Patriarchy, 1879–1919* (London: McGill-Queen's University Press, 1989), 189; Elinor Accampo, et al., eds., *Gender and the Politics of Social Reform in France, 1870–1914* (Baltimore: John Hopkins University Press, 1995).

CHAPTER 5

"Getting the Most Money Possible:" Women's Responses to the Implementation of Maternity Laws, 1916–1930

Marie Nordstrøm devoured her dinner and hurried off to the Kristiania (Oslo) meeting locale, *Bøndernes Hus*, to catch the last day of the maternity exhibition.[1] When Nordstrøm rushed down the basement stairs at *Bøndernes Hus* she was confronted with the organizers' staged depiction of a working-class family's home, an exhibit referred to as "the misery room."[2] Here dolls and props were used to display an exhausted mother sitting in front of a mattress full of holes and covered in dirty blankets. A baby pulled at the mother's skirt and two other children sat on the floor. Nordstrøm was moved by this "most realistic picture of the twentieth century's wretched homes" that displayed even the smallest details of working-class life, including half-eaten bread crusts lying on the table, worn-out boots strewn about, and a beer bottle that served as a candlestick holder.[3]

It was 1916 and Parliament had recently passed two of the most comprehensive pieces of maternity legislation to date: maternity insurance under the Sickness Insurance Law and public assistance for single mothers under the Child Welfare Act. Katti Anker Møller had worked tirelessly to pass these laws and to make sure they included clauses that could make compensation contingent on the recipient giving birth at a maternity home. Yet few municipal or state-run maternity homes existed in Norway at the time and the private maternity homes run by the Salvation Army and temperance societies did not have the capacity to meet the need such

© The Author(s) 2018

A. M. Peterson, *Maternity Policy and the Making of the Norwegian Welfare State, 1880–1940*, https://doi.org/10.1007/978-3-319-75481-9_5

legislation promised to create. So Møller and other feminists organized the maternity exhibition to try and push for the creation of state-funded maternity homes where working-class women could give birth.

The maternity home movement of the 1910s and 1920s stemmed from the 1915 passage of the maternity insurance law and the Castbergian Children's Laws. Feminists like Møller worked to take advantage of the political and public focus on maternity caused by the creation of these pieces of legislation. They seized the opportunity to further their goals of achieving hygienic births for working-class women's children through the establishment of publicly funded maternity homes. These homes were to be staffed by midwives and ensure that women received the best medical care. This feminist response to the implementation of the 1915 maternity laws was largely successful. Maternity homes were created throughout Norway and the rate of institutional births rose significantly in the interwar period.

Working-class mothers and midwives also responded to the laws' implementation. They negotiated the effects the policies had on their lives through interactions with medical and welfare officials. Both working-class mothers and midwives attempted to use these social programs for their own purposes and to their own benefit. Often their use of the laws contradicted the intentions policymakers and bureaucrats had to cultivate middle-class standards of motherhood among poor women. Through everyday engagement with the maternity insurance and Castberg Laws, these women indirectly influenced the formation and implementation of policy.

This chapter studies the ways in which these laws affected feminists, single mothers and midwives to reveal the broader implications and legacies of maternity legislation and also documents how the expansion of the state's role affected the law's targeted recipients and those charged with carrying out its implementation. In her study of the origins of the Norwegian social system, Anne-Lise Seip suggests that the Castberg Laws were merely "a declaration of principle" and indicates they had little real impact on people's lives.[4] In contrast, I find that this law and the maternity insurance signaled the state's emerging interests in protecting the health of women and children, and led to important changes in the relationship between feminists, working mothers and midwives and the state, their relationships with one another, and to the practice of midwifery.

This chapter also brings issues of control and agency into sharp focus, particularly in regard to the political and medical management of women's reproduction. Since the 1970s, scholars have argued that women were

"GETTING THE MOST MONEY POSSIBLE:" WOMEN'S RESPONSES...   125

often limited in their ability to mediate the effects of reproductive policies. These earlier works of scholarship often claimed that modern medical definitions of pregnancy and childbirth led to a reduction in women's reproductive choices and agency.[5] Barbara Duden found that this changed women's bodily experience of pregnancy and childbirth.[6] In addition, historians demonstrated the significant loss in power midwives experienced due to the medicalization of childbirth.[7]

More recently, research on this topic has argued that birthing women and midwives did not passively accept policy and medical dictates, but rather actively negotiated and at times encouraged developments in the increased management of childbirth.[8] This chapter supports these findings and argues that the maternity insurance and the Castbergian Children's Laws both affected and were affected by single mothers and midwives. In addition, this chapter demonstrates the extent and limits of different groups of women's agency in relation to state power. Policymakers may have written the laws with the intent of securing the health and wellbeing of poor women and children, but these policies held multiple meanings for the women they targeted. These women often worked to avoid the coercive aspects of the legislation while still being able to reap financial benefits. This was certainly not true for all working-class mothers, however, and many accepted state interference in their private lives in order to receive assistance and welcomed some of the developments in maternity services and care. Because of their financial and social position, as well as their relationship to the state, feminists and midwives benefited from the implementation of maternity legislation in ways working-class mothers were not able.

Maternity Laws and the Maternity Home Movement

Almost immediately following the passage of the maternity insurance and Castberg Laws in 1915, Møller set about working for the creation and use of maternity homes for the women affected by these laws. Møller thought that maternity homes were the safest places for working-class women to give birth and wanted the government to establish more municipal maternity homes to serve these women. Møller claimed that this was the only way to fulfill the maternity insurance's goal of "every birth tak[ing] place in hygienic conditions and infants [receiving] good care during their first days of life."[9] For Møller these maternity homes would be a good example of places where women helped other women. Midwives would run the homes and ensure that working-class women received the best care possible. Doing so would not only improve the health of working-class mothers and their children, but also secure midwives a place in the emerging institutionalized medical system.

Despite the fact that both laws allowed for benefits to be made contingent on women giving birth at government care facilities, few of these institutions existed, especially those solely devoted to maternity care. Møller and other feminists needed to capitalize on the political and public attention paid to maternity issues following the passage of the 1915 laws and place maternity homes on the political agenda.

Møller tried to make the need for maternity homes an issue of public health. After germ theory became widely accepted amongst medical professionals in Norway, both midwives and doctors voiced their frustration with trying to achieve aseptic conditions in women's homes.[10] When Nikoline Falck Ellertsen testified in favor of the maternity insurance law in 1913 she emphasized the benefits poor women would receive from extra care during labor and confinement. Ellertsen claimed that she had seen many cases where "the child lies wet and soiled from one day to the next, which led to it losing its skin as a result ... and a stench rose up from the mother's bed which meant that she was in danger."[11] Møller used stories such as these to argue that even well-trained and skilled midwives struggled to attain the necessary level of hygiene in working-class homes.[12] Møller emphasized the impact this could have on a woman's health, as doctors had found that increased hygiene during birth corresponded to fewer illnesses occurring during confinement. Møller also related this to Dr. Brandt's assertion that a hygienic birth significantly decreased a woman's chances of contracting other illnesses throughout her life.[13] Additionally, Møller was careful to highlight the benefit maternity home stays would have on children's health as well and claimed that maternity homes would help "bring children into the world with experts and quality childcare."[14] She argued that as a result both women and the nation as a whole would benefit from the creation of publicly funded maternity homes.

Møller ended up gaining support for her cause from a broad range of actors and organizations, including Castberg, medical professionals, and the *Norske kvinners nasjonalråd*, or Norwegian National Women's Council (NKN), *Norsk kvinnesaksforening*, or Norwegian Association for Women's Rights (NKF), and *Arbeiderpartiets kvindeforbund*, or the Women's Federation of the Norwegian Labor Party (AKF). She gave speeches to women's organizations, wrote articles on the subject for the newspapers and involved Castberg in her work.[15] Sometimes she ran into difficulties, as when the NKF was slow to warm to the idea of maternity homes as an issue they should support because they did not see how this strengthened women's rights.[16] The NKN, however, was supportive and asked Møller to spearhead a committee on maternity homes under its auspices. This committee was able to successfully lobby Parliament to provide a stipend to Dr. Marie Kjølseth in 1913 to study maternity homes in Denmark and Germany.[17] They intended for Kjølseth's study to later serve as model of how maternity homes could be run in Norway.

The AKF also supported Møller's work to create municipal maternity homes, because of the positive impact they believed maternity homes could have on working-class women's lives. In March 1914 the organization demanded that the Kristiania municipal council create maternity homes in working-class neighborhoods. These socialist women argued that their demands were based on their "intimate knowledge of the horrible conditions of working-class households."[18] The AKF mentioned the overcrowding that took place in working-class urban homes as evidence of these "horrible conditions" but they did not otherwise emphasize public health and hygiene in their proposal.

Instead the AKF stressed that because of their class position, working-class women deserved to give birth in maternity homes. When factory inspector Betzy Kjelsberg visited a maternity home in Göteborg, Sweden she claimed that a woman there had characterized her stay at the home as "like being on vacation."[19] The idea that a stay at a maternity home could be a vacation for working-class women was a major reason the AKF called for the creation of maternity homes. According to the AKF every woman should be entitled to a quiet place to rest after giving birth and related this to the significance of a woman's reproductive labor: "If there are days in a woman's life when she should be mercifully protected and her mind should have permission to rest in peace and quiet, it must be when she has fulfilled her biggest duty: birthing a new human."[20]

The AKF envisioned maternity homes as places where women could come and give birth without the added distractions and responsibilities of everyday life. This is why home care was an essential part of the AKF's demands. They wanted the municipality to pay for home care so that during a mother's stay at a maternity home, another person would care for her other children and run her household.

By 1915, Møller and other feminists had succeeded in getting Parliament to recognize the importance of institutional births and write them into the maternity insurance and the Castbergian Children's Laws, but the construction of maternity homes lagged behind the passage of the legislation. In response, Møller devised an innovative way to gain the attention and support of the Norwegian public: the creation of the maternity exhibition. For over a year Møller worked with a coalition of doctors, midwives and cultural and medical institutions to build an exhibition that would educate and entertain the public. The exhibition touched on a wide range of maternity issues. There were exhibits on the historic development of birthing assistance and infant care and lectures given by doctors, midwives, and Møller. Also included was a section showcasing baby pictures of powerful Norwegian statesmen.

The main purpose of the maternity exhibition was to get the public engaged in the issue and raise funds for the creation of municipal maternity homes. Baby pictures of the Prime Minister and the Minister of War certainly served to amuse attendees, but Møller also wanted people to be shocked by the conditions in which working-class women gave birth. This was the intention behind the "misery room." Under carefully staged conditions, people like Marie Nordstrøm could see for themselves how dirty and depressing working-class homes were, and how ill equipped they were to meet the medical criteria of an aseptic birth (Fig. 5.1). Møller further highlighted this point by juxtaposing the exhibit with one showcasing a birthing room at a maternity home, complete with all of the technological tools available to medical experts. This exhibit was bright, clean and airy and depicted the modern, scientific and hygienic birth that could take place in a maternity home.

All of the major Norwegian newspapers published pieces on the exhibition and recommended that people attend. *Dagbladet* emphasized the entertainment value of viewing pictures of statesmen as babies while simultaneously learning about the all-too-real circumstances most women gave birth in.[21] Other newspapers such as *Morgenbladet* and *Aftenposten* informed their readers about the educational opportunities the exhibition presented and how interesting it was to see the development of birthing assistance and infant care.[22] The socialist newspaper, *Social Demokraten*, devoted the most space to discussing the maternity exhibition and wrote several articles on its exhibits and the lectures.[23] In comparison to *Morgenbladet* and *Dagbladet*, *Social Demokraten* did not mention the more entertaining or humorous parts of the exhibition, but rather focused on the parts that had the most

Fig. 5.1 "The misery room," Arbeiderhjem på Sagene, Oslo. Courtesy of the Norwegian Museum of Science and Technology

relevance to working-class life. It defended the portrayal of working-class homes as realistic and argued that it left onlookers with the overwhelming conviction that "municipal maternity homes must be created!"[24]

This broad newspaper coverage, along with the opening of the exhibition by the king and queen, helped attract public attention to the exhibition.[25] By all accounts, people flocked to the maternity exhibition to experience the stark contrasts presented there. Some people went, perhaps, to learn more about scientific and technological advancements in the fields of obstetrics and pediatrics and see how these tools could be used in securing women access to safer births. Others paid the entrance fee to get a glimpse at a picture of General War Commissioner, Jens Kristian Meinich Bratlie, as a helpless infant lying in a cradle. A large segment of the middle and upper classes were likely also interested in viewing the "exotic" recreation of a working-class home.

For these and other reasons, the maternity exhibition was a success. The organizers discussed extending the number of days it was showcased at *Bøndernes Hus* and it eventually went on tour to select Norwegian cities.[26] As a result, a considerable amount of money was raised to help create a start-up fund for the establishment of a municipal maternity home in Kristiania.[27]

The maternity exhibition brought public awareness to the issue of maternity homes and the impact they could have on public health and ultimately led to the creation of Kristiania's first municipal maternity home in 1917. This birthing institution helped meet Møller's demands for hygienic birthing experiences for working-class women and enlivened the AKF's hopes that women could use the home as a type of vacation. After its opening, the AKF described the maternity home as "very hygienic and modern," but also as a place where mothers had no responsibilities, the nurses even placed a baby at its mother's breast.[28] Another municipal maternity home was in operation in Kristiania soon after in 1920. Møller's goal had been for every Norwegian town to have a maternity home, and while she did not achieve this, several other places initiated plans to build maternity homes based on Kristiania's model.[29]

By 1920 feminists such as Møller had been quite successful in using debates about medicine and public health to expand maternity policies and services for working-class women. Feminists were not satisfied with merely incorporating clauses into the maternity insurance and the Castbergian Children's Laws which allowed local authorities to make maternity benefits contingent on women giving birth at institutions. After the Laws passed, these women continued to argue that women's and children's health would not be secure until more mothers received expert care during birth and confinement. They used momentum from the passage of the laws to push for the creation of publicly funded maternity homes.

Their efforts contributed to the sharp rise in institutional births that took place in Norway during the interwar period. New medical and social beliefs about institutional births, the creation of more of these institutions and, perhaps most importantly, the tying of health insurance benefits and public assistance payments to maternity home stays, accelerated the transition from home births to births that took place at an institution. In Norway's second largest city, Bergen, for example, the number of home births decreased from 83% in 1914 to 64% in 1920. By 1930 this number had further decreased to 36% and in 1950 only 1% of births took place at home.[30] Similar trends occurred in other Western European countries, but with a national average of 74% Norway had one of the highest rates of hospitalization for births in Scandinavia.[31] This may have been because the connection between maternity benefits and assistance and hospital stays was stronger in Norway than in Denmark and Sweden.[32]

Feminists like Møller contributed to this massive shift in where Norwegian women gave birth. They had worked throughout the 1910s to convince politicians and the public that institutional births would be better for working-class women, their children, and the nation as a whole. They helped embed compulsory stays at institutions for birthing women into maternity legislation and facilitated the creation of publicly funded maternity home stays. In doing so, they not only aided the increase in institutional births, but also affected the lives and livelihoods of working-class women and midwives.

WORKING-CLASS MOTHERS AND THE 1915 MATERNITY LAWS

A significant number of working-class Norwegian mothers stood to benefit from the 1915 maternity insurance and the Castbergian Children's Laws. These laws provided women with and without work access to vital financial assistance. Previously, many working-class and poor mothers had to turn to poor relief to help them survive financially during the months surrounding birth. Until 1919, these women and all other recipients of poor relief were stripped of their citizenship rights. The maternity insurance and Castberg Laws provided women with economic assistance without costing them their rights, which was of increased importance after the implementation of women's suffrage in 1913. Even after the poor law was reformed in 1919, many working people considered poor relief as shameful and restrictive.[33] The maternity insurance and Castberg Laws represented an alternative for women who needed economic aid following the birth of a child but did not want to receive poor relief.

While the benefits these laws secured for women were real, and not to be underestimated, the terms under which they offered assistance frequently aimed to keep control in the hands of health and welfare officials. The laws were set to be administered at the local level where health and welfare officials were given the liberty to define certain eligibility standards and withhold assistance from women who did not meet these standards. With the maternity insurance, many working mothers and fathers lost out on their maternity benefits because local health insurance funds found their membership in the funds to be lacking. The implementation of the Castberg Laws included particularly stringent requirements aimed to secure the health and wellbeing of children by limiting women's autonomy.

132   A. M. PETERSON

To receive assistance under the Castberg Laws, women needed to fulfill the most recent medical dictates for childbirth and child-rearing, including birthing in an institution instead of at home and breastfeeding for a determined length of time following birth. Many women either could not, or did not want to, submit themselves to these requirements. As a result, the maternity insurance and Castberg Laws helped far fewer women than government officials originally anticipated.

Working-Class Mothers and Maternity Insurance

The national health insurance revision of 1915 promised more women than ever financial assistance during the time surrounding the birth of a new child. It included maternity provisions for both women who were directly insured because of their waged work and women who were indirectly insured through their husbands. For the woman member, the insurance provided 8 weeks of paid maternity leave and free midwifery care. The rate of pay was in accordance to her insurance class and represented a range of 1 to 2.70 kroner per day.[34] Instead of the maternity benefit, a member could receive free treatment and care at a maternity facility. The fund could decide whether to provide help for housekeeping and childcare while the member was staying at the maternity facility; up to 50% of the maternity benefit could be allocated in this way.

A member's wife was entitled to free midwifery care as well as a one-time cash benefit of 30 kroner. In place of free midwifery care and the cash payment, a member's wife could receive treatment and care at a maternity facility. During the woman's stay at the maternity facility, her family could receive up to 15 kroner to hire necessary housekeeping assistance. To receive these benefits, the member of the insurance (woman and man) had to maintain uninterrupted health insurance membership for 10 months prior to the birth of the child. This requirement was a safeguard put in place by parliamentarians to ensure that people did not misuse or take advantage of the maternity coverage in the health insurance by joining the fund because of an already known pregnancy.

When expanded maternity coverage was first proposed, health insurance fund managers worried that it would cost too much money and anger the already irritated compulsory members of the health insurance further. The director of Norway's largest health insurance fund in Kristiania, Marius Ormestad, cautioned the Ministry of Social Affairs against including members' wives in the policy as he believed this would necessitate an

"GETTING THE MOST MONEY POSSIBLE:" WOMEN'S RESPONSES... 133

increase in the premium workers paid. The insurance had recently increased the premium by 30%, and Ormestad stressed that "the health insurance has not been popular among people thus far. If we are to come with a new increase without a benefit for all there will be new difficulties."[35] While the government took these concerns seriously, they did not heed Ormestad's advice. The maternity insurance of 1915 went ahead as proposed.

Ormestad's worry was not misplaced. The maternity benefit for members' wives represented a substantial increase in maternity coverage and turned out to be the most expensive aspect of the 1915 maternity insurance. In 1918, 196,960 women workers were compulsory members of the sickness insurance. Between 1916 and 1918, on average only 1476 of them gave birth (0.07%) each year. Of those births, 569 were to married women, and 907 to unmarried women. The health insurance funds paid an average of 90,575 kroner each year for these births, representing 0.010% of total national expenditures.[36] While not unsubstantial, the effects varied by individual fund. For some, the maternity insurance coverage for women members did not significantly increase in the total percentage cost. For example, in Kristiania, the percentage of the budget paid to maternity benefits to women members decreased from 1.77% in 1915 to 1.68% in 1916.[37]

On average 141,765 married men were members of the sickness insurance from 1916–1918, and 15,923 of their wives gave birth each year. This cost the insurance an average of 703,337 kroner each year, nearly eight times the amount paid to directly insured mothers. The average budget of expenses nationally for Norwegian health insurance funds during these years was 8,610,225 kroner, meaning that maternity benefits paid to members' wives represented an additional 8.1% of the total budget. Together, the maternity benefits paid out in the years immediately following the implementation of the 1915 revision to the Sickness Insurance Law cost the funds 9.1%, or less than 10%, of their total expenditures.

Each year the number of women who received maternity benefits steadily increased. In 1922, health insurance paid out nearly 2 million kroner in maternity payments to members and members' wives. This is more than double what the funds paid out nationally in 1917. While this represents a substantial increase, it is important to note that the total percentage of maternity coverage in relation to the overall insurance budgets decreased over the years, from 7% in 1917 to 4.8% in 1922, as payouts for other medical expenditures such as medicine significantly increased during this period of time.[38]

134   A. M. PETERSON

The number of women who received financial assistance following the birth of a child under the Sickness Insurance Law was substantial. From the statistics we know that one of the main responses working-class women had to the implementation of maternity insurance was to apply for support. Directly insured women continued to apply for compensation for their maternity leave as they had been doing since 1911, and now they and their midwives also submitted receipts for reimbursements for midwifery assistance and care. Husbands had not previously been able to use their insurance coverage to benefit their wives during childbirth and confinement, but starting in 1916 they went to their local health insurance offices and submitted requests for free midwifery care and cash benefits for their wives. The greatest response working-class men and women had to the new law was to try and take advantage of the insurance coverage their premiums now granted them.

It is important to note, however, that the statistics only show how many mothers received maternity payments under the health insurance law. They do not reveal the vast number of cases where women and their husbands were denied maternity benefits, largely due to interruptions in their membership coverage.

When the Sickness Insurance Law originally passed in 1909, lawmakers debated the ten-month membership requirement for maternity benefits. M.P. Sæbø worried that this stringent requirement would prevent many needy women from receiving maternity coverage. Despite his objections, Parliament voted down his proposal for a decreased membership requirement of 6 months. In the 1915, the 10-month membership requirement withstood revisions to the law, but additional language was added that allowed for shorter interruptions of up to two weeks in membership coverage. Then the worry became that the membership requirement would no longer serve as a preventative measure against too many applicants. Ormestad believed the wiggle room represented by the allowance of shorter lapses in coverage would put the maternity insurance in "full force," implying that most, if not all, applicants would receive the benefit.

Ormestad was mistaken. Many of the working-class men and women who applied for maternity benefits throughout the 1910s and 1920s were denied due to lapses in their memberships. This did not, however, stop working-class men and women from applying and demanding what they believed was rightfully theirs. In many cases, men and women did not accept initial rejections of their applications for the benefit. They appealed decisions and sometimes even took their cases to court (Fig. 5.2).

Fig. 5.2 Two bureaucrats working at the welfare office in Hedmark county, 1923. Courtesy of Domekirkeodden Museum

Working-class men and women's tenacity and perseverance in regards to applying for the maternity insurance benefit is evident in the records from a small Buskerud health insurance office located in Røyken on the Oslo fjord. Also evident in this source material is the discretion local insurance offices had in deciding whether or not to award members the benefit they requested, regardless of the law.

A municipality of nearly 5500 inhabitants, Røyken, was home to a cement factory that employed over 580 workers in 1920. Its insurance office was small, but busy, likely due to the presence of such a large manufacturer. A ledger listing all incoming and outgoing correspondence shows that many members who applied for the maternity insurance benefit in the interwar period were denied by the Røyken health insurance board. At times, men and women did not accept this rejection and pushed the board to reconsider or appealed the decision. This determination could pay off, especially after a depression struck in the 1920s.

Of twenty-five applications submitted between 1915 and 1938, the health insurance office denied fourteen on the basis of the fact that the member did not meet the ten-month membership requirement. In six instances, the office initially denied members' applications, but after

136   A. M. PETERSON

further review awarded the maternity benefit. All but one of the six were applications put forth by male members. These cases mainly took place during the 1920s and the office approved applications in spite of memberships that at times lacked up to three months of coverage for the stated reason of "high unemployment."

These decisions surely gladdened the recipients who received money they desperately needed, but it caused problems for the insurance office. Word in this small municipality spread, and when Olaf K. applied for the maternity benefit for his wife in 1927 and was denied because of a lapse in membership, he complained of unfair treatment. He knew that others had been in similar situations and had received monies and he did not believe the insurance office could treat some members differently than others. These complaints worked and after reconsidering, the insurance office awarded him the benefit likely to save face in this small community. They noted in their meeting minutes that while they had been lax in adhering to the membership requirement because of the economic depression, this could continue no longer.

The insurance office held true to this statement for the next few applications, but again sympathy caused them to approve a request that according to the law should have been denied. In December of 1928, Harald S.'s wife, Valborg, gave birth to a baby girl in a maternity home. When the home wrote to the health insurance office requesting payment the office replied that Harald was missing 1 month of his 10-month membership requirement and the insurance would not be paying for Valborg's stay. Harald must have insisted, and/or begged and pleaded with the insurance office because in January the local board met and decided to compensate Harald for the maternity home stay despite his missing membership. Harald had told the board of his unemployment and how he and his newly augmented family had no income to live off. This tale of woe convinced the insurance office to go back to its previous ways and award the maternity benefit to people who were technically not entitled.[39]

It appears that after Harald S.'s case, the Røyken insurance office began to more stringently deny cases where applicants had not met the minimum membership requirements to receive the maternity benefit. Yet the people who received these rejections in the 1930s did not passively accept the insurance office's decision. Two of the 3 applicants who were denied benefits following Harald S.'s case appealed the insurance office's decision. In these instances, the applicant was informed that s/he should contact the National Sickness Insurance Office in Oslo within 28 days of notice of a denial to appeal the local office's decision.

"GETTING THE MOST MONEY POSSIBLE:" WOMEN'S RESPONSES... 137

This procedure revealed tensions between the local and insurance offices over interpreting the "shorter interruption" section of the maternity coverage membership requirement. Such was the case when the Røyken office denied Johan J's application for maternity coverage because he was only a member of the insurance fund for 4 months prior to the birth of his child. Johan appealed this decision and the National Health Insurance Office found him entitled to the maternity benefit. The local office was confused and frustrated by this result and wrote to the national office to complain that Johan J. clearly did not fulfill the minimum membership requirements.[40]

When the maternity insurance passed in 1915 many insurance fund managers worried that the policy was too expensive and could potentially lead to the funds' financial ruin. This fear did not come true. Many women and men did apply for and receive the benefits provided to them as members of the health insurance. To these working-class people, the aid they received was much more comprehensive and generous than any other maternity policy in existence. But many other working men and women were denied the benefit on the basis of insufficient membership length prior to the birth of a child. The official membership length of 10 months, with shorter interruptions of two weeks not taken into account, did not stop working-class women and men from applying for and in some cases demanding maternity insurance coverage. They saw the benefit as something to which they were entitled as premium paying members of the health insurance. As the records from the Røyken health insurance office demonstrate, when applicants were denied, they attempted to negotiate and cajole insurance boards into sympathizing with their situations and awarding them the benefit despite having lapses in insurance membership. When these efforts failed, some of them chose to go to the National Sickness Insurance Office to appeal the local office's decision.

Single Mothers and the Castberg Laws

For many unmarried and single mothers, a denial from the insurance office caused them to look to another law for help: the Castbergian Children's Laws' Child Welfare Act. When the Ministry of Social Affairs requested information in 1921 from all of Norway's health councils on the public assistance for single mothers offered through the Child Welfare Act, many reported that this law was being used by numerous women who should have qualified for the insurance benefit. The Oslo council identified the problem as being one related to the membership requirement:

"they haven't been members for an uninterrupted 10 months." The Faaberg health council specified this further, stating "Many [women] had apparently quit their positions because of pregnancy and gotten out of the health insurance fund without thinking that they would forfeit the maternity insurance benefit."[41] Nearly all the reports back to the Ministry of Social Affairs complained that the insurance law was not working and this caused an influx of applications for public assistance under the Castberg Laws' Child Welfare Act.

A significant number of poor Norwegian mothers stood to benefit from the Castberg Laws, including those who had been denied the maternity insurance benefit. Under the Child Welfare Act, for example, women could receive economic support for six weeks prior to giving birth and for up to six months afterwards. Even some married women who were eligible for this assistance, including those whose husbands were dead, had abandoned them, or those who had separated from their spouses for some special circumstances. The amount of support varied in accordance with city/town divisions and the decisions of local authorities, but the minimum rate of support was fairly substantial and may have allowed many women to refrain from waged work while receiving it.[42]

Funding for this assistance was split between the state and local governments, with the bulk of financing coming from municipal sources. In theory, the municipal budgets would not have been significantly burdened by the implementation of this law, because they were already supporting poor mothers and children through poor relief initiatives.[43] The laws merely funded this support through a different social program. This change may not have had a significant impact on municipal budgets, but it did significantly alter the legal status and social standing of poor women by keeping them off poor relief.[44]

While the law offered substantial economic support for poor mothers, just as with the health insurance, many women never received help under the Child Welfare Act. Politicians had predicted that 1400 married women would benefit from the law per year, but on average fewer than 60 married women received support in the years following passage of the law. More surprising was the fact that even unmarried women did not receive support at the rate anticipated. The government had anticipated that around 2500 unmarried women would receive this assistance per year, but on average fewer than 800 per year had done so by 1925.[45] In Kristiania, only 90 unmarried women received help prior to giving birth and 143 after giving birth in 1920.[46] These low numbers disappointed health and

"GETTING THE MOST MONEY POSSIBLE:" WOMEN'S RESPONSES... 139

welfare officials, women's rights advocates and other social reformers who had believed the legislation would significantly improve poor women's and children's health; this led them to work towards a revision of the law in the early 1920s.[47]

Politicians and women's rights activists argued that there were two main reasons women did not receive assistance: first, few women knew about the law and the number of applicants was therefore low; second, the bureaucratic administration of the law was ineffective and created obstacles for the women who did apply.[48] To solve this first problem, female factory inspector Betzy Kjelsberg worked to inform working women of the laws and the financial help they could receive.[49] Proposed revisions to the laws in the early 1920s also sought to simplify the application process.[50] Yet problems persisted and as late as twenty years later Katti Anker Møller's daughter, Dr. Tove Mohr, characterized the lack of use of the laws as a "shame for [women reformers]."[51]

It is difficult to know exactly why so few poor women received public assistance under the Castberg Laws' Child Welfare Act. Many may not have applied because of religious and social dictates that encouraged women who gave birth to children outside of wedlock to feel deeply ashamed. It is likely that these women did not apply for assistance because they did not want to draw attention to their situation and the resulting public scrutiny.

There is some evidence to suggest that other women did not apply because they did in fact not know about the existence of the laws, even as late as 1936. That year, a woman wrote to Dr. Mohr and thanked her for an article she had written on the Laws, because it helped the woman "understand [her] rights as it ha[d] gone over one year and [she] had not received support."[52] Armed with the information Mohr had included in her article, the woman reported that she went to the local welfare office and asked to be retroactively compensated. Her request was denied. Mohr claimed that she received many letters just like this one detailing the lack of knowledge poor women had of the Castberg Laws. For this reason, women's rights activists tried to educate poor women on the maternity benefits for which they were eligible.[53]

Other evidence suggests that even the women who knew about the assistance and applied for support faced difficulties meeting the scrutiny of local health councils, made up of medical doctors and civil servants from the community. The law had granted these health councils significant power in deciding who was eligible for assistance and how much support a woman

140   A. M. PETERSON

could receive. This local administration of the law meant that the members of the health councils often knew the women who applied for assistance and women's reputations could affect the status of their applications. This is what happened when Hilda E. applied for support in May 1924. Her local health council unanimously rejected her application because she was known in the community for being "immoral" and a "cheat."[54] Even though the Ministry of Social Affairs found these reasons "untenable," the Ministry found it best not to intervene in the case. Hilda E. ended up having to apply for poor relief.[55]

Cases such as Hilda E.'s suggest that administration of the law at the local level could entail extra obstacles for women. They not only had to overcome "the shame of [having their circumstances] known in their home villages," but also had to undergo review from members of their own communities.[56] This local administration made it difficult for authorities to judge an application impartially and consequently more onerous for some of the women who sought support.

Many of the women who applied for support were denied assistance because of the timing of their applications. These rejections occurred when a woman neglected to request assistance for a child before it was born, and if she did not apply for postpartum support within 3 months of a child's birth. Three women in Aure municipality, located on the western coast of Norway near Trondheim, experienced this denial when they applied for public assistance under the Child Welfare Act. Within months of one another, Anna S., Marta S. and Hanna E. all applied for pre- and postpartum support a month after their children were born. While the law was not entirely clear on whether or not a woman could receive the 6 weeks of prepartum assistance after the birth of her child, the Aure health council denied Anna, Marta and Hanna's applications. Despite the Ministry of Social Affairs' insistence that these women were in fact entitled to support, the Aure health council remained steadfast in their decision. Ultimately, Marta S. took her case to court on September 14, 1917.[57] Marta lost her case, and the court decision later led the government to clarify that in order to be eligible for assistance women had to apply for support prior to giving birth.[58]

Countless other women were denied partial or all of the 3 months' postpartum support because they did not request assistance prior to or immediately following the birth of a child. Local health councils interpreted §2 of the law: "the assistance shall be substantial enough so that she can keep the child in her care during the first three months of its life" strictly and only allowed women to receive support for the first three months of a child's life. For example, in 1926 the health council in Kristiansand had three women apply for 3 months of assistance between 6 weeks and 2 months after giving birth and all of the women had the period of time they waited to apply deducted from the 3 months of support.[59] This practice meant that in order to receive the full amount of assistance a woman needed to know about the policy prior to giving birth and apply immediately after her child was born. Otherwise she forfeited her right to the entire three months of municipal support. These women could, and often did, then apply for the "extended" additional three months of support, but this assistance was not a woman's legal right to receive and came with additional criteria.

In addition to the difficulties many women faced when applying for support, poor women may never have requested assistance because of the restrictions local health councils could place on the way they birthed and mothered their children. According to the law, the local health council could require that a woman give birth in an institution, such as a maternity home, in order to receive public assistance.[60] Many health councils took advantage of the clause and "use[d] the law to place the mother and child in a maternity home, because [they knew] the child [would] receive the necessary care [there]."[61] This must have been the attitude among the members of the Kristiansand health council in 1916 because nearly every woman who applied for assistance in that year was required to give birth in either a hospital or maternity home in order to be eligible.[62] The health councils' use of this section of the law reflected the fear that women who gave birth at home, away from medical supervision, would not use the assistance in the "correct" manner and that it would be "wasted" on what they perceived to be less-than-necessary purchases.[63] By forcing women to give birth at a governmentally controlled institution, health officials could better ensure that women gave birth in the type of environment congruent with their goals of protecting infant health.

Poor women did not always want to stay in maternity homes and some resisted this coercive aspect of the maternity support. Prior to the Second World War, few women gave birth in a place other than their own home.[64] Women, especially impoverished women who lived in rural areas, would not have been accustomed to the sterile nature of medical institutions.[65] While their advocates upheld maternity facilities as "hygienic" and "modern," many poor women were horrified by their "white coldness."[66]

Giving birth in a familiar and comfortable environment was important to many women and some of them were not willing to sacrifice this feeling of safety in order to receive public assistance. One woman wrote to Tove Mohr in 1934 complaining that the local health council denied her daughter maternity support because she refused to give birth in a maternity home. According to this woman, her daughter did not want to give birth in an unknown place when she had "it so good here at home." This mother found it disheartening that a poor woman who had already endured enough hardship should also be "forced from her home" and "not get what belongs to them [sic]."[67] The monetary assistance this woman's daughter could have gained by submitting to the local health council's requirement that she birth in a maternity home was not enough to persuade her to give birth in an institution.

Maternity homes could also be used to monitor and correct the ways poor women mothered their children. In birthing institutions, health officials collected information on infants' weight, measurements and general condition, which they sent to government authorities for statistical purposes. The health officials also used this information as a way to monitor and quantify how a mother cared for her child. The average length of stay at a maternity home was 14 days in 1917, and during this stay poor mothers were trained in "proper" childcare methods.[68] Mothers who had children whose statistics fell outside the range of "normal" received extra instruction.[69] Maternity homes could also be required by health councils to enforce a certain moral justice. For instance, the Bergen health council believed that women who gave birth to several children outside of wedlock should be "forced" to give birth at a maternity home as it was "good punishment for these [types of] mothers."[70]

Women who did not give birth at maternity homes but still received assistance were monitored by local health councils in other ways. For example, some single mothers were required to submit their children to regular medical checks that took place at infant control stations, or *spedbarnskontroll*. At the infant control stations, which had been modelled after Pierre Budin's practices at Charité Hospital in Paris, nurses and midwives weighed, measured and checked infants for illness.[71] The nurses and midwives staffing the station also instructed women in infant care and advised them to follow a strict feeding regime. Breastfeeding was almost always stressed as the only acceptable way for women to feed their children (Fig. 5.3).[72]

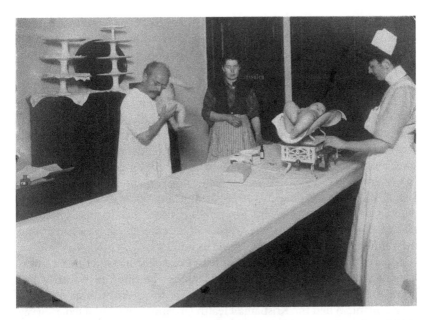

Fig. 5.3 Dr. Randers examines an infant at an infant control station, 1914. Courtesy of the Norwegian Museum of Science and Technology

Local health councils thought that infant control stations were a good way to ensure that poor women mothered their children according to the most recent medical standards of care, but the boards encountered difficulties getting women to attend the controls. In an effort to remedy this, the health councils in Bergen and Kristiania began to require women who received public assistance to bring their children to control stations or the office of the district physician in the 1920s.[73] One of the reasons the Kristiania health council implemented this practice was to have "more control over individuals who live at home and not in a maternity home."[74] The support payments were actually distributed at the infant control stations, and if a woman did not show up she risked forfeiting her assistance. The health councils also used in-home monitoring to help them ascertain whether a woman who received assistance was following the medical standards for childcare and housekeeping and breastfeeding her child.

For the women who had refused to give birth at maternity homes, infant control stations may also have been an unwelcome requirement. Many, but certainly not all, of the poor women who attended the control

144 A. M. PETERSON

stations disliked them because they felt them to be an intrusion in their private lives.[75] Some also resented the condescension they felt from doctors and nurses.[76] It is therefore possible that some women did not apply for or receive public assistance because they wanted to avoid having to bring their children to infant controls.

In order to receive extensions of their maternity support beyond the first three months, a woman also had to prove to the local health council that she breastfed her child. A section of the law specifically mentioned that only mothers of infants in poor health could receive the extended assistance, which was supposed to help ensure prolonged breastfeeding.[77] In conjunction with a circular sent to health councils by the Ministry of Social Affairs on October 29, 1915, local health councils were to require women to breastfeed beyond three months in order to be eligible for extended support.[78] For some women this requirement was something they either could not or did not want to fulfill.

Most of these women probably did not breastfeed beyond three months because they had to return to work. Despite returning to waged work, however, many women still needed assistance to cover the costs of caring for an infant. When the Kristiania Health Commission conducted a survey of unmarried mothers in 1912, they found that less than one-third of the women studied exclusively breastfed beyond three months.[79] Weaning their children was likely related to the fact that between 1918 and 1920, nearly 75 percent of the women supervised by the Kristiania health council returned to work within four months of giving birth.[80] This would have made it very difficult to continue to breastfeed and many women had to wean their infants between six weeks and two months after giving birth.

Local health councils did not have much sympathy for women who returned to waged work and stopped breastfeeding as a result. Many local health councils interpreted this practice as women *wanting* to be "done with [breastfeeding] as soon as possible to start work again."[81] Others characterized this practice as women's lack of caring for their children: "Some women care for their children very well but the majority want to wean the child and have someone else care for it so they can resume work."[82] Health officials did not perceive women who stopped breastfeeding as *needing* to do so in order to earn enough money to survive. For that reason, many women who could not continue to breastfeed their children past three months had to apply for poverty relief because health councils denied their applications for extended public assistance.[83]

Some women who did not breastfeed were able to still receive extended assistance if they could furnish proof that this was due to a medical condition. Every time the Kristiansand health council furnished an award of extended assistance to a woman, it specified that the monies were contingent on the mother breastfeeding. Even when a medical authority, such as a doctor, specified that a child's health warranted additional support, the board denied a woman's application if she did not breastfeed. This happened to Borghild K. in 1924. Katrine D.'s application for extended assistance was also denied initially in 1926 because she did not breastfeed. Yet after a midwife attested that Katrine's health would not allow her to breastfeed, the board consented to granting her 3 months of extended municipal support.[84] These cases suggest that while for the most part health councils stringently applied the breastfeeding requirement to mothers who applied for extended assistance, they could be flexible in instances where they believed a woman did not breastfeed because she physically could not rather than she merely chose not to.

While fewer women applied for or received public assistance under the Castberg Laws' Child Welfare Act than politicians had hoped, a significant number of women did benefit from the legislation. Between 600 and 800 poor women per year between 1915 and 1925 received maternity support from the Norwegian government to help them offset the costs of giving birth to and raising children.[85] Most of these women lived in Kristiania and were unmarried domestic servants, but many others lived throughout the Norwegian countryside and came from diverse marital and occupational backgrounds.[86] Many were unable to get support from their children's fathers and were ineligible to receive maternity insurance benefits because they did not fulfil the membership requirements.[87] For these women, the public assistance they received under the Castberg Laws' Child Welfare Act would have been a better, if not unproblematic, alternative to receiving poverty relief.

Some of the women who received assistance used the laws to exercise agency and citizenship rights. Such was the case with Marta S., who laid claim to public assistance benefits for mothers and infants as an entitlement in her case against the Aure municipality. Believing that the assistance was rightfully hers, Marta did not give up when her local municipality denied her application for support. In court, Marta and her lawyer argued that "the law afford[ed] her a right as an unmarried woman, a right that the municipality [was] required to pay."[88] While the court ultimately sided

146   A. M. PETERSON

with the Aure health board, Marta S.'s case demonstrates that some women not only knew about the law, they also felt it was their *right* as unmarried women to receive assistance.

Single Norwegian mothers negotiated, embraced, and resisted the various effects the 1915 maternity legislation had on their lives. Maternity insurance represented a substantial increase to working men's and women's insurance coverage and many of them eagerly sought to obtain the benefit. Unfortunately, local health insurance offices denied a significant percentage of applications due to insufficient membership lengths. These rejections did not stop working-class men and women from applying and at times pursuing appeals to these decisions.

When it came to the Castbergian Children's Laws' Child Welfare Act, many women never applied for the public assistance for which they were eligible and some who did had their applications denied. Even the women who did apply and receive support encountered restrictions on their freedom to choose where to give birth and how to mother their children. To escape the more coercive aspects of the law, many women sacrificed the support they could have received and refused to give birth in maternity homes, breastfeed past three months, and attend infant control stations. Other women like Marta S. saw the laws as an important right they had received and fought to claim their benefits. Women's reactions to the laws were frequently unanticipated by government officials and caused politicians and bureaucrats to re-interpret and re-evaluate the laws on maternity insurance and public assistance for single mothers in the Child Welfare Act throughout the interwar period.

MIDWIVES AND MATERNITY LEGISLATION

Single mothers were not the only group of women directly affected by the passage of these maternity laws. Midwives, too, were intimately involved in the implementation of the laws and stood to gain both economically and professionally from the legislation. Midwives were present at the majority of Norwegian births, and the state needed midwives to assist them with the bureaucratic implementation of the maternity insurance and Castberg Laws.[89] This need strengthened midwives' relationship to local and state authorities and created opportunities for midwives to bolster their professional status. Consequently, midwives became further incorporated in the state apparatus. This had substantial repercussions for midwives' professional lives and their relationships with birthing women.

The implementation of the maternity insurance and the Castberg Laws, along with other legal, medical, and social developments, also contributed to the institutionalization of birth in Norway. This marked increase in institutional births caused a crisis in midwifery. In response, midwives adapted their skills to changing ideas of pregnancy and infant care and became more involved in the state supervision of mothers.

As one of the main medical practitioners present at births, and one of the few governmental representatives in rural areas, the state needed midwives to help them carry out the maternity insurance law and the Castberg Laws. Many midwives were publicly employed and had important duties connected to their place in the state apparatus. These duties and services were expanded with the passage of the 1915 maternity legislation.

Under the maternity insurance law, midwives and local health insurance funds had to develop relationships with one another, work out rates and tariffs, and ensure the free midwifery services were available to all qualified members of the health insurance. Conflicts between the local insurance offices and midwives were common as midwives tried to negotiate higher rates and the duties they were expected to perform in order to receive pay. The *Journal of Midwifery* is full of notices throughout the interwar period that detail local midwifery associations' refusals to work with insurance offices who did not agree to their specified rates of payment. For example, in November 1922 the Sør Trøndelag association was not able to come to an agreement with the insurance office on their requested rate of 30 kroner per birth, so as mediator the county governor was tasked with deciding payment for each individual birth that took place in the county. In March 1923 the Vestfold county association cancelled their contract with the insurance office because the office would not increase their rate of pay by 5 kroner. Struggles between the insurance offices, individual midwives, and midwifery associations continued throughout the interwar period and wrought havoc on local administration.

Midwives also thought of the increased paperwork they needed to fill out for birthing women and the insurance funds as additional work and wanted more pay for working with insured people. In 1922 one midwife wrote to the editor of the *Journal of Midwifery* asking for advice because she had been denied payment from an insurance office because she did not make it to the birth in time to deliver the baby. A storm had prevented the midwife from arriving earlier, and once she did arrive she fulfilled her other duties of filling out the birth certificate and writing an attest for the birthing woman to receive her maternity insurance benefit.[90] The health insurance fund did not find the midwife deserving of payment because she had not been present for the birth of the child, while the midwife believed her job encompassed more than delivering babies. The state and insurance offices required additional duties of her, for which she demanded compensation.

When it came to the Castberg Laws, the government relied on midwives to help them with the bureaucratic logistics of implementation and supervision of poor mothers. For example, both the "Child Welfare Act" and the "Children Whose Parents are not Married" law required an unmarried woman who wanted maternity support from her child's father or the municipality to submit to a midwife's examination. During the examination the midwife would verify the existence of pregnancy and determine the approximate dates of conception and delivery. This information was then used to help establish paternity and decide when a woman was eligible to receive support payments.[91]

The Castberg Laws also charged midwives with establishing dates of conception and delivery, and midwives were additionally required to fill out detailed reports on illegitimate births for the authorities[92]—taking the power and duty of reporting illegitimate births out of the hands of unmarried mothers and into the hands of governmental officials. Prior to the Castberg Laws, unmarried mothers needed to report the births of their illegitimate children in order to initiate paternity suits. The passage of the Castberg Laws altered this practice. The government freed unwed mothers from the difficulty and shame of registering the births of their illegitimate children in order to get child support, but also took away their ability to choose whether or not to elicit support from their children's fathers.[93] The state wanted all fathers to be held financially accountable for their illegitimate children regardless of the wishes of unmarried mothers. This goal required that meticulous records of illegitimate births be kept. Midwives were essential to realizing this objective.

Some midwives struggled with this new role and the implications it had for their relationships with birthing women. Since the early nineteenth century midwives had fulfilled a bureaucratic role for the state by registering the live births they attended, and the reporting of illegitimate births was a part of this role.[94] After the passage of the Castberg Laws, the paperwork associated with an illegitimate birth became substantially more complicated. Previously, a midwife only had to indicate that a child was born outside of marriage by writing only the mother's name on the certificate instead of both the mother's and father's names.[95] After the passage of the

"GETTING THE MOST MONEY POSSIBLE:" WOMEN'S RESPONSES... 149

Laws, a midwife had to ask an unmarried birthing woman a series of questions about the pregnancy, possible dates of conception and the identity of the child's father.[96] This could lead to the birthing woman feeling interrogated by the person who was supposed to help and support her during a vulnerable time in her life.

Midwives could find themselves in difficult positions when their roles as birthing women's confidants and supporters clashed with their newly defined tasks of providing the state with information on illegitimate births. In 1919, "a country midwife" wrote to the *Journal of Midwifery* to ask for advice in a case where she felt that a birthing woman lied to her about when the woman had become pregnant in an effort to obscure the identity of the child's father.[97] This midwife thought it very difficult to discern whether she had an obligation to respect the birthing woman's statement or report her own expert opinion to the state.

Midwives could also be called into testify in paternity cases, and this made the midwife's role even more challenging. Midwives generally felt a duty to report the "truth" as they saw it, even if it meant discrediting a birthing woman. Despite the doubt the "country midwife" had regarding the veracity of the birthing woman's statement, the editor of the midwifery journal stressed the midwife's duty toward the woman as being more important than her duty to the state. The editor told the midwife that her thoughts on the identity of the child's father were immaterial and that she should relay only the mother's statement to the authorities. Further stressing this point, the editor stated that even if the midwife was asked to testify in court, she should be careful in asserting her own opinion as to whom the father might be.[98] The midwife was not satisfied by this answer and felt that she needed to act "according to her conscience and convictions" and not be made a "mouthpiece for a loose girl's coarse lies."[99]

Balancing allegiances between the state and birthing women was not easy, especially when legislation like the maternity insurance and Castberg Laws gave midwives increased power over poor mothers. Women now had to have midwives verify their pregnancies and were required to report intimate details of their lives, which often included their sexual histories, to midwives. The Castberg Laws' Child Welfare Act also included a clause that allowed local authorities to entrust a woman's public assistance payments to a midwife. In this way, the state gave midwives control over a poor mother's money to ensure that the payment was "used according to the best interests of the mother and child."[100] While parliamentarians had discussed having the maternity insurance payment to members' wives entrusted to midwives as well, this did not come to fruition, likely because the insurance benefit was a right working-class men and women were entitled to receive based on their premium payments.[101] These types of legislative decisions recognized and bolstered midwives' professional status, at the same time that they created distance between midwives and the women they attended.

The maternity insurance and Castberg Laws also contributed to the sharp rise in institutional births during the interwar period, in the face of which Norwegian midwives struggled to maintain their professional viability. The institutional model of childbirth called for fewer midwives to serve higher numbers of birthing women in institutional settings—it was not based on the one-to-one home birth model. These settings also threatened midwives' individual and collective authority and autonomy because they had to compete with (male) medical doctors and highly educated nurses as experts on maternity.[102]

Early on, midwives identified an institutional model of childbirth as placing the professional practice and status of midwifery in jeopardy.[103] They acerbically pinpointed the "genius idea of relocating births to clinics" as the reason there would "soon be no more midwives."[104] Worried that Norwegian midwives would become nothing more than a "saga," they sarcastically advised that would-be midwives might as well "report to the local poverty board" to receive assistance as go to midwifery school.[105]

Midwives did not passively accept this situation, which the Castberg Laws had helped create. They responded to the perceived threat of an institutional model of birth and expanded their professional domain. By the mid-1930s midwives believed their profession was in crisis and requested Parliament substantially revise the 1898 midwifery law. One of the changes midwives demanded was to be able to act as public health nurses in areas where they could not make a decent living from midwifery alone.[106] Parliament ultimately passed a law in 1937 that allowed midwives to act as public health nurses, but also granted them the ability to significantly expand their medical purview to encompass the care of infants and pregnant women, practice midwifery in maternity homes and hospitals and perform "other tasks within the public health system."[107]

The expansion of the boundaries midwives could operate within improved their ability to incorporate themselves into a modern, medicalized system of birth, but this shift did not occur immediately or without controversy.[108] Throughout the late 1920s and 1930s debates about whether or not midwives should practice anything but traditional midwifery took place in the pages of the *Journal of Midwifery*.[109] Some, such as Nikoline Falck-Ellertsen, worried that midwives would dilute their authority and "become servants for people" if they cared for pregnancy and infants.[110] Others such as a midwife who practiced in Nordland felt that the possibility of working as a public health nurse and infant care specialist represented a "lightening" of their dark situation.[111] By the time the revision of the midwifery law passed in 1937, midwives appear to have reconciled themselves to the prospect of acting in other capacities than childbirth assistants. Midwives argued that now that the law allowed midwives access to new positions as public health nurses, midwives actually needed to take advantage of this opportunity. In 1938 the Sogn and Fjordane Midwives Association, located on the western coastal region of Norway, recommended that midwives staff infant care stations or "be forgotten" and lose these jobs to nurses.[112] Even midwives living in remote areas further from hospital settings—such as these—believed that by retooling as experts in infant care and pregnancy midwives could prove their continued relevance and survive economically and professionally.

The move toward a more encompassing practice of midwifery may have helped midwives weather the storm of changing medical and social ideals, but it also affected midwives' relationships with birthing women. At infant control stations, midwives weighed and measured working-class women's children and advised these women on how best to care for their infants. This work further defined midwives' roles as supervisors of poor mothers and expanded the professional distance between them.

Midwives also responded to the heightened economic pressures they felt by trying to use their relationship to the health insurance funds and the services they provided in conjunction with the Castberg Laws to gain greater rates of compensation. Simultaneous to trying to negotiate higher tariffs with the insurance offices, midwives also attempted to use the Castberg Laws to re-interpret long-established laws that governed midwives attendance of poor women's births. The 1810 midwifery law required midwives to attend all birthing women regardless of whether these women could pay for midwifery services.[113] In cases where a birthing woman could not afford to pay a midwife for her services, the midwife could apply to the local and state governments to have her transportation costs and a fraction of her service fee reimbursed. Midwives often had to

152   A. M. PETERSON

struggle with local authorities to get them to pay for these services. Such was the case when Midwifer Gjernes in Aure received notice that the Aure poverty board refused to compensate her for the transportation costs she incurred when she assisted an impoverished woman because the birthing woman had fed her a meal while she attended the birth. Gjertnes had to get the district physician to mediate in this case. Getting paid the minimum rate they were due was difficult enough, and midwives encountered even more obstacles when they tried to obtain a raise in the rate in the 1930s.[114]

The Castberg Laws did not include free midwifery for unmarried women, but midwives claimed the legislation entitled them to a higher rate of compensation when helping unwed mothers. The Laws held an illegitimate child's father responsible for the costs of his child's birth. An attending midwife was supposed to receive compensation after a paternity case against the child's father was finished, but this could often take several months and in some cases the money never materialized.[115]

Similarly, the Child Welfare Act did not include any mechanism for the coverage of birth expenses or midwifery fees. Instead, the parturient woman was supposed to use part of the maternity support she received from the municipality to pay for a midwife. For many poor women paying a midwife out of an already small benefit was not feasible, and they often refused to pay midwives for their services or used the less-expensive *hjelpekoner* instead.[116] Midwives who did not receive payment had to go to the local authorities and ask to be reimbursed according to the 1810 midwifery law that required a midwife to attend all birthing women regardless of whether these women could pay for her services. This request could often be denied.[117]

In the 1920s and 1930s, midwives tried to argue that the Castberg Laws had radically altered unmarried women's status and thus midwives should not be required to serve them for less than their normal rate of pay. In 1929 *Den norske jordmorforening*, or Norwegian Association of Midwives (DNJ), wrote to the Ministry of Social Affairs demanding that midwives be compensated for the birthing assistance they provided to women covered under the Castberg Laws.[118] In this letter, the midwives' association maintained that the Castberg Laws had established that the maternity assistance poor women received was not to be considered poor relief. As the laws requiring a midwife to attend a birthing woman regardless of her ability to pay hinged on the woman's destitution and relationship to the poor relief board, the midwives' association argued that midwives were not obliged to assist women covered by the Castberg Laws. The Ministry rejected this interpretation of the law, but the DNJ continued to press this line of reasoning throughout the 1930s.[119]

Midwives' varied responses to the 1915 pieces of maternity legislation demonstrate the ways they accepted, adapted and challenged the impact these laws had on their lives and livelihoods. Under the legislation, the state required midwives to take an active role in executing the laws and ensuring that recipients of public assistance benefits mothered their children in ways that complied with state interests and wishes. Midwives had to report illegitimate births to the local authorities and question the women they attended about who the fathers of their children were. They could also administer the maternity support women received under the Castberg Laws. Additionally, as the government began to encourage, and at times coerce, women to give birth in maternity homes, midwives adapted their practices to accommodate the new system of institutional birth and care. Midwives began working in the infant control stations that were attended by some women under threat of having their support payments withheld. These developments had some professional advantages for midwives as well as consequences for the relationships midwives had with parturient women.

CONCLUSION

When Møller organized the maternity exhibition in 1916, the broader impact of the maternity insurance and Castberg Laws was yet to be seen. Legislators had written the laws in an attempt to protect and secure the state's interests in safeguarding Norwegian women's and children's health and wellbeing. They believed that one of the best ways to accomplish this was by strengthening the "health ... and the economic situation of the mother" and designed comprehensive maternity provisions to include in both the Sickness Insurance Law and the Castbergian Children's Laws.[120] Feminists used this political climate to push for the creation of maternity homes for working-class and poor mothers to give birth in. Their efforts helped spur the institutionalization of birth in the interwar period.

Policymakers did not anticipate the broad range of effects the laws would have on midwives, and working-class and single mothers nor were they able to accurately predict their responses to the laws' implementation. They ended up disappointed and dissatisfied by the low numbers of women who applied for and received maternity support in the years immediately following passage of the policies. Policymakers responded by seeking to educate more women about the existence of the laws and simplify the bureaucratic process women had to go through to apply for assistance. As a result, politicians discussed revisions to the Child Welfare Act throughout the 1920s. Additionally, when the health insurance law was revised in 1930, lawmakers provided more lenience in regards to membership length requirements and increased the "shorter interruptions" from two weeks to six weeks.[121]

These changes represent the indirect influence women had on policy decisions—by merely refusing or neglecting to apply for assistance, or applying but being rendered ineligible, women instigated discussions and actions on policy reform. Despite the clear resistance some women had to the more onerous and coercive aspects of the Castberg Laws, legislators did not, however, identify these elements of the Laws as being the reason so few women may have taken advantage of the assistance. Instead, local officials reacted to women's refusal to comply with certain criteria by implementing stricter measures and controls, such as requiring women who did not give birth at a maternity home to bring their babies to infant control stations in order to receive support.

Midwives attempted to use both laws to gain greater professional concessions from the government, but doing so complicated the relationship they had with birthing women. Midwives carried out the tasks and duties the state assigned them in conjunction with implementation of the maternity insurance and Castberg Laws even though this put some of them in conflict with the women they served. In addition to the professional advancement midwives realized under maternity legislation, they also encountered significant challenges. In conjunction with other legal and medical developments, the laws stimulated the growth of an institutional model of childbirth and threatened the livelihoods of midwives throughout Norway. Midwives were able to successfully navigate this shift by expanding their areas of expertise. This response to one of the effects of the Castberg Laws led to a significant change in the practice of midwifery and the place of midwives in the Norwegian medical system.

Studying women's responses to the Castberg Laws demonstrates the broader impact legislation has on women's individual and collective lives. It also illustrates the direct and indirect influence women had on policy implementation and development at both the local and national level. For working-class women and midwives, these changes were unintended.

They merely reacted to the impact the laws had on their daily lives. Yet, by doing so, they prompted large-scale changes that affected the shape of some of Norway's earliest and most ground-breaking social policies.

NOTES

1. Marie Nordstrøm, "Barselhjælputstillingen," *Kvinden*, June 1, 1916, 45.
2. Katti Anker Møller, "Om mødreforsikring," MS 4 2416:III, Håndskriftsamlingen, Nasjonalbiblioteket.
3. Nordstrøm, "Barselhjælputstillingen," *Kvinden*, June 1, 1916, 46.
4. Anne-Lise Seip, *Sosialhjelpstaten blir til: Norsk sosialpolitikk 1740–1920* (Oslo: Gyldendal, 1984), 198.
5. An excellent critique of the increased medical intervention in pregnancy and childbirth can be found in: A. Oakley, *Women Confined: Towards a Sociology of Childbirth* (Oxford, 1980).
6. Barbara Duden, *Disembodying Women: Perspectives on Pregnancy and the Unborn* (Cambridge, MA: Harvard University Press, 1993).
7. J. Donnison, *Midwives and Medical Men: A History of Inter-Professional Rivalries and Women's Rights* (London, 1977).
8. J. Leavitt, *Brought to Bed: Childbearing in America, 1750 to 1950* (New York, 1986); Regina G Kunzel, *Fallen Women Problem Girls: Unmarried Mothers and the Professionalization of Social Work, 1890–1945* (New Haven: Yale University Press, 1993); C. G. Borst, *Catching Babies: The Professionalization of Childbirth, 1870–1920* (Cambridge, MA, 1995); H. Marland and A.M. Rafferty, eds., *Midwives, society, and childbirth: debates and controversies in the modern period* (New York, 1997). For the Norwegian context, see: Ida Blom, *"Den haarde dyst": fødsler og fødselshjelp gjennom 150 år* (Oslo: Cappelen, 1988); T. Korsvold, *Sykehusfødselen tar form – med en nærstudie av E.C. Dahls stiftelse* (Oslo, 2001).
9. Katti Anker Møller, undated speech, "To foredrage uten tittel om mødreforsikring," MS 4 2416:III, Mødreforsikring Morstrygd, Håndskriftsamlingen, Nasjonalbiblioteket.
10. Midwives were especially concerned with how expensive aseptic practices were. As a result, they had been trying to get the municipality to cover the costs of antiseptics since the early 1900s. *Tidsskrift for jordmødre*, June and September, 1910.
11. Ot. Prp. Nr. 1, Appendix 5, "Skrivelse til Socialdepartementet av 5te september 1913 fra distriktsjormoren i Aarstad pr. Bergen," 69.
12. Katti Anker Møller, "Om barselutstillingen," MS 4 2416:V Kampen for kommunale fødehjem, Håndskriftsamlingen, Nasjonalbiblioteket.
13. Katti Anker Møller, "Om barselutstillingen," MS 4 2416:V Kampen for kommunale fødehjem.

156   A. M. PETERSON

14. Katti Anker Møller, "Krav om fødehjem og mødrehjem," MS 4 2416.
15. Blom, "*Den haarde dyst*," 159. Castberg also gave lectures on the subject. See: "Kommunale fødselshjem i hver kommune," *Kvinden*, April 1, 1914, 27.
16. Gina Krog to Katti Anker Møller, May 5, 1915, MS 2416:I Uegte Barn, Håndskriftsamlingen, Nasjonalbiblioteket.
17. "Kommunale barselhjem," *Nylænde*, November 15, 1915, 349; Stortingstidende forhandlinger i Odelstinget 1914, 218.
18. "Forslag om oprettelse av fødehjem indsendt," *Kvinden*, April 1, 1914, 26.
19. "Tale ved barselhjemutstillingens aapning April 26, 1916," *Nylænde*, June 15, 1916, 153.
20. "Forslag om oprettelse av fødehjem indsendt," *Kvinden*, April 1, 1914, 26.
21. "Store mænd i vuggen," *Dagbladet*, April 25, 1916.
22. "Barselhjemutstillingen," *Morgenbladet*, April 26, 1916; "Barselhjemudstillingen aabnes," *Aftenposten*, April 26, 1916.
23. Five separate articles were written on the exhibition. *Social Demokraten*: April 26, 1916, April 27, 1916, May 2, 1916, May 3, 1916.
24. Fernanda Nissen, "Barselhjemsutstillingen," *Social Demokraten*, April 27, 1916.
25. "Store mænd i vuggen," *Dagbladet*, April 25, 1916.
26. Fernanda Nissen, "Barselhjemsutstillingen," *Social Demokraten*, May 2, 1916; Ida Blom, "*Den haarde dyst*," 160–161.
27. The money the exhibition raised also went into a fund to help needy parturient women. In 1952 the director of *Kvinneklinikken* (Women's Clinic) distributed the interest from this money to women in need. See: "Katti Anker Møller fond for trengende barselkvinner," MS 2416:V Kampen for kommunale fødehjem, Håndskriftsamlingen, Nasjonalbiblioteket.
28. "Fødehjem," *Kvinden*, April 1, 1917.
29. By 1920, there were two municipal maternity homes in Kristiania and one in Sarpsborg. Bergen and Vestfold county had also started to make plans to build municipal maternity homes.
30. These statistics varied considerably across the country. In 1951, the national average of children who were born in hospitals was 74%. Blom, "*Den haarde dyst*," 48, 224.
31. In 1945 73% of all Swedish births and only 27% of Danish births took place in hospital. S. Vallgårda, Hospitalization of Deliveries: the Change of Place of Birth in Denmark and Sweden from the Late Nineteenth Century to 1970, *Medical History* 1996, 40, 173.
32. Ibid., 177.
33. Anne-Lise Seip, *Veiene til velferdsstaten: norsk sosialpolitikk 1920–1975* (Oslo: Gyldendal, 1994), 31–32.

34. Income class 1 (an income up to 300 kroner) received 1 kroner/day. Income class 2 (an income between 300 kroner and 600 kroner) also received 1 kroner/day. Income class 3 (an income between 600 kroner and 900 kroner) received 1.5 kroner/day. Income class 4 (an income between 900 kroner and 1200 kroner) received 2.1 kroner/day. Income class 5 (an income over 1200 kroner) received 2.7 kroner/day. The higher rates are in accordance with a higher premium paid.
35. Marius Ormestad, Kristiania Health Insurance Fund Report on "Mother Insurance," August 29, 1913.
36. Norges officielle statistikk, vi. 174 "Sykeforsikringen for årene 1916–1918," Riksforsikringsanstalten, 1920.
37. SAO/A-11489/A/Ac/Acc/L0003/0019—Oslo Trygdekontor, Bidrag til mødrehygienekontorets drift 1931–1932, Overview of the fund's position in 1916.
38. Norges officielle statistikk, vii. 94 "Sykeforsikringen for året 1922," Riksforsikringsanstalten, 1923.
39. Røyken Trygdekontor, Journaler 1915–1938, Statsarkivet i Kongsberg.
40. A response from the national office is not found in the records. Ibid.
41. Draft of Faaberg's health council protocol, July 26, 1921. Revisjon av forsorgsloven. RA/S-1279/D/L0020/0001 Barnevern: Forsorg for fattige mødre, Socialdepartmentet, Lovkontoret S, Saksarkiv.
42. This would have varied widely according to an individual woman's circumstances and whether or not she had to pay a midwife's fees with this money. The average minimum rate of support for the first month after the birth was 35 kroner. The average daily wage for a woman working in industry at the time was just over 2 kroner. For a servant, the average monthly wage in 1914 for a woman aged 20–24 was 18 kroner plus room and board. Statistisk sentralbyrå, Historisk statistikk, Daglønn, etter yrke, Bygder og byer, 1875–1920 and Månedslønn for hushjelp med kost og losji, etter alder, 1914–1948. See also Ida Blom, "Ingen mor maa til tidsfordriv sitte med sitt barn paa fanget": Konflikten mellom forsørgeransvar og omsorgsansvar blant ugifte mødre i Bergen, 1916–1940, in P. Fuglum and J. Simensen, eds., *Historie Nedenfra: festskrift til Edvard Bull på 70-årsdagen* (Oslo: Universitetsforlaget, 1984), 31.
43. Seip, *Sosialhjelpstaten blir til*, 140.
44. Establishing "worthy" aid separate from poverty relief was part of the modernizing and democratizing process in Norway. Ø. Bjørnson and Inger Elisabeth Haavet, eds., *Langsomt ble landet et velferdssamfunn: trygens historie, 1894–1994* (Oslo: Gyldendal, 1994), 29.
45. RA, G. Wiesener, Omkring barnelovene av 1915.

158   A. M. PETERSON

46. RA, Sosialdepartementet 2, Sosialkontor D, Barnevern, Forsorg og bidragssaker, 1919.
47. Ot. Prp. 18/1920.
48. Ot. Prp. 18/1920.
49. Nasjonalbiblioteket, Håndskriftsamlingen (heretter NBH), MS 2416:I Uegte Barn, Betzy Kjelsberg to Katti Anker Møller 15/4-1915.
50. Ot. Prp. 18/1920.
51. T. Mohr, Mødrenes kår, *Kvinden*, 1/8-1936, 20.
52. Ibid.
53. Betzy Kjelsberg tried to do this in her work as a factory inspector and the Norwegian National Council of Women also supported these initiatives. NBH, MS 4 2912:7, Norske kvinners nasjonalråd, Beretning 1907–1910.
54. RA, Sosialdepartementet, 2. sosialkontor D, Lov nr. 2 av 10 april 1915, barneforsorg, Case 5015/1924.
55. Ibid.
56. RA, Socialdepartmentet, Lovkontoret S. Barnevern: Forsorg for fattige mødre, Letter from Kristiania Underfogdskontor, 3/1-1918.
57. Aure helseraadutvalg, Fohandlingsbok, June 2, 1916 and April 3, 1917, Statsarkivet i Trondheim.
58. RA, Sosialdepartementet, 2. sosialkontor D. Lov nr. 2 av 10 april 1915, barneforsorg, Report from case nr. 71/1917.
59. Kristiansand Journal for Korrespondance vedk. Bidragssaker, 1916–1965. Stadslegen i Kristiansand, Kristiansand Helseråd, 351, Statsarkivet i Kristiansand.
60. Stortingsforhandlinger 1915, Forhandlinger i Odelstinget. Lov om forsorg for barn, 243.
61. RA, Revisjon av forsorgsloven, Barneforsorgskontoret i Kristiania to Barneforsorgsinspektøren, 11/6-1921.
62. Kristiansand Journal for Korrespondance vedk. Bidragssaker, 1916–1965. Stadslegen i Kristiansand, Kristiansand Helseråd, 351, Statsarkivet i Kristiansand.
63. RA, Revisjon av forsorgsloven. Reports from Sør Trøndelag fylke. 6/7-1921.
64. Blom, "*Den haarde dyst*," 121.
65. Poor women who lived in Kristiania would have been more familiar with birthing institutions because impoverished women could give birth for free at the Women's Clinic. This clinic was staffed by medical and midwifery students who used these poor women to practice their skills.
66. Fødehjem, *Kvinden*, 1/4-1917.
67. Letter sent to Tove Mohr in 1934 and reprinted in *Kvinden*, 1/8-1936, 20.

"GETTING THE MOST MONEY POSSIBLE:" WOMEN'S RESPONSES... 159

68. Statsarkivet i Oslo, Correspondence, Barselkvinners forpleiningstid, Kristiania Fattigstyre, Oslo Trygdekontor, 16/2-1917.
69. RA, Revisjon av forsorgsloven, Barneforsorgskontoret i Kristiania to Barneforsorgsinspektøren, 11/6-1921.
70. Medicinalberetning for Bergen Stadsfysikus, 1925, 17. Byarkivet i Bergen.
71. Many of the control stations were partially funded by the municipality and run by voluntary organizations such as the Norwegian Women's Sanitary Association, which hoped to use them to prevent the spread of communicable disease like tuberculosis. Voluntary organizations continued to take primary responsibility for the running of these clinics until the Public Health Station law in 1972 transferred full financial and staffing responsibility to municipalities. Ida Blom, "'How to have healthy children': Responses to the falling birth rate in Norway", c. 1900–1940, *Dynamis*, 2008, 28, 157.
72. Women who could prove that they were physically unable to breastfeed could receive help from "Milk Drops" organized by voluntary organizations. Blom, "How to have healthy children," 159.
73. KSK, 1920; Medicinalberetning for Bergen Stadsfysikus, 1924. Byarkivet i Bergen.
74. Ibid.
75. Blom, "How to have healthy children," 161.
76. Ibid.
77. Lov om forsorg for barn, 1915 §5.
78. RA, Socialdepartmentet, Lovkontoret S. Barnevern: Forsorg for fattige mødre, Revisjon av forsorgsloven.
79. Out of the 881 women studied, 259 or 29% breastfed beyond three months. Oslo byarkiv, Beretning fra Kristiania sundhetskommission (heretter KSK), 1913. Barn født utenfor egteskap i Kristiania i 1912 og deres forældre.
80. These data were collected by health council representatives who supervised these women. KSK, 1919, 1920, 1921.
81. RA, Revisjon av forsorgsloven.
82. RA, Revisjon av forsorgsloven, Reports from Bergen fylke.
83. RA, Revisjon av forsorgsloven, Barneforsorgskontoret i Kristiania to Barneforsorgsinspektøren, 11/6-1921.
84. Kristiansand Journal for Korrespondance vedk. Bidragssaker, 1916–1965. Stadslegen i Kristiansand, Kristiansand Helseråd, 351, Statsarkivet i Kristiansand.
85. RA, Sosialdepartementet 2, Sosialkontor D, Barnevern, Forsorg og bidragssaker, 1919; RA, G. Wiesener, Omkring barnelovene av 1915.
86. KSK, 1916–1940.

160   A. M. PETERSON

87. RA, Socialdepartmentet, Lovkontoret S. Saksarkiv, Revisjon av forsorgsloven, Barnevern: Forsorg for fattige mødre, Correspondence.
88. RA, Sosialdepartementet, 2. sosialkontor D. Lov nr. 2 av 10 april 1915, barneforsorg, Report from case nr. 71/1917.
89. In 1911, midwives attended more than 86% of all births. Ot. Prp. 1/1914, 11.
90. *Tidsskrift for jordmødre*, March 1922.
91. Women could only receive payment after a doctor or midwife attested to the fact that the birth would take place within six weeks from the date of the report. *Norsk lovtidende*, Lov om forsorg for barn, 1915, 146.
92. Rundskrivelse fra det kgl. social og industri departement, *Tidsskrift for jordmødre*, 1/8-1916, 89.
93. Paternity case records indicate that many women resisted this change because they did not want to name their children's fathers and/or register their children as illegitimate.
94. Since 1902 the state had charged midwives with following certain rules when reporting births, including reporting whether or not a child was born within marriage. Blom, "*Den haarde dyst*," 34.
95. Schema 2a and 2b in P.M. Drejer, *Lærebog for Jordmødre* (Kristiania, 1906), 272–273.
96. Rundskrivelse fra det kgl. social og industri departement, *Tidsskrift for jordmødre*, 1/8-1916, 89.
97. Brevkasse, *Tidsskrift for jordmødre*, 1/4-1919, 67.
98. Ibid., 68.
99. Jormødrene og barnefarspørsmål, *Tidsskrift for jordmødre*, 1/5-1919, 90.
100. *Norsk lovtidende*, Lov om forsorg for barn, 1915, 146.
101. Ot. Prp. Nr. 1, 1914, 22.
102. *Tidsskrift for jordmødre*: Jordmødre-deres kår, arbeidsfelt og utdannelse, Kontrollstasjoner- jordmødre-jordmor utdannelse, Jordmødre, har dere overveiet hvad det betyr?, 1/2-1939, 17–29.
103. N. Falck Ellertsen, *Jordmødre som konsulenter* (Bergen, 1920), 8–9.
104. Er den norske jordmor snart en saga?, *Tidsskrift for jordmødre*, 1/6-1933, 63.
105. Ibid.
106. Reprinted in Ot. Prp. 58/1937, 1.
107. Norges lovtidene, "Lov om forandring i lov om jordmødre av 19 desember 1898 med tilleggslover," 25 June 1937, 19–20.
108. For example, midwives remain crucial to the running of infant control stations in Norway today, and this work is considered the domain of midwives, not nurses or doctors.

"GETTING THE MOST MONEY POSSIBLE:" WOMEN'S RESPONSES... 161

109. See for example: N. Falck Ellertsen, "Jordmoren på sin rette plass," *Tidsskrift for jordmødre*, 1/4-1931, 50; Våkn op jordmødre, *Tidsskrift for jordmødre*, 1/7-1938, 109.
110. *Tidsskrift for jordmødre*, 1/4-1931, 50.
111. *Tidsskrift for jordmødre*, 1/1-1937, 46.
112. *Tidsskrift for jordmødre*, 1/7-1938, 119.Våkn op jordmødre, *Tidsskrift for jordmødre*, 1/7-1938, 109.
113. Reglement for Gjordemodervæsenet, Indretning og Bestyrelse i begge Riger, 1810.
114. This was one of the demands midwives voiced in 1934 when they asked Parliament to revise the 1898 midwifery law. Reprinted in Ot. Prp. 58/1937: 1. *Tidsskrift for jordmødre*, 14/6-1899; RA, Sosialdepartementet, 2. medisinalkontor L. Jordmorvesenet.
115. RA, Sosialdepartementet, 2. medisinalkontor L. Jordmordvesenet.
116. RA, Sosialdepartementet, 2. medisinalkontor L. Jordmordvesenet.
117. RA, Sosialdepartementet, 2. medisinalkontor L. Jordmordvesenet.
118. RA, Sosialdepartementet, 2. medisinalkontor L. Jordmordvesenet, Fødselshjelp til ugifte mødre 1929–1939, the den norske jordmorforeningen to the Socialdepartement, 12/12-1929.
119. RA, Sosialdepartementet, 2. medisinalkontor L. Jordmordvesenet, Fødselshjelp til ugifte mødre 1929–1939.
120. Ot. Prp. 5/1914, 1.
121. This was contingent on the insured having the first 2 months of membership uninterrupted. Law on Health Insurance, §13, 7. Norsk Lovtidene, 1930.

CHAPTER 6

"Mothers' Freedom Is the Key to Women's Emancipation:" Feminist Efforts to Expand Maternity Legislation in the Interwar Period

In February 1939 over 200 women working at the Oslo Social Welfare Office received an unusual internal memo.[1] The memo contained a poem that informed them they were now eligible for twelve weeks of paid maternity leave:

> It is <u>leave</u> that she needs
> From her career and her husband
> At least 8 weeks before and 4 after should be the length
> And <u>with pay</u> of course
> It is not an exorbitant use of resource
> To create a child—it takes a lot of strength
> …
> Hundreds of career women are employed here
> Who can have tons of children without any fear
> If that is what they desire the office will provide the funds
> The board did what was necessary
> As it decided yesterday
> To provide pay for a total of 12 weeks, when all is said and done…[2]

All of the women employed at the Oslo Social Welfare Office, regardless of whether they were members of the sickness insurance and despite the fact that public servants were not usually covered by the Employment Protection Act, were eligible to receive this benefit.

© The Author(s) 2018
A. M. Peterson, *Maternity Policy and the Making of the Norwegian Welfare State, 1880–1940*, https://doi.org/10.1007/978-3-319-75481-9_6

163

The creative way the Oslo Social Welfare Office had informed its workers of its decision to implement paid maternity leave caught the attention of the press.[3] Dagny Bjørnaraa, editor of the feminist periodical, *Norges Kvinder*, was particularly impressed. She congratulated Director Marius Ormestad with helping women employees successfully become a "combination [of] career woman/wife/mother."[4]

The decision to provide all of the women employees at the Oslo Social Welfare Office with twelve weeks of paid maternity leave reflected a new way of thinking about maternity support that had gained strength in the 1920s and 1930s and was heavily influenced by feminist demands. Throughout the course of the early twentieth century, women's rights activists had worked to define motherhood as a service women preformed for the state, a service that deserved recognition and compensation. Their work built on the Castbergian Children's Laws and the maternity insurance laws that had established the state's interests in women's reproductive labors. These earlier pieces of legislation, however, focused on protecting vulnerable social groups and targeted mainly poor, working-class mothers, many of whom were unmarried. In the interwar period diverse groups of feminists sought to expand these laws to include more women, especially middle-class, married women. In doing so, they transformed maternity support from a form of economic protection, one that in many cases was tainted by a rhetoric of dependence and included means-testing, to an economic right.

During the interwar period, most European feminists operated in a conservative political and social climate hostile toward women's rights, a time Karen Offen refers to as "feminism under fire."[5] In this environment, European feminists focused their efforts on achieving greater economic rights for women under the guise of policies perceived to be more moderate, mainly family-centered policies. This context helps explain the feminist push for universal maternity or child allowances in countries such as France, Britain, and Sweden during this period.[6]

While some historians have interpreted this strategy as a sign of feminism's nadir, Ann Taylor Allen argues that the rights of mothers actually provided a vehicle for feminists to call for the end of women's economic subordination and dependency.[7] Such was the case in Norway, where the interwar period was a time marked by feminist achievements. Labor feminists, equality-rights feminists, and maternal feminists all met success in realizing greater economic recognition and rights for mothers in the home and the workplace, ultimately enhancing women's social and economic rights.

In an era marked by economic depression, European feminists concentrated on issues they believed would bring women greater economic security and equality. While feminists agreed on this goal, they disagreed, at times vehemently, over the best way to achieve it. The existing divide between feminists who sought women's rights as individuals and feminists who emphasized women's rights as mothers grew into a schism in the interwar period.[8] During this time, "difference" squared off against "equality" as the cited reason for women's emancipation. Nowhere was this division more evident than in Britain where Eleanor Rathbone's work for the endowment of motherhood clashed with feminists who wanted to do away with all legislation specifically designed for women.[9]

Like their European counterparts, Norwegian feminists were also divided over the best way to achieve greater economic rights for women. They came into conflict over many issues, but of central concern was whether they believed the key to women's emancipation was in the home or in the workplace. One faction, led by Katti Anker Møller, called for motherhood to be compensated for by the state. Like Rathbone, feminists such as Møller tried to gain support for paid motherhood by framing motherhood as an occupation. These feminists argued that pregnancy, childbirth, and childcare were reproductive labors that women performed for the benefit of the state and society. As such, they thought mothers should be entitled to compensation. This had little to do with protecting impoverished parturient women and their children from the consequences of industrialization and social conditions. Instead, this was about economic rights to which every mother should be entitled. These types of arguments stimulated discussions of mothers' pensions, mother wages and family wages during the interwar period and led to their eventual implementation.

Other feminists disagreed with this method and thought that women's ability to combine motherhood with paid employment outside the home was the path to women's economic independence. They lobbied the state to assume some of the responsibilities of motherhood, including pushing for better and more comprehensive forms of maternity leave that could enable all mothers to work outside the home without suffering economic discrimination. Typically, equal rights feminists were behind many of these initiatives, but maternal feminists also supported efforts to increase women's rights in the workplace, especially those related to maternity. Norwegian feminists in the *Norsk kvinnesaksforening*, or Norwegian Association for Women's Rights (NKF), and the *Arbeiderpartiets kvindeforbund*, or Women's Federation of the Norwegian Labor Party (AKF), lobbied the state in the interwar period to make maternity leave a right that all women who worked for wages could choose to receive.[10] If women decided to take the leave, feminists demanded that they be protected from being fired. Their efforts resulted in the passage of generous and comprehensive maternity leave legislation in 1936 and also influenced initiatives like those taken by the Oslo Social Welfare Office.

The 1936 revision of the maternity leave policy was the last piece of maternity legislation passed in Norway before the outbreak of World War Two. In the decades leading up to its passage, a diverse group of feminists, midwives and working women concurrently articulated demands for women's increased rights in the home and in the workforce. Their efforts contained dual approaches to motherhood and led to the creation of policies that bolstered women's ability to stay at home with their children, including public assistance for single mothers and municipal mothers' pensions, and legislation to help strengthen women's ability to combine motherhood and waged labor, including labor protection acts and sickness insurance laws. The legislative framework women helped create would be instrumental in shaping Norwegian parental leave policies after 1945.

THE ECONOMIC, POLITICAL AND SOCIAL CLIMATE IN INTERWAR NORWAY

Norwegian feminists had been trying to achieve economic emancipation for women since the nineteenth century, but their greatest breakthroughs did not occur until the 1930s. Their successes in the 1930s were largely due to the political climate that developed in Norway during the interwar period. Despite remaining neutral throughout World War One, the war affected Norway economically, politically and socially. This significantly influenced Norwegian social policy in the 1920s and 1930s. Some developments—such as the economic crisis—stalled women's efforts, while others—such as the ascent of the Labor Party and focus on family politics—created a climate amenable to feminist demands for greater economic rights for women.

Norway's neutrality in the war also softened the effect of some elements of the interwar period that made feminists' work in other parts of Europe so embattled. In Norway the demographic anxieties and strength of pronatalist arguments never held as much sway as in war-torn European countries. For the most part Norway was also spared the gender conflicts that took place in other parts of Europe during the interwar period.

The political climate in Norway was less divisive and oriented against women's emancipation than elsewhere. This more amenable political environment allowed Norwegian women's organizations to more easily create political alliances than elsewhere in Europe and helped directly shape legislative actions after the war.[11]

Norway's neutrality did not spare it economic devastation, and economic catastrophe prevented many social reforms from being realized during the interwar period. Increased demands for shipping during the war had brought economic prosperity to Norway, and at the war's end in 1918 the Norwegian state had a substantial amount of money that could be used for public expenditures.[12] Two years later, in 1920 the economic bubble burst. Prices began to fall and unemployment rose. At the economic depression's height in the early 1930s, around 30 percent of Norwegians were without work and hundreds of thousands of people lived in poverty. Many turned to poor relief and other forms of public assistance in order to survive. This situation affected the development of social policies, including maternity legislation. Norway was in a severe economic depression and the government was reluctant to pass any social policies that could cost the state money it did not have. On the other hand, the scope of the crisis also increased politicians' willingness to support social reforms after the depression had ended in the 1930s.[13]

The economic situation in the 1920s affected feminists' ability to achieve their goals of expanded rights and benefits for mothers. The crisis had dire consequences for married women's employment in particular. Political parties and employers actively tried to discourage married women from working in order to protect men's jobs. This contributed to a marked decrease in married women's employment during the interwar period.[14] As a result, the antagonism towards married women's work, and the general economic climate, made it very difficult for feminists to argue for the expansion of maternity leave protections and rights for women. Efforts to strengthen women's economic position in the home also met with limited success due to the state's reluctance to spend money. Instead, feminists focused on trying to achieve things at the municipal level. They also worked to cultivate political support for expanded rights and benefits for mothers that would be realized in the 1930s after the economy had recovered.

The political climate during the interwar period was also marked by the growth of the Norwegian Labor Party *(Arbeiderparti)*. The Norwegian Labor Party gained a larger percentage of the vote and influence in Parliament in the 1920s and 1930s, and this affected feminist organizations' abilities to achieve their objectives. By 1927 the Labor Party had become the largest party in Norway and exercised considerable political power.[15] In many cases, the Party supported feminist objectives, especially the goals of social democratic feminists.

Social democratic feminists operated within the Labor Party, and the Party often took up their concerns on its party platforms. The Labor Party likely had the largest number of women members of all Norwegian political parties in the interwar period due to their long history of having a women's division (AKF).[16] This helped social democratic feminists achieve many of their objectives to help improve the condition of motherhood at both the municipal and national level in the interwar period.

All political parties began to pay more attention to women's demands in the interwar period because of women's recent enfranchisement. In the years since Norwegian women won the vote in 1913, it became clear that women actually did use their vote in large numbers and were a constituency all political parties needed to take into consideration when designing their platforms. Women rapidly mobilized and participated in parliamentary elections at a high rate.[17] Just two years after universal suffrage passed in 1915, women cast over 45 percent of all votes.[18] They continued to turn out at the polls in large numbers throughout the 1920s and 1930s.[19]

Women's high rate of voter participation caught the attention of political parties and strengthened women's individual and collective ability to shape policy decisions.[20] While feminists had successfully lobbied the state to implement maternity and family centered policies without the vote, both in Norway and elsewhere in Europe, women's suffrage gave feminists political leverage they did not previously possess.[21] In order to successfully win parliamentary elections, political parties recognized that they needed to appeal to women voters.[22] Feminist organizations saw this as an opportunity to bolster their claims that women's interests had political significance.

Feminists used the real and imagined power of women's voting rights to influence the passage of maternity legislation in the early twentieth century. Already in 1914, when Odelstinget debated maternity insurance, Castberg argued that politicians had to take women's preferences into consideration because "the majority of the Norwegian people and the majority of the Norwegian voters are women" and women had "already risen up and will continue to rise up with steadily more strength to demand that more is done for the families, the mothers and the young children in [Norway]."[23]

Feminists cultivated the idea of women's political power by attributing legislative victories to the political influence women now wielded. For example, when maternity insurance and the Castberg Laws passed in 1915 feminists credited this as being the "first ripe fruit of women's vote."[24] In the 1930s then-leader of the NKF, Margarete Bonnevie, asserted that the right to vote allowed women to achieve their political demands without the help of men.[25] According to Bonnevie, women no longer needed men's assistance in getting legislation passed, they only needed to use their vote. By connecting women's increased political rights to their ability to push through significant pieces of legislation, feminists argued that politicians had no choice but to pay attention to their demands. A large portion of these demands centered on increasing rights and benefits for mothers.

In order for the characterization of women's voting power to be more than just a rhetorical illusion, feminists needed to get women to vote in a way that supported their goals. Soon after the vote was won the AKF's periodical, *Kvinden*, re-published a Swedish article that argued that Norwegian working-class women had a responsibility to use their vote to support issues like maternity insurance.[26] Møller also encouraged women to use their vote to achieve more rights and benefits for mothers. In the early 1920s, she called on women to use "[their] power to push for an expansion" of maternity benefits.[27] Sometimes feminists directly mentioned which parties women should vote for. By the 1930s the Labor Party had gained more power in Parliament and included many feminist demands on their party platform. As a result, Møller's sister, Ella Anker, called on women to "vote for the Labor Party which supports" mother and child welfare.[28] It is difficult to know to what extent these pleas led women to vote in favor of certain political parties, but one thing is certain: the threat that women might vote for particular issues, and therefore specific political parties, influenced Norwegian party politics during the 1920s and 1930s.[29]

Women's enfranchisement also aided feminists' use of a rhetoric of rights in their call for more generous maternity legislation during the 1920s and 1930s. After universal suffrage was implemented, women entered into a relationship with the state based on the rights and duties of citizenship. As such, women's rights activists could argue that Norwegian laws should not place women in a state of dependency. Legislation that targeted women because they were women should not be restrictive and punitive. Instead, the few instances where women had special legal protections, such as the maternity leave clause in the Factory Act, should benefit

170   A. M. PETERSON

women and be characterized as a right. This argumentation was influential in the 1936 revision of the maternity leave clause and debates about a mother's wage.

The Population Question

Norwegian politicians also became more focused on women's rights because of domestic and international population anxieties. The human devastation of the war exacerbated European politicians' fear about population quantity and quality. While other European countries had taken note of this marked decrease in births much earlier, the Norwegian birth rate did not start to drastically decline until later in the 1920s.[30] By the 1930s Norwegian politicians had also become increasingly alarmed about falling fertility rates, and this bolstered the strength of women's demands for "family friendly" policies.

By the 1930s the word *familievennlig* or "family friendly" had become ubiquitous in Norwegian political discussions.[31] This occurrence was influenced by international developments, including the 1934 publication of Alva and Gunnar Myrdal's *Kris i Befolkningsfrågan* (*Crisis in the Population Question*). The Myrdals' work reflected some of the acute pronatalist attitudes present in Sweden in the interwar period. These anxieties did not have nearly the same resonance in Norway, but their work did instigate discussions amongst politicians and reformers about whether population politics were necessary in Norway.[32] Many Norwegian politicians agreed with the following assessment of the Myrdals' work written in *Kvinden*: "It doesn't matter how many people live in Norway but rather how they live and if they have a good life."[33] This was about quality of life, not quantity of population.[34] Now the thinking was that governmental planning was required in order for the population have a certain quality of life.[35] Women were able to use this focus on population concerns to lobby for increased economic rights for mothers.

KATTI ANKER MØLLER AND THE CONCEPT OF MOTHER WORK

One of the strategies feminists employed in the interwar period to achieve their goal of greater economic rights for women was to argue that mothering was work and like any other occupation deserved compensation. Women's rights activists claimed that the reproductive labor women preformed benefitted society and the state and therefore the state should bear the responsibility of ensuring payment to mothers for their services. These claims challenged the patriarchal family system. By arguing that motherhood was also a form of productive labor that deserved payment, feminists tried to undermine patriarchal structures and give women financial independence from men. Their solution involved transferring this power to the bureaucratic state.[36] In doing so, feminists encouraged the state to intervene in the private life of the family.

Møller was perhaps the most vocal Norwegian proponent of what the English termed the "national endowment of motherhood."[37] Influenced by her connections to British and German women's movements, Møller gave a series of lectures introducing her thoughts on motherhood as an occupation in the 1920s and 1930s.[38] In these public lectures, Møller argued that paid motherhood was essential to both the emancipation of women and the continuation of society. Many of the ideas Møller presented were quite radical and created tensions within and amongst women's rights organizations.

The basis of Møller's argument for paid motherhood rested on her construction of motherhood as an occupation. According to Møller, women's reproductive labor was some of the most grueling, dangerous and taxing work: "If we are talking about difficulty of work then what is the long and arduous period we call pregnancy?!—not to mention labor and delivery and confinement and breastfeeding and then comes the raising of this child."[39] On other occasions Møller referred to pregnancy as a "nine-month-long work day."[40] Møller framed women's reproductive and domestic labors as equal to if not exceeding the mental and physical requirements of other forms of waged work, and this allowed her to call for the similar compensation and protection of mother work.

Møller built on precedents set in the 1915 maternity insurance to push for greater compensation for women's mother work more broadly. She argued that married women's incorporation into the maternity insurance section of the Sickness Insurance Law established that mothers should be paid for their reproductive work.[41] Now Møller wanted the state to take the next step and pay women during their pregnancies and to then stay home with their children until their children reached working age, because until then children were "only a burden on their parents."[42] This characterization of children as financial burdens served to distance motherhood from unquantifiable emotion work and instead tie it to something monetarily quantifiable. It also reflected new ways of thinking about children as an economic burden, not an economic asset.[43]

Møller wanted all mothers to be compensated for this work and demanded that the state assume the costs. Møller stressed that motherhood was of importance to not only individual women's lives but also to the collective, stating that women's reproductive work was responsible for "the very existence of society."[44] Due to the significance of mother work women "[did] not need to be shy of our demands ... a mother is the most important person in a society ... and we need to dedicate a sum to the people who grow the Norwegian populace."[45] She argued that mother wages should be funded through national taxes because of the enormous importance women's reproductive labors had for the vitality and viability of the Norwegian state.

Møller believed that motherhood was not a duty that could be required of women, but rather an occupation that women could choose to undertake.[46] Above all, Møller thought that motherhood had to be truly voluntary—there should be open access to birth control information for married women and abortion should be legal.[47] Motherhood was a choice in Møller's mind and she argued that women would perform this work only if it received the recognition and remuneration it deserved.

Møller caused a stir in 1919 when she called on Norwegian women to go on birth strike in a lecture she gave at the Liberal Party's and the Labor Party's women's association meetings. In her talk, Møller criticized her audience and chastised them for deluding themselves into thinking that "pretty platitudes about the sacred call of motherhood" would be enough to convince people that women's reproductive work had economic worth. Instead, Møller adamantly stated that "all sentimentality must be put to an end." She framed reproduction as a political and social act that had economic consequences and argued that it was now time for "mothers to stop providing work without pay" because "when someone can get labor for free, who would be so stupid to start paying for it?"[48] Møller claimed that only by getting the fertility rate below 10 per 1000 inhabitants (it was 25 at the time) would the government heed women's demands about mother work.[49]

While many of Møller's ideas about mother work had resonated with the goals of women's organizations, her speech on reproductive politics incited a public debate about motherhood. One of Norway's most famous women authors, Sigrid Undset, criticized Møller's economic characterization of motherhood in a response essay entitled "*Begrepsforvirring*," or "Conceptual Confusion." For Undset, "Being a mother [was] not work ... motherhood [was] life."[50] Marie Michelet from *Hjemmenes Vel*, a conservative women's organization, also spoke out against Møller's proposals for state-provided wages for mothers. Michelet believed that this was a call for state-supported matriarchy and an effort to exile fathers from their own families.[51] The radical nature of Møller's call for the politicization of motherhood additionally caused an uproar in the Liberal Party's women's association where Møller first presented these ideas, and the Norwegian National Women's Council refused to allow Møller to speak on the topic at their national meeting.[52]

Møller's call for a birth strike and her characterization of reproduction as an economic act was more welcome in social democratic organizations. Almost immediately the Labor Party published Møller's speech on Women's Reproductive Politics as a pamphlet. Their support of Møller's conceptualization of paid motherhood was not absolute, however. Augusta Aasen was one of the driving forces behind the AKF periodical, *Kvinden*, in the late 1910s and her Marxist beliefs shone through in this role.[53] Yet even Aasen had reservations about Møller's materialization of motherhood because she found it "unappetizing to think of motherhood as a site of production."[54] In spite of that, Aasen did agree with many of Møller's other points and encouraged *Kvinden*'s readers to read the pamphlet the Labor Party had printed of Møller's speech on women's reproductive politics.[55]

The social democratic women were also supportive of Møller's other ideas about increased economic rights for housewives and mothers. Starting in 1905 the Norwegian Confederation of Trade Unions (*Landsorganisasjonen*) focused on incorporating women's trade unions into its umbrella organization and these initiatives were largely successful. More and more women's trade union activists left the AKF and joined that national confederation of trade unions instead. As a result, married, working-class housewives came to dominate the AKF by 1907.[56] These married, working-class housewives were particularly interested in strengthening women's position in the family.

After 1907, the AKF increasingly focused its political work on the improvement of motherhood. *Kvinden* bears the marks of this. In *Kvinden*'s first issue in 1909, editor Fernanda Nissen listed the purpose of the periodical as convincing married, working-class housewives "that in order to protect their homes their thoughts have to extend beyond the living room and into politics."[57] As a result, many of the articles written for *Kvinden* politicized women's work in the home as housewives and mothers. In this way, the AKF had maternalist-feminist tendencies that fit

174 A. M. PETERSON

well with Møller's ideas and initiatives. The organization wanted women's particular needs as women to be recognized and met. Included in these demands was the state support of motherhood, because as the AKF argued throughout the 1910s and 1920s, "raising a child [was] not a private matter but a social matter."[58]

THE COMPENSATION OF MOTHER WORK: THREE INITIATIVES

Inspired by Møller's concept of mother work, Norwegian feminist organizations, including the AKF, the NKF and the *Norske kvinners nasjonalråd*, or Norwegian National Women's Council (NKN), lobbied for the greater compensation of motherhood in the 1920s and 1930s. While feminists wanted to achieve the same goal, they disagreed on what strategy to employ. Social democratic women, with their desire to increase support for working-class mothers in the home, focused on crafting policies that rewarded women for their domestic labors. They adopted Møller's ideas and articulated demands for mothers' pensions and a mother's wage. In contrast, bourgeois women's rights organizations argued for the creation of a family wage for breadwinners. Conservative feminist associations, such as the NKN, supported this initiative because they thought it rewarded mothers' contributions in the home and fathers' contributions in the workplace. Equal rights organizations, like the NKF, agitated for the family wage for a different reason. These feminists believed that a gender-neutral family wage would strengthen women's opportunities to work outside the home. In spite of these differing opinions, all of these feminist groups wanted to greatly expand the number of women who benefitted from reform.

Mothers' Pensions

The AKF was responsible for one of the first initiatives that sought to remunerate women for the work they performed as mothers. This was in large part achieved because of the AKF position within the Labor Party. These social democratic feminists wanted to build on the support for single women created in the Child Welfare Act that granted public assistance for mothers and children in 1915. The 1915 law gave financial assistance to women only for a short period prior to and following childbirth. Women in the Labor Party wanted to significantly expand this legislation to include single mothers who had children up to the age of fifteen. This support was referred to as *morstrygd*, or mother's pension.

Social democratic women wanted mothers' pensions implemented to help secure a woman's right to remain in the home and care for her children. They argued that a woman could not "abandon her small children to work outside the home."[59] *Kvinden* also blamed the women who left their children in other people's care to go out and work as "ripping apart" the working-class family.[60] Yet, single mothers did not have a breadwinner and they either had to work or rely on poor relief, which resulted in the loss of their citizenship rights. Members of the AKF thought the solution to this problem was for the government to give all single mothers a stipend to enable them to stay at home with their children. Initially, however, they presented a modified claim for widows to receive mothers' pensions because they believed that this was more politically feasible.

The social democratic women's demands led the Oslo City Council to establish a committee to investigate the question of mothers' pensions. The committee, which was dominated by Labor Party representatives, went even further than the feminists' initial requests for pensions for widows and suggested that all single mothers receive support.[61] This included unmarried mothers and divorced women. This proposal met resistance from non-social democratic municipal representatives who thought that it would be better to give the support to only "deserving" mothers such as widows. They also objected to the notion that the state should not replace the father and assume his responsibility to provide for his children. Ultimately, the social democratic proposal won out, not least because it would decrease single mothers' dependence on municipal poor relief and protect their citizenship rights.[62]

In 1919 Kristiania (Oslo) municipality implemented mothers' pensions for all single mothers under a certain income with children under the age of fifteen. This social policy was to be paid out of municipal taxes.[63] Mothers' pensions were a radical initiative, but the impact they had on women's lives is debatable. First of all, social democratic women's goal of allowing women to refrain from waged work was not realized with this policy. The amount of support was to be only a supplement to a woman's income and relied on a mother earning additional income. Secondly, many women were not eligible for a mother's pension because they had not lived in Kristiania (Oslo) for the required fifteen years prior to applying for support. Lastly, the assistance came with municipal supervision. All women who received a pension were to be monitored by women inspectors. Women who failed these inspections risked not only losing their support, but also their children.[64]

Social democratic women were also disappointed that mothers' pensions were implemented only at the municipal level, likely because policies implemented at the local level tended to be more conservative and affected many fewer people. The AKF lobbied the state to implement mothers' pensions at the national level and called it the "most important of all social reforms" in the 1930s.[65] While the Labor Party did include mothers' pensions on their party platform in 1927, a national law on support for single heads of household was not realized until the 1970s.[66] Instead, different cities and towns adopted mothers' pensions throughout the 1920s and 1930s. Starting in Oslo, the mother's pensions spread to over twenty-eight municipalities by 1935.[67]

The adoption of mothers' pensions at the municipal level meant that significantly fewer women were helped by the policies than the AKF had intended. The number of women who received support was quite small and most of them lived in Oslo. In 1935, 1637 women received a mother's pension and over 80 percent of those women lived in Oslo. Additionally, many municipalities did not follow Oslo's example and grant mothers' pensions to all single mothers. The vast majority made support only available to widows.[68] Even in Oslo, over 46 percent of mothers' pensions went to widows.[69] The AKF did not like this bourgeois discrimination against unmarried mothers. They argued that supporting these supposedly "immoral" women would "keep them away from that which is referred to as "street traffic" or living off of that type [of occupation]."[70] These arguments were not successful and municipalities continued to prioritize the support of widows over other single mothers.

While the results of the mothers' pensions may have been negligible, on the immediate level they established a precedent that women should receive support for their mother work beyond the time surrounding childbirth. Social democratic women were able to use their connections to male labor politicians in municipal government and pass policies that would come to benefit thousands of single mothers. The support these single mothers received allowed them to work less outside the home and was a form for public compensation of women's work in the home. Feminists would try and build on this support for mothers when they started to lobby for a mother's wage in the 1920s and 1930s.

A Mother's Wage

Women active in the Labor Party supported Møller's ideas about mother work and worked to have mothers' wages realized. They aimed to build on and expand the mothers' pensions that had been implemented in Oslo in 1919 and broaden this assistance to cover married women. By doing so, they believed working-class women's position in the home would be secured and their work as mothers duly recognized.

In the 1920s social democratic women were still uncertain how best to support women's work in the home. Many women believed that establishing a mother's wage was the best option as it would decrease women's economic dependence on their husbands. Mothers' wages would also be protected from instabilities in the labor market, including unemployment, strikes and wage cuts. This would be a service to the working-class and as Sigrid Syvertsen said, "aid the class struggle."[71] Yet not all social democratic women believed that mothers' wages were the only way to compensate women for mother work.[72] Møller's sister, Ella Anker, became one of the most vocal proponents of the combination of a family wage and a mother wage in the social democratic movement. Anker argued that wages needed to compensate fathers at a higher rate than single workers because of the important work mothers did in the home. Only then would a "child's right to his mother and the mother's right to her child" be secured.[73]

Many working-class activists found the issue of a family wage problematic and in conflict with socialist goals. The trade unions, for example, were against the idea of a family wage because they thought it would lead to an overall decrease in wages.[74] Others argued that a family wage would not protect mothers and children in instances of strikes or lock-outs. Many members of the labor movement were also concerned that a family wage would destroy the principle of equal pay for equal work.[75]

At the behest of women in their party, the Norwegian Labor Party created a committee to discuss the subject of mothers' wages in 1923. Many high-ranking members of the Labor Party, including Inge Debes, Sigrid Syvertsen and Ella Anker, participated on this committee. While the committee never reached total agreement on all aspects of the issue, they did determine that the best way to solve the issue of compensation for mothers was through a mother's wage and not a family wage. They did not figure out, however, how this should be financed or how many women should be eligible to receive the benefit. Some advocated a finance system partially based on the sickness insurance model, which would include contributions from the state, county and employer but not the individual. Others believed that it should be tax financed. By 1930 this issue had been worked out and the Labor Party recommended that a mother's wage should involve cash allowances paid for out of national taxes. The Labor Party had still not decided if all mothers should receive a mother's wage or if only poor mothers should benefit.[76]

In trying to gain support for their initiative, women active in the Labor Party stressed the importance of mothers' wages for child welfare. Anker wrote a series of articles for *Kvinden* that reflected this belief. Echoing her sister's earlier writings, Anker argued that each child represented a financial burden for a woman for which she was not compensated, and if the state wanted women to give birth to strong and healthy children, it needed to recognize that the raising of children was a social concern, not a private one.[77] She claimed that women either, "do not want to or cannot give birth to children under [current] circumstances" and linked this to a decrease in birth rates.[78] If the state really valued children and wanted to strengthen the family then it needed to subsidize women's mother work.[79] Anker called for the state to support "the replenishment of the people, [its] nourishment and care" and argued that the best way to do that was to recognize motherhood as having the "greatest national economic value."[80] These arguments fit well with contemporary political concerns about falling birth rates and the economic health of the family.

By 1930 the strategy of highlighting the impact a mother's wage would have on birth rates and the well-being of children led the Labor Party to rename its proposal for a mother's wage to a child welfare allowance. In 1930 the Labor Party placed child allowances on its party platform.[81] The Party knew that it wanted mothers to receive recognition and compensation of the work they performed in the home, but there were still a number of uncertainties about how exactly this would work.

A Family Wage

While social democratic women worked to get their version of compensation for mothers passed, bourgeois women's organizations lobbied the state to create a family wage system.[82] The family wage would result in greater pay for heads of households. Conservative feminist organizations like the NKN supported a family wage because they thought it recognized and remunerated women's work in the home by paying men who were heads of household more than single men. In contrast, the NKF embraced the family wage because they saw in it the ability to better argue for equal pay for men and women.

In 1925 the NKN set up a committee to discuss wage reform. The committee was primarily focused on figuring out how to best achieve a family wage for those involved in the public sector, but they also considered how this could be implemented for those employed in private industry. There were disagreements amongst members of the committee, but the majority of them believed that a family wage would rectify the injustice of single workers receiving the same pay as the fathers of families.[83] For the NKN, a family wage was one of the basic foundations of "family friendly politics."[84] Yet due to internal disagreements on the committee, the NKN never passed a resolution on the subject of family wage reform.[85]

The NKF also supported the implementation of a family wage, but for a very different reason. Bonnevie thought that a family wage was a means to increase women's rights in the labor market. This was mainly due to the fact that employers often paid men more than women for the same work because they perceived men to be the ones who had families to support. With the implementation of a family wage only supporters of families would receive this higher wage, and it would be easier to achieve equal pay for all single workers regardless of their sex. Bonnevie also pushed for the wage to be gender-neutral and apply to all parents, both fathers and mothers. In this way women could "work outside the home and maintain their mother work in a way that does not hurt home life or their wages and working conditions."[86] Under a family wage system a mother would receive extra pay which would allow her to join the workforce and pay for someone else to take care of her domestic duties. According to Bonnevie, the Labor Party's suggestion of a mother's wage was "fascist" because it tied women to the home instead of encouraging women to choose where they wanted to work.[87] In comparison, Bonnevie argued that the family wage would enhance women's ability to choose their occupation.

The varying perspectives on a mother's wage compared to a family wage made it difficult for any single feminist group to reach internal consensus and they asked Parliament to set up a governmental commission on the issue. Their requests eventually led to the creation of the Commission on Child Allowances in 1934. Many of the feminists who had pushed for the compensation of mother work sat on this commission, including Syvertsen and Bonnevie.

180   A. M. PETERSON

In 1937 the Commission on Child Allowances concluded that the best way to strengthen the family was to grant an allowance to all families with more than one child. This was to be financed out of national taxes and paid directly to mothers. In many ways this reflected the proposal developed by the Labor Party Committee back in the 1920s. Bonnevie had tried to push for her vision of the family wage, but this remained the minority opinion.

The Commission's proposal was not particularly pronatalist. Instead, it followed Anker's recommendation that the best way to secure the nation's progress was "not to increase the birth rate at the expense of mothers' health, but rather prevent morality and sickness by strengthening the resources of the family."[88] Neither the minority nor the majority position wanted to encourage women to have as many children as possible by restricting the allowance to families over a certain size. In fact, several members of the commission even suggested decreasing the amount of support for large families.[89]

Due to complicated discussions that took place after the report's release, Parliament did not discuss the proposal for a mother's wage, or child allowance as it was then called, prior to the outbreak of World War Two. Germany's occupation of Norway from 1940 to 1945 stalled any further discussion of the initiative until after liberation. Yet the very first social reform passed in the postwar period was the law on child allowances.[90]

When the law on child allowances passed in 1946 it introduced universalism to Norwegian social policy. All mothers were to receive support from the government to help them raise their children. It is not surprising that Norway's first universal welfare measure targeted mothers and children. Since the late nineteenth century, feminists and their allies in Parliament and the social reform movement had worked to get motherhood recognized as a legitimate area of public concern. They started by pushing for greater maternity benefits for women workers and were able to successfully place maternity and mother's rights on the public agenda. Women had incorporated maternalism into social policy.[91]

Møller was one of the main actors involved in this political development. It was her conceptualization of mother work that inspired women in the Labor Party to take up the fight for a mother's wage during the 1920s. These feminists were able to gain support for their ideas from members of the Labor Party and successfully placed compensation for motherhood on the public agenda. Unfortunately, Møller died in 1945 and was not alive to see the law she had so greatly influenced pass.

An Alternative Approach: Strengthening Women's Employment Rights

As we've seen, not all Norwegian feminists agreed that strengthening women's economic position in the home was the best method to achieve greater economic rights for women. Many equal-rights based feminist groups, including the NKF, saw women's economic participation outside the home as key to women's emancipation, and they worked to improve women's position in the workplace.[92] Both of these alternatives challenged the male breadwinner model, but for many people, encouraging women's work outside of the home was even more radical. This was due to the fact that if a woman worked for wages then she was financially independent of both the patriarchal family and the patriarchal state. In addition, working mothers were not able to care for their children full time, which further threatened the complementary gender order.[93]

The issue of women's work outside the home divided working-class and middle-class feminists. Throughout the early twentieth century the AKF competed with bourgeois feminist organizations, including the NKF, to speak on behalf of women workers. Prior to the rise of the Labor Party, bourgeois organizations like the NKF had greater access to political powerbrokers and received many more opportunities to advise not only the Norwegian government, but also international women's organizations on the status of working-class women's wants and needs. This upset leaders of the AKF, especially because the NKF's equality-based feminism stood in opposition to many of the rights and protections the AKF wanted implemented for working-class women.

The NKF's and AKF's divergent perspectives on women's rights were glaringly evident in debates over special protections for women workers in the 1910s and 1920s. The NKF and the AKF agreed women should receive maternity leave as long as it was compensated, but they disagreed over whether the state should restrict women's working hours and the types of occupations they held. The AKF believed that women's reproductive capabilities entitled them to certain workplace protections. The social democratic women wanted the government to protect women workers because they believed that women's "constitution" demanded it.[94] They wanted the law to "recognize [that] women are created to be mothers!"[95] and that their "physical weak[ness]"[96] necessitated special protections. The NKF, on the other hand, fought to keep any special protections, or what they termed restrictions, for women workers out of the Factory Act.

NKF leaders thought that such restrictions would infringe on a women's right to earn a living and compromise her equal treatment in the workplace because: "What employer will employ a woman if he has to take into account special laws?"[97] These different approaches to the issue of the protection of women workers reflected the AKF's greater adherence to a difference-based feminism and the NKF's commitment to equality-based feminism. Ultimately, in spite of the AKF' resistance, the NKF was quite successful at keeping special protections for women beyond maternity leave out of the Norwegian Factory Act.[98]

The AKF also tried to discredit bourgeois women's ability to voice an opinion on the matter of protections for working-class women. For AKF leaders, middle-class women had no right to speak on working-class issues because they did not understand the realities of working-class life. When Dr. Dagny Bang spoke on behalf of the NKF in front of Parliament in regards to workplace protections for women, the AKF commented: "Can you think of anything more ridiculous than an upper-class woman—who has never in her whole life worked in a factory—standing up and involving herself in an issue that she does not have the slightest clue about—it is unbelievable how far these women go in their eagerness."[99] This opposition to bourgeois women's representation of working-class women's interests also extended to Norwegian factory inspector Betzy Kjelsberg. When Kjelsberg attended the International Congress of Working Women's meeting in Washington, D.C. in 1919, the AKF recommended that Kjelsberg "have a meeting with [them] before the next conference" so that they could inform her of working women's real interests and needs.[100]

The NKF did try to initiate some meetings with working-class women and listen to their demands, which they often described as being concerned with women's role in the home.[101] Yet it is unclear to what extent the NKF incorporated the perspectives of working-class women in their work, especially when it came to contested issues like special protections for women workers. These antagonisms, however, did not necessarily prevent working-class and middle-class women's rights associations from working together on other issues related to women's work, particularly where motherhood was involved.

It was important to the NKF to improve women's economic rights more broadly. While this included efforts to improve women's rights in the workplace, members of the NKF also expressed sympathy for the work women performed in the home. In 1897 Gina Krog published two letters to the editor in *Nylænde* that characterized women's domestic labor as "work" and initiated a conversation about the entitlements women should receive because of this work.[102] Many members of the NKF were also concerned that women should have more economic rights in marriage. After the Castberg Laws passed and unmarried mothers were eligible to receive more financial assistance from the government than married women, some NKF members worried that this disadvantaged married women. They wanted married women to have just as much "economic independence" as an unmarried woman.[103] For the NKF, one of the ways to achieve more financial independence was to not only improve married women's rights in marriage and at home, but to also ensure their equal treatment in the workplace. This is one of the reasons they opposed special protections for women workers and lobbied for compensation of state-mandated maternity leave.

The different strategies and goals of women's rights organizations influenced their approach to the issue of greater economic rights for mothers in the interwar period. During the 1920s and 1930s there were three major legislative initiatives born out of feminists' desire to decrease women's economic dependence on the patriarchal family: mothers' pensions, mothers' wages and expanded maternity leave provisions. The social democratic women's organization and the middle- and upper-class women's associations had divergent opinions on these issues.[104] At times, these perspectives came in conflict with one another and led these groups to pursue alternative visions of how mothers' economic independence could best be achieved.

The Combination of Wage Work and Motherhood: Feminist Efforts to Expand Maternity Leave

Feminists who wanted to strengthen women's position in the workplace believed women's ability to combine paid work with motherhood was key to their emancipation. Paid maternity leave was crucial to this vision, and organizations such as the NKF worked to expand paid maternity leave into a right all women workers could benefit from in the interwar period.

After maternity insurance passed in 1915, Norwegian women were eligible to receive eight weeks of paid maternity leave and free midwifery if they were members of the sickness insurance. The wives of male members were eligible to receive a lump-sum maternity benefit and free midwifery services. In the interwar period, feminists saw this law as limited in its ability to bolster women's economic rights. The law did not protect women from being fired for taking maternity leave and was also fairly narrow in scope. Many women who worked in middle-class occupations such as civil servants, teachers, and retail workers were not included in the class of workers covered by labor protection or sickness insurance laws. Additionally, the law characterized maternity leave as a state-mandated requirement rather than a woman's right. Feminists in the NKF wanted to change these elements of the legislation and worked to transform maternity leave from a restriction to a benefit.

Women's rights activists wanted to make maternity leave more beneficial to a greater number of women, but this was not an easy task in the 1920s and early 1930s. The economic crisis made it particularly difficult to push for increased social expenditures. Due in part to this poor economic climate, Norway had been out of compliance with the international standards set by the International Labor Organization (ILO)'s 1919 Maternity Protection Convention. This convention required that member states' maternity leave include the following: (1) prohibition of women's work for six weeks after giving birth, (2) right to maternity leave for six weeks prior to giving birth, (3) right to monetary support during the maternity leave and right to free medical treatment, (4) right to breastfeeding breaks from work, (5) protection from termination in conjunction with the leave.[105] The NKN and Møller worked together in the 1920s to try to get Parliament to follow the convention's recommendations for maternity leave policies.[106] Though Parliament discussed implementation of these guidelines in 1921 and 1927, they did not find it economically feasible to pass any legislation that required a significant amount of state funding.[107]

In fact, politicians were so concerned about the economic crisis that they contemplated reducing the amount of money already budgeted for maternity benefits. In 1928 the Social Committee put forth a legislative proposal to decrease spending on maternity insurance and sickness insurance more generally. The National Sickness Insurance Office reported that the most expensive portion of the maternity insurance at that time was the benefit members' wives received. The insurance office therefore recommended completely doing away with the benefit for members' wives, but offered an alternative in which the government could reduce the amount of support from 30 kroner to 20 kroner.[108] The Committee ultimately did not find this necessary and chose to keep the support at 30 kroner. Elsewhere in Europe, maternity benefits did not always fare as well in budgetary discussions. In Britain insurance bodies consistently avoided paying maternity insurance because of financial worries and in 1932 married women officially lost their entitlement to the maternity sickness benefit.[109] This example demonstrates the difficulty women's rights activists had in to trying to push for expansions to maternity policies, especially those financed by the state.

The 1930s signaled a shift in attitudes toward social expenditures in general and maternity policies in particular in Norway. During this time, Norway regained economic strength and employment rates began to reach pre-depression levels. The improved economic climate, along with a renewed focus on population politics, helped Norwegian feminists realize some of their goals for women's economic rights.

Discussions about population and family politics helped ameliorate the political situation and bolster feminists' demands for the expansion of maternity leave during the 1930s. Feminists, including members of the AKF and NKF, wanted maternity leave to be a *right* for women.[110] They also wanted women to be protected from being fired from their jobs for exercising this right.[111] The NKF was particularly concerned that maternity leave coverage be expanded to include larger groups of women, including members of the middle class and married women. These initiatives would allow more women to combine motherhood with waged labor and achieve a feminist goal of realizing greater economic independence for women.

By changing maternity leave from a mandated requirement to a woman's right, feminists highlighted the importance of women's freedom of choice in matters of social policy. Previously, the maternity clause of the Factory Act emphasized that women were prohibited from working during the time surrounding childbirth. Feminists, including members of the NKN, thought that this wording was discriminatory. According to the NKN, women should not be "prohibited" from working but rather should have the opportunity to take advantage of their "right" to maternity leave should they so choose. Only by presenting maternity leave as a right would women be able to compete equally in the labor market and be free from workplace discrimination.[112]

The prevention of women's potential discrimination in the workplace was of utmost importance to feminists. If a woman was to successfully combine work and motherhood, she needed to be protected from unequal treatment in the workplace. This is one of the reasons factory inspector Kjelsberg did not recommend that Norway implement the section of the

186   A. M. PETERSON

Maternity Protection Convention that allowed women breastfeeding breaks at work when the Convention was discussed by Parliament in 1927. She thought that this would be too difficult for women to do without losing their jobs.[113]

Protecting women from losing their jobs due to the demands of motherhood was a major concern of feminists. As early as 1897 *Nylænde* reported that women might be fired from their positions for taking the mandated maternity leave. This continued to be a worry for feminists as neither the Factory Act nor the Labor Protection Act prevented an employer from firing a woman who took maternity leave. The NKF opposed this oversight and tried to get Parliament to add a sentence in the law that would make it illegal for an employer to terminate a woman who took maternity leave.

The NKF wanted married women and women who worked in middle-class occupations to benefit from maternity legislation as well. These feminists not only wanted maternity leave to be a right that a woman could take without fear of being fired, they also wanted more women to be eligible for these rights. Bonnevie argued in a letter to the Ministry of Social Affairs that this was a matter of fairness: "It must be seen as harmful to society that a woman who does something as natural as gets married and has a child should lose her job. Just like a man every woman should be able to trust that even if she is married or not, and even if she has a child or not, as long as she performs her work in a satisfactory way she should keep her job."[114] To Bonnevie and others, married women had just as much of a right to expect fair treatment in the workplace as unmarried women and men. They claimed that all women had the right to choose to combine motherhood with work and if an employer discriminated against women for this choice, then society could not count on women to continue to have children. This argumentation fit well with politicians' and reformers' population concerns in the 1930s.

Parliament took up feminist demands for greater maternity benefits for working women in the mid-1930s. Norway had regained some economic stability, and the Labor Party had also experienced a major upswing of electoral approval in the late 1920s and came to dominate parliamentary politics.[115] Ideas about population policy and family politics circulated around Europe and influenced many political initiatives in Norway as well. The Labor Party was especially supportive of these types of policies.[116] Norway was also embarrassed by their incompliance with ILO guidelines, especially after Germany ratified the Maternity Convention in 1927. The coalescence of these factors, combined with pressures from women's rights organizations, led to important changes in Norwegian maternity leave legislation in the late 1930s.

Maternity Leave Becomes a "Right"

In the mid-1930s the Norwegian Labor Party won a majority of seats in Parliament and began fulfilling its platform promise of expanding labor protection laws.[117] The maternity leave clause was one of the areas that parliamentarians proposed to revise substantially to fall in line with feminist demands and international standards. For example, when the government first introduced the proposed revisions in 1935, it emphasized that the suggested changes to the maternity clause would allow them to accede the ILO's Maternity Convention.[118] Following these international guidelines, the government proposed Norwegian maternity leave be extended in length, women receive breastfeeding breaks at work, and perhaps most significantly, employers be prohibited from firing women who took maternity leave.[119]

The Parliamentary Social Committee largely supported the proposed changes to the maternity clause, with some important exceptions out of concern for the rights of employers. The Committee wanted women to have to provide their employers with at least three-days' notice before they had the right to take six weeks of leave prior to giving birth. This was to give employers a chance to find replacement labor.[120] Concerns about how the legislative changes would affect employers also led to the inclusion of a clause that would allow women's temporary employment to be terminated if the work was completed prior to her return from maternity leave.[121] These changes were meant to balance the rights and protections women gained with the new maternity leave clause with the needs and wants of employers.

In 1935 legislators decided to change the language of the law so that it no longer characterized maternity leave as mandatory for women workers. The Social Committee suggested that the wording be changed from "must" take leave to "should" take leave. They believed this would indicate that women could decide for themselves whether or not they wanted to take maternity leave, a decision that represented a triumph for feminist demands.[122] Karl Frimann Dahl (*Arbeiderparti*, Labor Party)[123] protested this change as he argued that mandatory maternity leave was necessary to protect both the health of the mother and child. His point of view did not win out as he was

188   A. M. PETERSON

the only one to vote against this change.[124] Instead, the law "left it up to the woman herself to determine to what extent she wanted to use the leave the law secured her."[125] By 1936 parliamentarians believed that maternity leave should not be a mandate, but rather a benefit that women could choose to receive.[126]

When the Employment Protection Act passed in 1936 it included a maternity section that guaranteed women workers more rights and protections than ever before in Norwegian history. Feminists had succeeded in getting a law passed that economically benefitted a larger number of women and was characterized as a right. According to the law, with at least three-days' warning a women had the right to be free from work for the six weeks prior to giving birth. Following the birth, a woman was recommended to take leave from work for six weeks, which could be extended an additional six weeks if her health required it. The law secured the woman a right to her job even if she took this leave unless the work was temporary. In addition, a woman who breastfed could "demand the freedom that she needs" to facilitate this, and the law guaranteed her at least two half-hour breaks from work.[127] Compensation for the leave was to be administered under the Sickness Insurance Law and supported by the 1915 Child Welfare Act which granted public assistance for mothers and children. The Employment Protection Act solidified the fact that any public support a woman received in conjunction with maternity leave would not be considered poor relief.[128] Nearly all occupations were covered by the law and it represented a significant step away from a social policy that targeted only "dangerous" groups such as unmarried, impoverished women to a more universalist policy that encompassed all working women[129]

Maternity Leave for Whom?

The law was comprehensive and covered nearly all types of work, but women who worked in the public service sector were not included. Due to this and subsequent interpretations of the Sickness Insurance Law, most of the women who worked in public administrative positions did not receive paid maternity leave. This included teachers, telephone operators and the women who worked in the Oslo Social Welfare Office.

There were discussions at the municipal level in Oslo during the late 1920s about whether women public servants should receive paid maternity leave. Many public administrators were confused as to what the Employment Protection Act, Sickness Insurance Law, and Law on Public

Servants dictated in regards to maternity leave for public servants. At that time it was determined that maternity leave for public servants was not covered under any of those laws, mainly because "childbirth was not an illness."[130] This directly contradicted what had been established in the 1909 Sickness Insurance Law and the inclusion of maternity in that piece of legislation.

Public service was quite different from other types of work in that it employed the upper echelon of Norwegian society, and many male bureaucrats did not want pregnant women or young mothers to work in governmental positions.[131] This was especially true of teachers who were encouraged to take leave at least three months before giving birth, seemingly to keep women's pregnant bodies out of the classroom.[132]

Director Ormestad of the Oslo Social Welfare Office reported that the women who worked for him normally took leave for six months, but without pay "of course."[133] Ormestad lamented the short length of this leave, however, because he did not think that young mothers should return to work so soon after giving birth. In his opinion, having an infant at home "distracted [a woman] in her work and she could not be considered fully capable of work."[134] Between 1927 and 1939, Ormestad must have had a change of heart because he decided to do away with this extended unpaid leave and implement a shorter, paid version for his women employees.

Ormestad's change in opinion may have been due to pressure from women's rights organizations. In the late 1930s the NKF demanded of both Parliament and the Oslo municipality that women public servants receive paid maternity leave.[135] The NKF wanted the state and municipality to offer their employees three months of maternity leave at full salary, which was much more generous than other women workers received at the time. They argued that the Sickness Insurance Law had already established that maternity was an illness and that this applied to public service as well. In the NKF's opinion, "it was directly hostile to the family to take women's resources from them during the time that they fulfill the socially beneficial and necessary task of birthing children."[136] The state agreed with this and met the NKF's demands in June 1937. The Oslo municipality, however, continued to grant maternity leave without pay and on an individual basis for its workers.

When the Oslo Social Welfare Office granted twelve weeks of paid maternity leave to women employees in 1939 it did so without the consent of the National Welfare Office or municipal authorities. Instead, these bodies found out about this decision from the extensive press coverage that ensued.[137] They demanded that the Oslo Social Welfare Office present the policy to the municipality and National Social Welfare Office for approval and admonished the Oslo office for implementing a policy that conflicted with the national Sickness Insurance Law (Fig. 6.1).

The Oslo Social Welfare Office acted as it had to ensure that all of its women workers received equal maternity leaves. It did not meet the NKF's demands for a three-month long maternity leave, but consciously followed the length of time established in the 1936 Employment Protection Act.[138] Ormestad responded to the municipal authorities by stating that if he and the office board had followed the guidelines set in the sickness insurance, that only 68 out of the 211 women who worked for him would receive paid leave. These women worked in the office's administration and were covered by the law. The remaining women, many of whom worked as secretaries, nurses and cleaning staff, would not have been covered by this law.

The Oslo Social Welfare Office's decision to have a maternity policy apply to all their workers reflected a new way of thinking about welfare policies and was influenced by NKF demands. Ormestad told the munici-

Fig. 6.1 Reception Hall at the Oslo Social Welfare Office, 1945–1950. Courtesy of Oslo Museum

pality that he did not believe that having different policies for different groups of workers was wise.[139] As Director of one of the largest employers of female public servants, Ormestad did not think his workers should experience differential treatment when it came to maternity leave. Cleaning staff as well as nurses and office secretaries should receive the same amount of maternity leave.

In addition to the petitions of feminist organizations, the Oslo Social Welfare Office's implementation of maternity leave for all of its women workers was also likely influenced by the demands of the women who worked there. Prior to 1939, when confronted with women's requests for maternity leave, the law and municipal policy were quite ambiguous. It would have been much easier for the office to have a concrete policy to follow in all cases of petitions for maternity leave. Ormestad used the example of Mrs. Signe Berg, a cleaner who worked for the welfare office, when he explained how difficult it was to determine which policy applied to her case.[140]

The welfare office may have also encountered personnel difficulties from having a lack of maternity leave policies. Prior to 1939 many women chose to quit their jobs at the welfare office when they received notice that their petitions for pay during maternity leave would not be granted. Other women tried to extend the length of their unpaid maternity leave and when this was denied they resigned from their positions.[141] It is possible that these women's reactions to the lack of adequate and paid maternity leave influenced the Oslo Social Welfare Office's decision to grant its workers twelve weeks of paid maternity leave.

The Oslo Social Welfare Office's implementation of twelve weeks of maternity leave for all of its women workers represents the shift in thinking about maternity policies that took place during the 1930s, largely at the behest of feminist organizations. Parliament passed legislation that made it much easier and less shameful for women to take maternity leave from work. Women received the right to twelve weeks of maternity leave and were protected from being fired for choosing to take this leave. This legislation covered nearly all occupations and would have applied to women working outside of the classical "vulnerable" jobs of domestic service and industrial work. Women who worked in retail and private offices would have also had a right to maternity leave. This encompassed a whole new group of women workers, namely, those from the educated middle classes. Public servants were not included in this legislation, however, and this led to difficulties for women teachers, nurses, and public administrators.

192   A. M. PETERSON

The Oslo Social Welfare Office saw this lack of maternity leave as a problem and took the initiative to heed the demands of feminists and working women themselves and implement maternity leave for its workers.[142] They helped these women successfully combine being a "career woman/wife/mother"[143] and secured the welfare office the labor of a new type of women worker. The office not only offered this leave to "pink collar" workers, but also to cleaning staff. This further sowed the seeds of universalist thinking about labor protections and benefits as something all women workers should receive.

CONCLUSION

By 1940 more women than ever before were able to benefit from Norwegian maternity policies. Both married and unmarried women had access to maternity support from the government during their confinements. More middle-class women also started to receive maternity provisions. The state also recognized the mother work women preformed as something of economic value. In addition, women gained more rights in the workplace. Maternity leave became a right that women were entitled to, instead of a mandated requirement, and even some women not covered in the Sickness Insurance Law were able to receive compensation for this leave. Such was the case with the women who worked at the Oslo Social Welfare Office.

In order to achieve these results, feminists had to cultivate support for this new way of thinking about motherhood and employment. They built on previous maternity legislation that had established motherhood as a public concern and expanded these policies both in content and in scope. In Norway, as elsewhere, this approach followed two paths. One, supported by Møller, social democratic feminists, and other maternal feminists, advocated increased economic rights and benefits for the work mothers performed in the home. These ideas formed the foundation of the implementation of municipal mothers' pensions in 1919. They also shaped the content of what is considered Norway's first welfare state measure: the child allowance policy that Parliament passed in 1946. Other feminists, most notably Bonnevie and members of the NKF and NKN, tried to strengthen women's ability to combine motherhood with waged labor. Their efforts resulted in substantial revisions of maternity leave legislation and policies in the late 1930s.

Norwegian feminism may have followed a similar trajectory as other European feminist initiatives in the interwar period, but Norwegian feminists were able to achieve more favorable outcomes than their European counterparts. As was the case elsewhere in Europe, Norwegian feminists focused on family-centered policies in the interwar period. They were also similarly split over the issue of pursuing women's individual rights as workers or advocating for women's rights as mothers.

Yet, Norwegian feminists operated in a political and social environment more amenable to their demands than was the case in many parts of Europe. Norwegian feminist efforts were aided by the fact that Norway's neutrality in the First World War largely spared Norwegian politics and culture the extreme divisiveness that was present in countries like Germany, France, and Britain. There was less gender conflict and the accompanied backlash against women's emancipation in Norway than in combatant countries. Norwegian feminists also benefitted from working in a country with one of the longest histories of women's suffrage in Europe. Women's exercising of their political rights had proven significant in Norway and feminists tried to use this, as well as their relationship with the Labor Party, to their advantage. The Labor Party's political ascendency during this period also helped feminists achieve their demands as the Labor Party was particularly interested in developing social programs and benefits. Social democratic feminists in particular were able to use their connections to the Labor Party to accomplish their objectives.

Women's efforts to gain state support for all mothers are an essential part of the history of the development of the Norwegian welfare state. In many ways these discussions were a part of larger debates about universal rights and entitlements. Feminists wanted the state to pay all mothers, regardless of their economic conditions, for the work that they did as mothers. By arguing for women's rights as mothers, regardless of their economic standing, women helped shape debates about the state's duty to ensure its citizens a certain standard of living. This was no longer about protecting vulnerable groups in society or promoting "help to self-help" but rather the beginnings of a universalist welfare state. These discussions would continue after the Nazi occupation of Norway ended in 1945 and throughout the postwar period.

NOTES

1. A 1924 law officially restored the medieval name of "Oslo" to the city, effective January 1, 1925. I follow this chronology and refer to the city as "Oslo" after January 1, 1925 and "Kristiania" prior to this date.
2. Translation is my own. Underlined in original. S1939/27 Permisjon under nedkomst, Oslo Trygdekontor, Sakserie Personal og ansettelsessaker 1939–1943, Statsarkivet i Oslo.
3. See for example: *Morgenposten*, February 10, 1939 and February 28, 1939; *Dagbladet*, February 11, 1939; *Norsk Handels-og Sjøfartstidende*, February 21, 1939; *Norges Kvinder*, February 24, 1939.
4. Dagny Bjørnaraa to Director Ormestad, February 20, 1939, S1939/27 Permisjon under nedkomst, Oslo Trygdekontor, Sakserie Personal og ansettelsessaker 1939–1943, Statsarkivet i Oslo.
5. Karen Offen, *European Feminisms, 1700–1950: a Political History* (Stanford, CA: Stanford University Press, 2000), 272.
6. Gisela Bock, and Pat Thane, eds., *Maternity and Gender Policies: Women and the Rise of the European Welfare States, 1880s–1950s* (New York: Routledge, 1991), 11.
7. Ann Taylor Allen, *Feminism and Motherhood in Western Europe 1890–1970: The Maternal Dilemma* (New York: Palgrave Macmillan, 2005), 142.
8. Offen, *European Feminisms*, 277.
9. Offen, *European Feminisms*, 282.
10. In 1923 *Arbeiderpartiets kvindeforbund* was dissolved and replaced by *Arbeiderpartiets kvinnesekretariat* later called *Landssekretariatet* in 1927. This organization was not separate from the Labor Party, but was rather a committee that fell under the Labor Party's Executive Committee.
11. Silke Neunsinger, *Die Arbeid der Frauen, Die Krise der Männer: Die Erwerbstaetigkeit verheirateter Frauen in Deutschland und Schweden, 1919–1939* (Uppsala: Uppsala University Press, 2001), 89–94.
12. Anne-Lise Seip, *Veiene til velferdsstaten: norsk sosialpolitikk 1920–75* (Oslo: Gyldendal, 1994), 19.
13. Ibid., 19–25.
14. The number of married women who worked in the 1920s was half of the levels in the 1910s. See: Ida Blom, and Sølvi Sogner, eds., *Med kjønnsperspektiv på norsk historie: fra vikingtid til 2000-årsskiftet* (Oslo: Cappelen akademisk forlag, 1999), 345.
15. For an excellent discussion of Labor politics during the interwar period see: David Redvaldsen, *The Labor Party in Britain and Norway: Elections and the Pursuit of Power Between the World Wars* (London: I.B. Tauris, 2011).

16. This is not completely accurate for this period, but Kari Melby has argued this based on what evidence is available in Blom, *Med kjønnsperspektiv på norsk historie*, 248.
17. For a good overview of women's participation in Nordic politics see Elina Haavio-Mannila, Drude Dahlerup, Maud Eduards, et al., eds., *Unfinished Democracy: Women in Nordic Politics* (New York: Pergamon Press, 1985).
18. Statistisk sentralbyrå, "Stortingsvalg, Personer med stemmerett, avgitte stemmer og valgte representanter," http://www.ssb.no/a/histstat/tabeller/25-2.html, Accessed April 17, 2013.
19. The percentage of women voters did not slip below 45 percent throughout the 1920s and 1930s and in 1936 over 50 percent of voters were women. Statistisk sentralbyrå, "Stortingsvalg, Personer med stemmerett, avgitte stemmer og valgte representanter," http://www.ssb.no/a/histstat/tabeller/25-2.html, Accessed April 17, 2013.
20. There were also small numbers of women representatives in parliament. In 1921, Karen Platou was the first elected to parliament and by 1933 there were three women representatives in parliament. Statistisk sentralbyrå, "Stortingsvalg, Personer med stemmerett, avgitte stemmer og valgte representanter," http://www.ssb.no/a/histstat/tabeller/25-2.html, Accessed April 17, 2013.
21. Bock, *Maternity and Gender Policies*, 6.
22. Kari Melby, "Husmorens epoke, 1900–1950," in *Med kjønnsperspektiv på norsk historie*, eds. Ida Blom and Sølvi Sogner (Oslo: Cappelen Akademisk Forlag, 1999), 247–248; Synnøve Hinnaland Stendal, "'…under forvandlingens lov': en analyse av stortingsdebatten om kvinnelige prester i 1930-årene" (PhD diss., University of Lund, 2003), 280–283.
23. Stortingsforhandlinger, forhandlinger i Odelstinget, June 5, 1914, 219.
24. "Mødreforsikringen," *Nylænde*, August 1, 1915, 229.
25. Margarete Bonnevie, "Hva kan gjøres for å sikre kvinners lønn, arbeidsvilkår og avansement," NKN Foredrag ved 11 landsmøte Oslo September 1938. MS 4 2912:7, Håndskriftsamlingen, Nasjonalbiblioteket.
26. "Rostratt – ansvar," *Kvinden*, February 1, 1912.
27. Katti Anker Møller, "Om kommunal morspensjon," MS 4 2416:III, mødreforsikring—morstrygd, Håndskriftsamlingen, Nasjonalbiblioteket.
28. Ella Anker, "Barnetrygd," *Kvinden*, February 1, 1930.
29. Kari Melby, "Husmorens epoke, 1900–1950," in *Med kjønnsperspektiv på norsk historie*, 247–248.
30. There was a marked decrease in the birth rate from 26 per 1000 births in 1920 to 19 in 1925 and 17 in 1930. Statistics Norway, http://www.ssb.no/a/histstat/, Accessed June 9, 2013.
31. For an example of this, survey the headlines of *Kvinden* in the late 1920s and 1930s.

196   A. M. PETERSON

32. Gro Hagemann, "Maternalism and Gender Equality," in *Reciprocity and Redistribution: Work and Welfare Reconsidered*, ed. Gro Hagemann (Pisa, Italy: Pisa University Press, 2007), 80.
33. *Kvinden*, August 1, 1936, 17.
34. This also included discussions of eugenics. Most of the feminists studied here carefully separated eugenics from their demands for maternity benefits for women. For a good overview of the relationship between eugenicism and social policies in Scandinavia see: Gunnar Broberg and Nils Roll-Hansen, eds., *Eugenics and the Welfare State: Sterilization Policy in Denmark, Sweden, Norway, and Finland* (East Lansing, MI: Michigan State University, 1996).
35. This was inspired by the Myrdals' ideas about social engineering and applied to the family, social, and economy. Inger Elisabeth Haavet, "Milk, Mothers and Marriage: Family Policy Formation in Norway and its Neighboring Countries in the Twentieth Century," in *The Nordic Model of Marriage: A Historical Reappraisal*, eds. Niels Finn Christiansen, Klaus Petersen, Nils Edling, and Per Haave (Copenhagen: Museum Tusculanum Press, 2006), 205.
36. For a discussion of the affects of this state intervention in private life see: Jacques Donzelot, *The Policing of Families*, trans. Robert Hurley (London: The Johns Hopkins University Press, 1979); Detley J.K. Peukert, *Grenzen der Sozialdisziplinierung: Augstieg und Krise der deutschen Jugenforsoge, 1878–1932* (Cologne: Bund Verlag, 1986).
37. Allen, *Feminism and Motherhood*, 64. Katti Anker Møller's papers also contain a pamphlet detailing the English version of these demands. MS 4 2416:VI National Endowment of Motherhood, Håndskriftsamlingen, Nasjonalbiblioteket.
38. Ida Blom, "Voluntary Motherhood," in *Maternity and Gender Policies: Women and the Rise of the European Welfare States, 1880s–1950s*, eds. Gisela Bock and Pat Thane (New York: Routledge, 1991), 29; Inger Elisabeth Haavet, "Hvor mye er en mor verd? – Mødrenes forkjemper 125 år," in *Katti Anker Møller: Mødrenes forkjemper 125 år* (Bergen: Senter for humanistisk kvinneforskning, 1994), 9.
39. Katti Anker Møller, "Om mødreforsikring," MS 4 2416:III.
40. Katti Anker Møller, "Mødrehjælp," Kvindernes Enhetsfront Oplysningsarbeide, June 7, 1925, MS 4 2416:VI, Håndskriftsamlingen, Nasjonalbiblioteket.
41. Katti Anker Møller, "Om mødreforsikring," MS 4 2416:III mødreforsikring—morstrygd, Håndskriftsamlingen, Nasjonalbiblioteket.
42. Katti Anker Møller, "Om mødreforsikring," MS 4 2416:III mødreforsikring—morstrygd.

"MOTHERS' FREEDOM IS THE KEY TO WOMEN'S EMANCIPATION... 197

43. For a classic discussion of this, see: Viviana Rotman Zelizer, *Pricing the Priceless Child: The Changing Social Value of Children* (New York: Basic Books, 1985).
44. Katti Anker Møller, "Mødreforsikring," MS 4 2416:III Håndskriftsamlingen, Nasjonalbiblioteket.
45. Katti Anker Møller, "Krav om fødehjem og mødrehjem," MS 4 2416:I.
46. Katti Anker Møller was a proponent of "voluntary motherhood" and led the birth control movement in Norway. She opened a Mother Hygiene Office in Oslo in 1924 that dispersed contraceptive information and birth control devices. Møller also supported the revision of the abortion law and wanted women to have the legal option of terminating their pregnancies.
47. To this end, Møller opened the Mother Hygiene Office in Oslo. Katti Anker Møller, "Moderskapets frigjørelse, foredrag holdt 1. gang i Kristiania 1915," in *Katti Anker Møller: Mødrenes forkjemper 125 år* (Bergen: Senter for humanistisk kvinneforskning, 1994), 91.
48. Katti Anker Møller, "Kvindernes fødselspolitik, Venstrekvinnelaget, Kristiania, 1919" in *Moderskapets frigjørelse. To foredrag-fra 1915 og 1919*, ed. Katti Anker Møller (Oslo: Tiden, 1974).
49. Ibid., 40.
50. Sigrid Undset, "Begrepsforvirring," (1919) reprinted in *Essays og artikler 1910–1919*, ed. Liv Bliksrud (Oslo, 2004), 329–346.
51. Katti Anker Møller to Mrs. Michelet, MS 4 2416:VI Kvinnenes fødselspolitikk, Håndskriftsamlingen, Nasjonalbiblioteket.
52. "Venstrekvinnelaget," *Nylænde*, 1919, 126. Møller later felt vindicated when she was able to present her speech on mothers' wages at the International Women's Conference held in Oslo in 1920.
53. The periodical even changed its name from *Kvinden*, or *The Woman*, to *Arbeiderkvinnen*, or The Working Woman, during her reign.
54. Augusta Aasen, "Kvindernes Fødselspolitik," *Kvinden*, June 1, 1919, 42.
55. Ibid.
56. Kirsten Hofseth, "Fra stemmerettskrav til kvinneregjering: et historisk studiehefte" (Oslo: Det norske arbeiderpartiet, 1988), 5.
57. *Kvinden*, September 1, 1909.
58. "Likelønnsystemet supplert med barnetillegg," *Kvinden*, March 1, 1928.
59. *Kvinden*, October 1, 1924, 2.
60. "Arbeiderklassen på skilleveien: Hjem eller fabrikker?" *Kvinden*, May 1, 1929, 66.
61. Anne-Lise Seip and Hilde Ibsen, "Family Welfare, Which Policy? Norway's Road to Child Allowances," in *Maternity and Gender Policies: Women and the Rise of European Welfare States, 1880s–1950s*, eds. Gisela Bock and Pat Thane (New York: Routledge, 1991), 42–43.

198   A. M. PETERSON

62. Anne-Lise Seip, *Veiene til velferdsstaten: Norsk sosialpolitikk, 1920–1975* (Oslo: Gyldendal, 1994), 176.
63. Inger Elisabeth Haavet, "Befolkningspolitikk og familiepolitikk," in *Langsomt ble landet et velferdssamfunn: trygdens historie, 1894–1994*, eds. Øyvind Bjørnson and Inger Elisabeth Haavet (Oslo: Gyldendal, 1994), 120.
64. Seip, *Veiene til velferdsstaten*, 177.
65. "De fraskilte kvinners kår," *Kvinden*, nr. 7, 1937, 2.
66. Det norske Arbeiderparti program 1927, Norsk sammfunnsvitenskapelig datatjeneste, www.nsd.uib.no, Accessed April 16, 2013; Haavet, "Befolkningspolitikk," 121.
67. *Statistiske Meddelelser* (Oslo: Det statistiske centralbyrå, 1936), 142.
68. 24 out of the 28 municipalities gave mothers' pensions to widows only. Ibid.
69. Ibid.
70. "Omsorgen for de enslige mødre," *Kvinden*, June 1, 1926, 42.
71. Den norske arbeiderpartiets protokoll, 1935, 35–36.
72. In fact, many social democratic women supported initiatives to grant family wages to civil servants even though this did not affect members of their own social class. Seip and Ibsen, "Family Welfare, Which Policy," in *Maternity and Gender Policies*, 46.
73. Ella Anker, "Frem med kvinnesakene!" *Kvinden*, July 1, 1929, 100.
74. This is because many people argued that the current wage was already a family wage, and if the family wage system was implemented single workers would see their wages reduced. See: Seip, *Veiene til velferdsstaten*, 183.
75. Seip and Ibsen, "Family Welfare, Which Policy," 48.
76. Ibid., 45–47.
77. Ella Anker, "Likelønnsystemet supplert med barnetillegg," *Kvinden*, March 1, 1928, 26.
78. Ibid.
79. Ella Anker, "Mødrenes arbeidsforhold," *Kvinden*, July 1, 1927, 83.
80. Ella Anker, "Barnetrygd," February 1, 1930, 19.
81. Det norske arbeiderpartis program 1930, Norsk sammfunnsvitenskapelig datatjeneste, www.nsd.uib.no, Accessed April 16, 2013.
82. In 1913 parliament created a committee on family subsidies for civil servant wages. This was put into practice during the First World War to help compensate for price increases. The economic crisis during the 1920s led to discussions of abandoning this practice. See: Seip, *Veiene til velferdsstaten*, 181.
83. Seip and Ibsen, "Family Welfare, Which Policy," 48.
84. Norske Kvinners Nationalraad 7th landsmøte 1925, 12. MS 4 2912:7, Håndskriftsamlingen, Nasjonalbiblioteket.

"MOTHERS' FREEDOM IS THE KEY TO WOMEN'S EMANCIPATION... 199

85. Seip and Ibsen, "Family Welfare, Which Policy," 47.
86. Margarete Bonnevie, "Hva kan gjøres for å sikre kvinners lønn, arbeids-vilkår og avansement," NKN Foredrag ved 11 landsmøte Oslo September 1938. MS 4 2912:7, Håndskriftsamlingen, Nasjonalbiblioteket.
87. Child Allowances Bill, 1937, 77.
88. Ella Anker, "Likelønnsystemet supplert med barnetillegg," Kvinden, March 1, 1928, 26.
89. Seip and Ibsen, "Family Welfare, Which Policy," 50.
90. Ibid., 40.
91. Hagemann, "Maternalism and Gender Equality," 77.
92. This included work for "equal pay for equal work." Most often their efforts focused on middle-class women's occupations such as teachers, but the NKF was also concerned with workplace regulations for industrial women workers.
93. The complimentary gender order had its roots in the Enlightenment. See Thomas Laqueur, *Making Sex: Body and Gender from the Greeks to Freud* (Cambridge, MA: Harvard University Press, 1990).
94. "Kvindens retslige stilling," Kvinden, April 1, 1910.
95. "1ste. Mai," Kvinden, May 1, 1910.
96. "Saerbeskyttelse for kvinder," Kvinden, August 1, 1914.
97. "Nogle ord om arbeiderbeskyttelse og særlov for kvinder," Nylænde, June 1, 1908.
98. See: Gro Hagemann, "Protection or Equality? Debates on Protective Legislation in Norway," in *Protecting Women: Labor Legislation in Europe, the United States, and Australia, 1880–1920* (Chicago: University of Illinois Press, 1995).
99. "Saerbeskyttelse for kvinder," Kvinden, August 1, 1914.
100. "Kvinderne og Washingtonkonferansen," Kvinden, February 1, 1920.
101. Norsk kvinnesaksforening: Kons. Til brev og møtereferater inntil 1922, Norske Kvinneforening 1904–1915, Randi Blehr, Riksarkivet.
102. Nylænde, February 1, 1897 and March 1, 1897.
103. "I anledning av Kvindernes fødseslpolitik," Nylænde, May 15, 1919, 150.
104. Of course, there were also conflicting opinions within these feminist groups, but the focus here will be on the official stance of the organizations.
105. Maternity Protection Convention, 1919 (No. 3) Convention Concerning the Employment of Women Before and After Childbirth, http://www.ilo.org/dyn/normlex/en/f?p=1000:12100:0::NO::P12100_ILO_CODE:C003, Accessed March 30, 2013.
106. St. prp. nr. 27 (1921) and St. prp. nr. 70 (1927); Norske kvinners nas-jonalråd, årberetning 1922. MS 4 2912:65 Arbeidervernloven, Håndskriftsamlingen, Nasjonalbiblioteket.

200   A. M. PETERSON

107. St. prp. Nr 70 (1927), "Om vedtakene fra de Internasjonale Arbeidskonferanser," 14.
108. Ot. Prp. nr. 46 (1928), "Om endringer i lov om sykeforsikring," 3.
109. Susan Pedersen, *Family, Dependence, and the Origins of the Welfare State: Britain and France, 1914–1945* (Cambridge: Cambridge University Press, 1993), 135–178.
110. "Kvinners og barns erhervsmessige arbeide: svangre kvinners fabrikkarbeide," *Kvinden*, July 1, 1927, 50.
111. Norsk Kvinnesaksforening II, Korrespondanse og henvendelse, Ms fol. 3868:6, Håndskriftsamlingen, Nasjonalbiblioteket.
112. NKN to Kommunal og Arbeidsdepartement, undated, MS 4 2912:65 Arbeidervernloven, Håndskriftsamlingen, Nasjonalbiblioteket. An article printed in *Kvinden* on July 1, 1927 also supported this argumentation.
113. St. prp. Nr. 70 (1927), "Om vedtakene," 11.
114. NKF to Ministry of Social Affairs, January 27, 1939, Norsk Kvinnesaksforening II. Korrespondanse og henvendelse Ms fol. 3868:6, Håndskriftsamlingen, Nasjonalbiblioteket.
115. Statistisk sentralbyrå, "Stortingsvalg, Valgte representanter, etter parti, 1906–2001," www.ssb.no/a/histstat/aarbok, Accessed March 26, 2013.
116. Redvaldsen, *The Labor Party in Britain and Norway*, 74.
117. The Norwegian Labor Party received just over 40 percent of the vote in 1934. Statistisk sentralbyrå, "Stortingsvalg, Valgte representanter, etter parti, 1906–2001," www.ssb.no/a/histstat/aarbok, Accessed March 26, 2013; Det Norske Arbeiderpartis arbeidsprogram 1933, Norsk sammfunnsvitenskapelig datatjeneste, www.nsd.uib.no, Accessed April 14, 2013.
118. Stortingsforhandlinger 1935, Ot. prp. Nr. 31, 38.
119. Ibid., 38–40.
120. Stortingsforhandlinger 1936, Instillinger til Odelstinger Inst. O. VI, 20–21.
121. Stortingsforhandlinger 1936, Forhandlinger i Odelstinget, 266.
122. This did conflict with the ILO maternity convention, however, and was eventually changed back to "must" in the 1950s to coincide with international requirements. See: Bjørnson and Haavet, eds., *Langsomt ble landet et velferdssamfunn*, 127.
123. Karl Frimann Dahl was not an elected member of parliament. He was a Supreme Court Justice who starting filling in for Alfred Martin Madsen (*Arbeiderparti*) on the Social Committee in 1935. Norsk sammfunnsvitenskapelig datatjeneste, www.nsd.uib.no, Accessed April 14, 2013.
124. Stortingsforhandlinger 1936, Instillinger til Odelstinger, Inst. O. VI, 20–21.

"MOTHERS' FREEDOM IS THE KEY TO WOMEN'S EMANCIPATION... 201

125. Ferdinand Rømcke, *Lov om Arbeidervern av 19. juni 1936* (Oslo: Olaf Norlis Forlag, 1936), 81.
126. For some parliamentarians this may have been for no other reason than that it would be difficult to police such a prohibition of parturient women's work. Stortingsforhandlinger 1936, Instillinger til Odelstinger, Inst. O. VI, 20–21.
127. These breaks were to be in addition to other legally-mandated breaks but it was left up to the employer to decide whether breastfeeding breaks were to be paid.
128. Rømcke, *Lov om Arbeidervern av 19. juni 1936*, 80.
129. Almost all occupations were covered by the law except for the fishing industry, the airline industry, certain types of agriculture, and public administration.
130. Correspondence, November 14, 1927, Oslo trygdekontor, Personalet, Spørsmål om lønn under nedkomst, Statsarkivet i Oslo.
131. Civil servants have typically been the most powerful people in Norway, because the royal family and aristocracy were quite weak.
132. Some of these teachers received salary for this leave, but were expected to pay for their substitutes out of this salary.
133. Correspondence, October 24, 1927, Oslo trygdekontor, Personalet, Spørsmål om lønn under nedkomst, Statsarkivet i Oslo.
134. Ibid.
135. Norsk Kvinnesaksforening II. Korrespondanse og henvendelse, Ms fol. 3868:6, Håndskriftsamlingen, Nasjonalbiblioteket.
136. NKF to Oslo Municipal Chairman, January 29, 1938, Norsk Kvinnesaksforening II. Korrespondanse og henvendelser, Ms fol. 3868:6, Håndskriftsamlingen, Nasjonalbiblioteket.
137. Oslo Municipality to Oslo Social Welfare Office, March 1, 1939, Permisjon under nedkomst, Oslo Trygdekontor, Sakserie Personal og ansettelsessaker 1939–1943, Statsarkivet i Oslo.
138. The extensive press coverage may have been the reason that the Oslo Social Welfare Office was not forced to reverse this policy decision. See: Oslo Social Welfare Office board meeting, February 15, 1939, Permisjon under nedkomst, Oslo Trygdekontor, Sakserie Personal og ansettelsessaker 1939–1943, Statsarkivet i Oslo.
139. Oslo Social Welfare Office to Oslo Municipality, March 10, 1939, Permisjon under nedkomst, Oslo Trygdekontor, Sakserie Personal og ansettelsessaker 1939–1943, Statsarkivet i Oslo.
140. Oslo Social Welfare Office board meeting, February 15, 1939, Permisjon under nedkomst, Oslo Trygdekontor, Sakserie Personal og ansettelsessaker 1939–1943, Statsarkivet i Oslo.

202   A. M. PETERSON

141. Oslo trygdekontor, Personalet, Spørsmål om lønn under nedkomst, Statsarkivet i Oslo.
142. The Oslo Social Welfare Office continued to be an anomaly in regards to granting this paid leave to its female public servants until long after World War Two. "Barselkvinnen 1937–1957," Arbeidstilsynet, juridisk avdeling, Riksarkivet.
143. Dagny Bjørnaraa to Director Ormestad February 20, 1939, S1939/27 Permisjon under nedkomst, Oslo Trygdekontor, Sakserie Personal og ansettelsessaker 1939–1943, Statsarkivet i Oslo.

CHAPTER 7

Conclusion

Maternity policy is still fiercely debated in Norway today. While current discussions of maternity policy focus on gender equality more broadly, the rhetoric of women's rights and duties that feminists, midwives, and policy recipients used to frame maternity policy in the early twentieth century continue to mark these debates. In Fall 2017 the Norwegian government proposed to significantly change how parental leave is distributed between mothers and fathers. The current policy allocates 10 weeks of leave to the mother of a child and 10 weeks of leave to the father with the remaining weeks to be divided between the two parents as they see fit. Though the shared portion of the leave can be taken by either the mother or the father, mothers are the primary users of the leave.[1] The proposed revision would significantly alter this practice. Paternity leave would be doubled by reducing the portion of shared leave. The resulting policy would equally distribute parental leave between mothers and fathers, with mothers retaining an exclusive right to an additional 3 weeks preceding the birth and 6 after for medical reasons.

This proposal has stimulated much discussion, especially regarding parental leave's impact on women's and children's health, women's rights, men's rights, and gender equality. Those in favor of the proposal argue that equally dividing parental leave between fathers and mothers will increase gender equality. Gender Equality and Anti-Discrimination Ombud, Hanne Bjurstrøm, claims, for example, that the current allocation of leave strengthens traditional gender roles and divisions of labor in the home. She believes

© The Author(s) 2018   203
A. M. Peterson, *Maternity Policy and the Making of the Norwegian Welfare State, 1880–1940*, https://doi.org/10.1007/978-3-319-75481-9_7

that the proposal to equally divide the leave is a "new and bold reform" that will emphasize that raising children is an equally shared task between mothers and fathers.[2] To critics who allege that the proposed change to parental leave will ultimately harm children by limiting the time they spend with their mothers, Bjurstrøm responded by saying that this is an antiquated position: "Fathers are important to their children, and one expects something completely different of fathers today than before."[3]

While supporters of the proposal have said that equally dividing parental leave will increase gender equality, detractors argue that gender equality is not the same as gender equity. Medical professionals have been particularly critical of the proposal, arguing that women's biological difference from men must be taken into account when deciding who should get what amount of parental leave. They believe that equally dividing parental leave between mothers and fathers ignores this difference and will adversely affect women's rights and women's and children's health. The role of breastfeeding is central to their position.

Outspoken breastfeeding advocate and pediatrician, Dr. Gro Nylander, for instance, views maternity leave as an essential prerequisite for women's economic rights. Nylander strongly advocates for women receiving at least 8 months of maternity leave and has described women's ability to combine breastfeeding with a career as an achievement of the Norwegian women's rights movement.[4] For Nylander, the maternity leave has allowed "women to participate in both production and reproduction."[5] She further believes that while "paternity leave is great," its introduction has meant that "young women have had to let go of privileges it has taken generations of fighting to achieve," directly referencing women's historical struggle to make maternity leave a benefit to which women were entitled.[6]

Compared to other European countries, the lines between maternity, paternity, and parental leaves are blurred in Norway just as they are in other Nordic countries.[7] Though maternity and parental leave is nearly ubiquitous in Europe, very few countries exclusively reserve leave for fathers beyond a customary two-week paternity leave immediately following the birth of a child. Norway was the first country to introduce paternity quotas in 1993 and has increased the length of duration of this leave exclusively reserved for fathers in the decades since. Despite being a frontrunner in the implementation of parental leave reserved specifically for fathers, the current debate in Norway indicates that the more leave granted to fathers at the expense of, rather than in addition to, the leave granted to mothers is seen by some as a threat to women's rights and the health and wellbeing of women and children.[8]

The 2017 Proposed Parental Leave Policy in Light of the Longer History of Maternity Policy in Norway

The arguments for and against the proposed change to parental leave in 2017 are entwined in the historical legacies of policy development. As detailed in this book, feminists, midwives, and the intended policy recipients played an early role in linking maternity policy to discussions of women's and children's health, the social and economic value of women's work in the home, and the greater need for women's rights in the workplace. The rhetorical devices women used to advance their particular visions of maternity policy formed a complicated framework that reformers had to operate within after the Second World War.

Entrenched in early maternity policies was the belief that men and women were biologically different. Women of various economic positions and ideological persuasions used this belief to argue that this biological difference necessitated greater recognition and protection of women's reproductive role in the family and the nation. Over time, these women tied the fight for women's equality to arguments for the expansion of maternity policy. By the 1940s, feminists, midwives, and the intended policy recipients had successfully framed maternity policy as a benefit rather than a restriction. They argued that women not only needed time off from work, medical assistance during pregnancy and childbirth, and financial support to raise young children, but that they deserved it. Maternity policy had become a hallmark of women's rights by the mid-twentieth century in Norway.

This book's central argument is that women were intimately involved in this process and shaped maternity legislation to fit their various wants and needs. Feminists, midwives, and the intended policy recipients often approached maternity policies from divergent perspectives and wielded varying levels of political influence. This led to the incorporation of a diverse set of interests into early welfare policies that targeted women and the family.

Women pursued different types of policy initiatives and outcomes based on their ideological, professional and class backgrounds and the perceived effect maternity legislation might have on their lives. Depending on their ideological and class backgrounds, feminist organizations and individuals had differing goals for maternity policies. Bourgeois feminist organizations, such as the Norwegian Association for Women's Rights and Norwegian

206 A. M. PETERSON

National Council of Women, often pursued versions of maternity policies designed to strengthen women's economic rights in the workplace. Social democratic feminist organizations, such as the Women's Federation of the Norwegian Labor Party (AKF), mainly focused their efforts on obtaining state support for the work mothers preformed in the home. The degree to which feminists were able to achieve these goals often depended on their political connections, which party had power in parliament, and the level of popular support they were able to cultivate for their ideas.

Of all the women studied, feminists were best able to access channels of political power. Sometimes this was through personal connections. Many bourgeois feminists were related to or had close relationships with men who sat in Parliament, including Katti Anker Møller, Gina Krog, Fernanda Nissen and Margarete Bonnevie. Feminist associations also had the advantage of being recognized as legitimate organizations that represented the interests of Norwegian women. This meant that the government often relied on them to give opinions on legislative issues that affected women, such as maternity leave. Due to this relationship, feminists had the greatest ability to shape maternity policies to fit their particular goals. The feminist organization that had the greatest ability to shape the content of debates about maternity leave often depended on which political party was in power in parliament. This shifted with time and as the power of the Labor Party increased over the course of the early twentieth century, so too did the influence of the AKF.

Midwives also had a keen interest in the content and form of maternity policies, because they stood to gain economically and professionally from their implementation. In contrast to feminists, midwives did not have as much access to the locus of political power. Midwives lived throughout the Norwegian countryside and did not organize into a national body until the early twentieth century. Even after they formed the Norwegian Association of Midwives, midwives' direct political influence remained marginal. Politicians perceived doctors as possessing superior medical knowledge and expertise and often sought out the opinion of doctors as opposed to midwives on issues related to maternity. In spite of this, midwives did help shape maternity policies, particularly in the way they were implemented at the local level.

As the main targets and beneficiaries of maternity policies, working women also contributed to the content and scope of maternity legislation. Though in contrast to midwives and feminists, working women did not have the same ability to directly influence policy. Women's labor unions do not appear to have engaged in the issue of maternity legislation, and the AKF was dominated by women with middle-class backgrounds and working-class housewives.[9] As such, working women were further removed from people in positions of political power at the national level and not collectively represented in political debates about maternity. Instead, working women wielded the greatest amount of influence at the individual level.

The greatest influence working women had on maternity policies occurred through the interactions they had with state authorities at the local level. In their interactions with bureaucrats and midwives, working women adapted maternity policies to fit their individual needs and interests. This often caused midwives and bureaucrats to interpret policy in ways unintended by legislators. Though the locus of working women's influence was mainly at the individual level, they also had a type of group influence. When enough individual women made the same decision, such as not taking advantage of a benefit available, these individual actions were interpreted as collective action. Through these actions, working women framed debates about maternity legislation at the national level and influenced the types of policy revisions that took place.

Feminists, midwives and working women were able to exert influence over maternity policymaking because they promoted ideas about maternity that resonated with the major concerns of the time. At the turn of the twentieth century, this involved debates about infant mortality rates and public health. Women used the focus on these issues to push for compensatory maternity benefits for women, leading to more comprehensive maternity policies for working-class women under the Sickness Insurance Laws and Castbergian Children's Laws.

By the start of the Second World War, maternity leave was perceived as a pillar of women's rights in Norway, demonstrating the strength and diligence of the Norwegian feminist movement. In the interwar period, feminists from the Norwegian Association for Women's Rights, Norwegian National Council of Women and Women's Federation of the Norwegian Labor Party framed maternity benefits as an issue of women's rights. They tied women's recently won citizenship rights to the need for women's increased economic and social rights. They also drew upon the idea that motherhood was a service women preformed for the state and likened motherhood to an occupation deserving of pay and workplace protections. These ideas fit well with the concerns of a newly independent nation state and the interwar focus on birth rates and the family. The growth of the Labor Party in the interwar period

208   A. M. PETERSON

also bolstered the political saliency of many of these claims. Consequently, feminists succeeded in getting the government to pass comprehensive maternity policies in the 1930s that strengthened women's economic position at work and in the home.

The types of rhetoric women used to advance maternity politics affected policy outcomes. When focusing on the effect increased maternity provisions could have on infant health, the results were policies that were more restrictive for women. Such was the case with the Castbergian Children's Laws where women were required to fulfill certain requirements as a mother in order to receive public assistance. By broadening this focus to encompass public health more generally, women succeeded in expanding the number of women covered by maternity policies and increasing the amount of benefits they received. Yet tying maternity benefits to discussions of public health also contributed to the institutionalization of women's birth experiences, an aspect of maternity policy that many women resisted. In the interwar period, women's articulation of maternity benefits as a right to which all women were entitled stimulated the creation of the most generous maternity policies to date.

Women's influence on the development of maternity policy in Norway has had lasting effects on the Norwegian welfare state. Feminists, midwives, and working women effectively made maternity a political issue, one that warranted state protection and support. By doing so, they made mothers and children a primary focus of early welfare policies. It is therefore not surprising that the first universal policy passed in Norway was the Child Benefit Act in 1946 that gave support to all mothers with young children. Though this law was passed after the war, it built on ideas that had been developed by women during the early twentieth century.

Feminists, midwives and working women had successfully incorporated the needs and interests of a variety of women in Norwegian maternity policies and their achievements would continue to frame discussions of maternity long into the postwar period. While bolstering mothers' rights in the home may have been the main focus of these initiatives, women also made considerable efforts to increase mothers' rights in the workplace. This led to the creation of policies that strengthened women's ability to choose where they wanted to work. Women could stay at home with their young children and receive assistance from the state, or they could combine motherhood with work outside of the home and benefit from the protections and support provided for working mothers. In 1940 this choice would still not have been without its limitations. Important measures for working

CONCLUSION 209

women, such as childcare, remained largely unavailable and impeded women's choices to work outside the home. Yet women had made significant advances in the case of state-supported maternity. They contributed to the crafting of a Norwegian welfare state that contained dual paths to economic support for mothers, which continues to characterize the maternity policies in place in Norway today.[10]

Regardless of whether or not Norway decides to pass the proposal put forth in 2017 to equally distribute parental leave between mothers and fathers, it is likely that maternity policies will continue to elicit debate. Women's early and diverse influence on the policymaking process helps explain why debates over parental leave policies continue to be punctuated by discussions of women's and children's health, women's rights, as well as gender equality over 75 years later.

NOTES

1. In 2011, only 10 percent of all eligible fathers took leave beyond the allocated paternal quota. Berit Brandth and Elin Kvande, "Norway Country Note," in *International Review of Leave Policies and Research*, 2016, accessed November 22, 2017, http://www.leavenetwork.org/lp_and_r_reports/.
2. Hanne Bjurstrøm quoted in Eirik Husøy, "Likestillingsombudet vil todele foreldrepermisjonen," *Aftenposten*, September 29, 2017.
3. Ibid.
4. Gro Nylander, "Del permisjonen til barnets beste!," *Aftenposten*, August 8, 2016.
5. Gro Nylander quoted in Heidi Borud and Sofie Gran Aspunvik, "Kvinner bør ha minst åtte måneders permisjon," *Aftenposten*, February 6, 2013.
6. Ibid.
7. Peter Moss and Sheila B. Kamerman, "Introduction," in *The Politics of Parental Leave Policies: Children, Parenting, Gender, and the Labour Market*, eds. Sheila Kamerman and Peter Moss (Bristol: The Policy Press, 2009), 3–4.
8. Berit Brandth and Elin Kvande, "Norway: The Making of the Father's Quota," in *The Politics of Parental Leave Policies: Children, Parenting, Gender, and the Labour Market*, eds. Sheila Kamerman and Peter Moss (Bristol: The Policy Press, 2009), 203–205. In spite of assertions that paternity leave increases gender equality and ultimately bolsters women's rights and position in society, critics fear that paternity leave pits the wellbeing of men against the wellbeing of women. Studies have shown that the paternity quota enhances fathers' lives and children's lives by strengthening fathers' relationships with their children. The paternity quota has not

necessarily led to a more equal division of labor in the home between men and women and fathers indicate their primary use of the quota is not to increase gender equality. See Berit Brandth and Elin Kvande, "Masculinity and Child Care: The Reconstruction of Fathering," *The Sociological Review* 46, no. 2 (1998): 293–314.

9. Two of the most influential members of the Women's Federation of the Norwegian Labor Party in the early twentieth century came from prominent Norwegian families. Fernanda Nissen, for example, came from a family of diplomats, she was married to a newspaper editor, and the sister-in-law of cultural elite, Erik Werenskiold. Ella Anker, sister of Katti Anker Møller and sister-in-law with Johan Castberg, also came from a prominent family and was a well-published journalist.

10. For a discussion of the ambivalence and dualism that characterizes Norwegian family policies today, see: Anette Borchorst, "Woman-friendly Policy Paradoxes? Childcare Policies and Gender Equality Visions in Scandinavia," in *Gender Equality and Welfare Politics in Scandinavia: The Limits of Political Ambition?* eds. Kari Melby, Anna-Birte Ravn, and Christina Carlsson Wetterburg (Bristol: The Policy Press, 2009); Berit Brandth, Brita Bungum, and Elin Kvande, "Innledning: Valfrihet I omsorgspolitikken," in *Valgfrihetens tid. Omsorgspolitikk for ban møter det fleksible arbeidslivet*, eds. Berit Brandth, Brita Bungum, and Elin Kvande (Oslo: Gyldendal Akademisk, 2005).

INDEX[1]

NUMBERS AND SYMBOL

1907 report, 59n101, 67, 94n18, 105

A

Aasen, Augusta, 173, 197n54
Abortion, 172, 197n46
Abrahemsen, Lars Kristian, 73
Aftenposten, 83, 128, 156n22, 209n2, 209n4, 209n5
Ameln, Henrik, 85–88
Angel-makers, 50
  See also Englemakere; Foster mothers
Anker, Ella, 169, 177, 178, 180, 195n28, 198n73, 198n77, 198n79, 198n80, 199n88, 210n9
Antepartum care, 67
Arbeiderdemokratene, 56n45, 63, 73, 96n55
  See also Radical People's Party
Arbeiderpartiet, 59n98, 197n56, 198n71
  See also Norwegian Labor Party

Arbeiderpartiets kvinneforbund, 15
  See also Women's Federation of the Norwegian Labor Party
Arup Seip, Jens, 31, 55n33
Auclert, Hubertine, 13

B

Bakke, David Olson, 90
Bang, Dagny, 70, 95n31, 182
Berg, Signe, 191
Biological difference between men and women, 204, 205
Birthing traditions, 88
Bjørnaraa, Dagny, 164, 194n4, 202n143
Bjørnson, Bjørnstjerne, 29, 200n122
Bjurstrøm, Hanne, 203, 204, 209n2
Bøndernes Hus, 123, 129
Bonnevie, Margarete, 169, 179, 180, 186, 192, 195n25, 199n86, 206

[1]Note: Page numbers followed by 'n' refer to notes.

© The Author(s) 2018   211
A. M. Peterson, *Maternity Policy and the Making of the Norwegian Welfare State, 1880–1940*, https://doi.org/10.1007/978-3-319-75481-9

212 INDEX

Brandt, Kristian, 68, 69, 72, 77, 81,
    85, 91, 94n22, 94n23, 97n70,
    105, 126
Bratlie, Jens Kristian Meinich, 129
Breastfeeding, 50, 52, 61, 68, 69,
    94n22, 103, 105, 106, 111,
    112, 114, 115, 118, 132,
    142–145, 171, 184, 186, 187,
    201n127, 204
  mandates, 201n127
Breast milk, 68, 69
  substitutes, 105

C
Castberg, Johan, 4, 17, 22n38, 34,
    56n45, 61–65, 70, 71, 75, 77,
    78, 81, 82, 84–92, 96n51,
    96n52, 96n53, 96n54, 97n71,
    97n74, 102–106, 109–112, 116,
    117, 121n33, 126, 127,
    168, 210n9
  work with Katti Anker Møller, 4,
    17, 22n38, 62–65, 77, 81, 82,
    90–92, 96n51, 96n52, 96n53,
    96n54, 97n71, 97n74,
    102–106, 109, 110, 117,
    121n33, 125
Castbergian Children's Laws,
    1915 (CCL)
  influence on how women mothered
    children, 113
  maternity support in, 102
  provision of public assistance for
    single mothers, 9, 102, 112,
    114, 115, 123, 137, 146, 166
  responses to, 119, 153, 154
  See also Castbergske barnelover
Castbergske barnelover, 121n27
CCL, see Castbergian Children's Laws
Central Statistical Agency,
    67, 115
  See also Sentral statistiske byrå

Child allowances, 119, 164, 178,
    180, 192
Childbirth
  assistance, 8, 15, 42, 44, 48, 52,
    60n116, 62, 65, 79, 83, 87,
    112, 132, 134, 152
  assistance procedures, 44
  breech, 44
  control, 153, 172
  home, 130, 150
  hygiene, 76, 91, 113, 126, 127
  illegitimate, 29, 47, 108, 148,
    149, 153
  as an illness, 65, 70, 189
  institutional, 124, 128, 130, 131,
    147, 150, 153
  institutionalization of, 12, 13, 114,
    147, 153, 208
  as an intimate affair, 42
  medicalization of, 12–13, 68, 125
  professionalization of, 114
  rate, 1, 18n3, 86, 159n71, 170,
    178, 180, 195n30, 207
  safe, 83, 113–114
Childcare policies, 9
Children
  equal naming of (see Castbergian
    Children's Laws)
  health of, 124, 126, 187
  inheritance rights for (see
    Castbergian Children's Laws)
  legal equality for, 104
  public assistance for, 9, 102, 110,
    112, 113, 153, 174, 188
  of single mothers, 9, 101–119, 123,
    124, 137, 142, 146, 166,
    175, 176
  See also Illegitimate children
Children's health, 203–205, 209
  state interest in, 104, 153
Child support, 7, 27, 30, 39, 40,
    50–52, 55n25, 111, 148
  provision, 51

INDEX 213

Child Welfare Act 1915, 112, 114, 115, 119
  Knowledge of, 130
  See also Lov om forsorg for barn 1915; Castbergian Children's Laws
Christensen, Peder, 61, 65, 92–93n2, 93n3
Christianity
  doctrine, 29
  practice, 29
Citizenship
  benefits, 33
  rights, 32, 33, 50, 117, 118, 131, 145, 169, 175, 207
Clinical scrutiny of women's reproductive processes, 68
Commission on Child Allowances of 1934, 179
Confederation of Trade Unions (*Landsorganisasjonen*), 173
Confinement, 28–30, 44, 50, 70, 75, 78, 83, 91, 110, 111, 126, 130, 134, 171, 192
Conservative Party, 3, 35
  See also Høyre
Contraception, 109, 197n46
Crise de Natalité, 7, 118

D
Dagbladet, 83, 98n89, 120n3, 128, 156n21, 156n25, 194n3
Dahl, Karl Frimann, 187, 200n123
Debes, Inge, 177
Delivery, 54n13, 59n92, 71, 74, 75, 77, 79, 87, 106, 148, 171
Den hvide baand, 107
  See also White Ribbon Maternity Home
Denmark, 7–9, 21n30, 26, 127, 130, 156n31
  maternity policies in, 7, 8, 26, 130

Den norske jordmorforening (DNJ), 15, 82, 152, 153, 161n118
  See also Norwegian Association of Midwives
Disease, 44, 67, 159n71
Divorce, 4, 102
Doctors
  operative interventions, 44
  relationship with midwives, 12, 41, 43–45

E
Ebbell, Thea, 40, 58n69
Economic depression, 136, 165, 167
  effects on feminist goals, 38, 185
Economic security and equality
  disagreements over, 179
  for women, 165
Eftestøl, Olav Andreas, 72, 73
Ellertsen, Nicoline Falck, 82, 83, 91, 126, 151, 160n103, 161n109
Employment Protection Act of 1936, 188
  See also Lov om arbeidervern, 1936
Endowment of Motherhood, 103, 119, 165
Englemakere, 50
  See also Angel-makers; Foster mothers
Equal pay for equal work, 38, 41, 177, 199n92
European labor activists, 27
European maternity legislation, 5–8

F
Factory
  inspectors, 48, 59–60n105, 127, 139, 158n53, 182, 185
  laws, 35, 37–39, 46, 51, 61, 78
  regulations, 25, 26
  work, 16, 31, 48, 67

214 INDEX

Factory Law, 1909, 61
Factory Protection Act, 1892, 34, 36, 38, 41, 65, 70
Familievennlig ("family friendly"), 170
Family politics, 166, 185, 186
Family structure, 9
   traditional, 9
Family wage, 165, 174, 177–180, 198n72, 198n74
Fathers
   accountability of, 30, 108, 112, 118, 148
   payment of, 150
   responsibilities of, 102, 109, 175
   unsupportive, 30
   See also Paternity
Feminist movements, 3, 5, 37–39, 207
Feminist organizations
   bourgeois, 181, 205 (*see also* Norwegian Association for Women's Rights; Norwegian National Council of Women)
   social democratic, 206 (*see also* Women's Federation of the Norwegian Labor Party)
Feminists
   conservative, 15, 174, 178
   individualist, 15, 38, 39
   maternalist, 62, 173
   relational, 14
   relationship with politicians, 27
   Scandinavian, 3
   social democratic, 168, 174, 192, 193, 206
   socialist, 15
   See also Norwegian feminist movement
Fetus, 44, 108
First working-class movement, 31
   See also Thrane, Marcus, Thrane Movement
Fløistad, Guttorm, 86, 115

Forceps, 45, 59n92, 59n93
Foshaug, Meyer Nilsen, 85, 90, 98n87
Foster care, 51, 75, 105
Foster homes, 50
Foster mothers, 50
   See also Angel-makers; *Englemakere*
France, 7, 13, 20n24, 23n48, 26, 62, 65, 86, 93n7, 93n11, 94n19, 114, 118, 120n5, 164, 193
   maternity policies in, 7

G
Gender equality, 1, 8, 9, 203, 204, 209, 209n8
Gender roles, 203
   traditional, 203
Germany, 21n31, 21n32, 23n48, 25, 26, 32, 34, 35, 53n3, 65, 88, 93n11, 97n69, 127, 180, 186, 193
   maternity policies in, 21n31, 23n48, 25, 34
Germ theory, 66, 126
Good of the child, the, 72
Governmental care facilities, 116, 117, 126

H
Halvorsen, Otto Bahr, 116
Hansson, Andreas, 73
Health councils, 5, 113–116, 137, 138, 140–142, 157n41, 159n80
Health Officials, 76, 141, 142, 144
Health of the nation, 62, 66, 74
Helping wife, 42
   See also Hjelpekone
Hjelpekone, 15, 42, 152
   See also Helping wife
Høidal, Anne Marie Ellingsdatter, 61, 92n1

INDEX 215

Hospitals, 13, 16, 68, 116, 117, 130, 141, 150, 151, 156n30, 156n31
Høyre, 3, 35, 85, 109, 110, 116
  See also Conservative Party

I
Illegitimate children
  1907 report, 54n16
  deaths, 104
  rights, 64, 77, 104, 106, 108–110
Immorality, 7
Industrialization
  effects of, 2, 6, 31, 32
  labor, 31, 33, 36, 51, 74
Infant care and wellbeing, 68
Infant control stations
  (*spedbarnskontroll*), 142, 143, 146, 151, 153, 154, 160n108
International Congress of Working Women, 182
International Council of Women, 38
International labor conferences, 6
International Labor Organization (ILO), 184, 186, 200n122
International worker congress, 34
Interwar period, 7, 9, 21n30, 119, 124, 130, 135, 146, 147, 150, 153, 163–193, 207, 208

J
Jail, 61, 62, 65, 92, 92n1, 106
Johannessen, Axel, 72, 77, 81, 91, 96n59, 97n72, 105
Johnsen, Josef, 35, 36
Jordmødre, 41
  See also Midwives
Journal of Midwifery, 48, 81, 94n22, 147, 149, 151
  See also Tidsskrift for jordmødre

K
Kjelsberg, Betzy, 48, 49, 59n105, 127, 139, 158n49, 158n53, 182, 185
Kjølseth, Marie, 127
Klavenes, Fru, 43, 58n80, 59n87, 121n35
Koht, Paul, 35
Konow, Didrik, 108, 121n21
Konow, Wollert, 4
Kragtorp, Ludvig Larsen, 25, 73, 86, 89
Kristiania Health Commission, 144
Kristiania, Norway, *see* Oslo, Norway
Krog, Gina, 14, 37–40, 57n57, 77, 109, 121n24, 121n26, 156n16, 182, 206
Krohg, Christian, 29

L
Labor
  gender-specific policies, 27
  policies, 6, 27
  protections, 39, 166, 184, 187, 192
  unions, 59n98, 207
Landskvinnestemmerettsforeningen, 38
  See also National Association for Women's Suffrage
Larsen, Lina, 50, 60n112
Liberal Party, 3, 4, 15, 172
  See also Venstre
Lillestrøm, Norway, 101
Local Sickness Insurance Funds, 91
  discretionary power, 88
Lov om arbeidervern, 1936, 163, 188, 190
  See also Employment Protection Act of 1936
Lov om forsorg for barn 1915, 115
  See also Child Welfare Act 1915; Castbergian Children's Laws

216 INDEX

M

Male domination, 14
Marriage, 7, 47, 62, 72, 78, 80, 102, 104–106, 108, 109, 111, 112, 148, 160n94, 183
Marxism, 173
Match Worker Strike, 1889, 47
Maternal dilemma, 11
Maternalist, 14, 22n38, 62
Maternity
  as a condition in need of state protection, 27, 103, 208
  medical conceptualizations of, 28
Maternity care, 126
  state-driven, 119
Maternity compensation, 37, 66, 71, 74, 89, 92
  minimum rate of, 90
Maternity home
  issues, 116, 126, 127, 130
  privacy, 123
  stays, 79, 114, 126, 127, 130, 131, 136, 141, 142
Maternity insurance
  acceptance of, 72
  coverage, 7, 133, 134, 137, 146
  expansion of, 79 (*see also* Møller, Katti Anker)
  expense of, 87
  as important for health of future generations, 85
  membership requirement, 145
  as needed to ensure better military defense, 86
  premium, 80, 108
  proposal, 75, 77, 80–82, 84, 85, 90, 184
  transportation fees, 88
Maternity laws
  1892, 5, 7, 17, 34, 38, 40, 51, 53
  1909, 17
  1915, 17, 119, 124, 131–146
  1936, 166

Maternity leave
  efforts to expand, 75–78
  evasion, 47
  industrial, 29
  legislation, 26, 41, 57n65, 166, 187, 192
  mandatory, 6, 21n30, 25, 28, 48, 187
  medically-dictated length of, 73
  optimal length, 35
  paid, 74
  policies, 9, 25, 26, 30, 34, 51, 166, 184, 191
  prohibitions, 31
  six-week minimum, 73
Maternity leave as a benefit *vs.* restriction, 92, 103
Maternity Policy, 2, 5–17, 19n17, 28, 47, 93n10, 118, 119, 130, 137, 185, 190–192, 203, 205–209
  underuse of, 75
Maternity Protection Convention 1919, 184
  See also International Labor Organization
Means-testing, 17, 103, 164
Medical care
  birth, 79
  gynecology, 28, 68, 72
  obstetrics, 28, 68, 72
  postpartum, 40, 44
  pregnancy, 68, 112
Medical interventions, 28
  forceps, 45, 59n92, 59n93
Medical professionals, *see* Doctors; Midwives
Medical supervision
  of maternity benefits, 114
  of mothers, 87
Michelet, Marie, 172, 197n51
Middle-class women, 37, 38, 41, 43, 94n15, 182, 192, 199n92
Midwife–doctor relationships, 45
Midwifery

districts, 43
free, 5, 17, 66, 76–79, 81–85,
   87–91, 103, 132, 134, 147,
   152, 183
as a higher calling, 43
law 1898, 27, 37, 41, 42, 44, 45,
   150, 161n114
reforms, 26
regulations, 52
school, 15, 42, 150
Midwives
control over mothers, 149
economic lives, 46
educated, 15, 42–45, 54n13,
   58n78, 150
as individuals, 15
as one body, 46, 206 (*see also Den
   norske jordmorforening*;
   Norwegian Association of
   Midwives)
professionalization of, 41
relationship to state, 44
role, 15
salary, 41, 42, 58n78
social position of, 87, 125
Sogn and Fjordane Midwives
   Association, 151
tasks, 41, 44, 149, 154
uneducated, 42
use by the state, 69
working conditions, 41, 42, 45, 69
See also Jordmødre
Ministry of Health, 83, 85
Ministry of Justice, 78
Ministry of Social Affairs, 78, 82, 86,
   111, 112, 114, 132, 137, 138,
   140, 144, 152, 186
Mohr, Tove, 139, 142, 158n51, 158n67
Møller, Katti Anker
protection of children and mothers,
   103, 106
vision of maternity insurance, 81
work with feminists, 66, 75

work with Johan Castberg, 62, 102
See also Maternity insurance,
   expansion of
Morality
arguments, 8
of maternity, 8
Morality debate, 29
See also Sedelighetsdebatten
Morgenbladet, 83, 128
Mortality
infant, 26, 28, 33, 52, 54n16,
   56n46, 67, 69, 73–75, 94n19,
   104–106, 111, 114, 207
maternal, 28, 44, 45, 51–52, 85
Motherhood
as an occupation, 165, 171
paid, 1
politicization of, 173
voluntary, 172, 197n46
Mother
new, 5, 7, 27, 29, 36, 39
pensions, 7, 9, 119, 165, 166,
   174–177, 183, 192
pregnant, 30
rights, 30, 93n7, 208
role, 14
separated from children, 50
working, 2, 4, 39, 50, 51, 124, 131,
   147, 151, 165, 171, 172, 174,
   176, 178–180, 188, 189, 192,
   193, 206, 208
Municipal assistance, 50
See also Poverty board
Myrdal, Alva, 170
Myrdal, Gunnar, 170, 196n35

N
National Association for Women's
   Suffrage, 40, 57n57
See also
   Landskvinnestemmerettsforeningen
National factory inspectorate, 36

218 INDEX

Nationalism, 3
influence on maternity policy, 10, 11
National Sickness Insurance
Office, 184
Neonaticide, 29, 30, 55n20, 101,
106, 111
state responsibility, 101
Netherlands, the, 7, 72, 118
maternity policies in, 7, 118
Newborns, 18n6, 25, 28, 29, 33, 39,
61, 84, 104, 110, 120n2
Night Work, 4, 6, 27, 33, 38,
53n7, 70
Nissen, Fernanda, 156n24, 156n26,
173, 206, 210n9
Nordstrøm, Marie, 123, 128,
155n1, 155n3
Norsk kvinnesaksforening (NFK), 29,
37, 70, 95n30, 106, 109, 126,
165, 199n101, 200n111,
200n114, 201n135, 201n136
See also Norwegian Association for
Women's Rights
Norske kvinners nasjonalråd (NKN),
15, 76–78, 96n50, 109, 121n24,
126, 127, 158n53, 174, 178,
179, 184, 185, 192, 195n25,
199n86, 199n106, 200n112
See also Norwegian National
Women's Council
Norwegian Association for Women's
Rights (NKF), 15, 29, 30, 37–41,
43, 44, 57n57, 70, 71, 75, 77,
106, 109, 126, 127, 165, 169,
174, 179, 181–186, 189, 190,
192, 199n92, 200n114,
201n136, 205, 207
See also Norsk kvinnesaksforening;
Women's organizations
Norwegian Association of Midwives
(DNJ), 5, 15, 46, 82, 152,
153, 206
See also Den norske jordmorforening

Norwegian Crafts and Industrial
Associations, 37
Norwegian Factory Protection Act
1892, 34, 36, 65
1909, 59n105, 72, 74
1915, 65
Norwegian feminist movement, 37
See also Feminists
Norwegian Labor Party, 3, 15, 41, 80,
81, 90, 126, 127, 130, 165–167,
169, 173–177, 181, 182, 185,
187, 200n117, 206, 207, 210n9
growth of in the interwar period,
167, 168, 207
See also Arbeiderpartiet
Norwegian Medical Association, 28,
35, 37, 46
Norwegian National Council of
Women (NKN), 15, 76–78, 109,
126, 127, 158n53, 173, 174,
178, 179, 184, 185, 195n25,
199n86, 200n112, 206, 207
See also Norske kvinners nasjonalråd
Norwegian public health
movement, 66
Norwegian women's rights
movement, 204
See also Norwegian feminist
movement
Norwegian Workers' Commission,
32–34
Norwegian working class, 31, 36, 169
Nylænde, 38, 40, 44, 55n22, 55n23,
55n24, 57n55, 57n59, 57n60,
57n61, 57n62, 57n64, 57n66,
57n67, 58n68, 58n69, 58n81,
58n82, 58n84, 60n115, 70, 83,
93n4, 95n30, 95n31, 106, 108,
109, 120n15, 121n20, 121n26,
156n17, 156n19, 183, 186,
195n24, 197n52, 199n97,
199n102, 199n103
Nylander, Gro, 204, 209n4, 209n5

O

Old-age homes, 116
Ormestad, Marius, 74, 79, 80, 96n45, 97n63, 132–134, 157n35, 164, 189–191, 194n4, 202n143
Oslo, Norway, vii, 4, 16, 19n16, 22n36, 22n37, 23n41, 24n51, 50, 54n11, 54n12, 54n15, 54n19, 55n26, 55n27, 55n28, 55n29, 55n30, 55n31, 55n32, 55n33, 56n36, 58n72, 59n86, 59n98, 59n99, 60n106, 60n109, 60n112, 60n113, 60n116, 94n16, 94n20, 94n23, 95n25, 96n45, 96n46, 97n63, 97n65, 97n67, 107, 120n1, 120n9, 123, 135–137, 155n4, 155n8, 156n33, 157n37, 157n42, 157n44, 159n68, 159n79, 163, 164, 166, 175–177, 188–192, 194n1, 194n2, 194n4, 194n12, 194n14, 195n22, 195n25, 197n46, 197n47, 197n48, 197n50, 197n52, 197n56, 198n62, 198n63, 198n67, 199n86, 201n125, 201n130, 201n133, 201n136, 201n137, 201n138, 201n139, 201n140, 202n141, 202n142, 202n143, 210n10
See also Kristiania, Norway
Oslo Social Welfare Office, 163, 164, 166, 188–192, 201n137, 201n138, 201n139, 201n140, 202n142

P

Parental leave, 1, 166, 203–209
Parliament
committee on social affairs, 82, 86
Odelstinget, 115, 116
See also Storting
Parliamentary democracy, 3, 4

Paternity
definition of, 104
leave, 203, 204, 209n8
Patriarchy, 171, 181, 183
Pederstuen, Karen, 30, 55n28
Penal reform, 61, 62
revision of the penal code, 1921, 62
Petersen, Kristian Friis, 85
Pettersen, Othilie, 101, 104, 106
trial of, 101
Polytechnic Association, 37
Poor houses, 116, 117
Poor relief
denial of, 49
poverty board, 48, 50, 60n116, 150, 152 (see also Municipal assistance)
requirements, 48–50
Poor women, 10, 48, 51, 52, 60n116, 75, 102, 103, 112, 114, 116, 118, 124–126, 138, 139, 141–143, 145, 151, 152, 158n65
Population policy, 36, 66, 86, 114, 170, 186
Postpartum allowances, 7
See also Maternity leave
Pregnancy
hygienic approaches to, 68
as an illness, 65, 70, 72, 81, 189
as medical condition, 27, 68, 71
as natural, 68, 81
scientific management of, 68
Pronatalist, 166, 170, 180
Public assistance
cost of, 113–115
supervisory mechanisms, 113
for vulnerable groups, 113
Public health movement, 62, 66, 67, 91
Public servants, 163, 188, 189, 191, 202n142
law on, 188–189

220 INDEX

R

Radical People's Party, 63, 73, 77, 93n8
 See also Arbeiderdemokratene
Rathbone, Eleanor, 165
Religious teachings, 29
Røyken, Norway, 135–137, 157n39
Rural Districts, 90, 116, 117
Rygg, Nicolai, 47, 54n16, 59n101, 67, 73, 94n18, 94n19, 95n26, 95n42, 105, 120n11, 121n36
 1907 report, 54n16

S

Sæbø, Lars Olsen, 71, 95n33
Scandinavia
 farmers movement in, 3
 maternity policy in, 8
 sonderweg particular to, 8
Scandinavian Model of Welfare, 8–9, 11, 21n33
Schuler, Fridolin, 33
Sedelighetsdebatten, 29
 See also Morality debate
Sentral statistiske byrå, see Central Statistical Agency
Sex, 7, 40, 72, 179
 outside wedlock, 40
Sexual double-standard, the, 107
Sickness Insurance
 cost, 81
 denial of, 136, 137
 directors of, 78
 inclusion of midwives, 76, 82
 inclusion of wives, 80
 local administration, 147
 obligatory, 70, 80, 96n45
 office in Oslo, Norway, 136
 premiums, 79, 80, 89, 108, 134, 150
Sickness Insurance Laws
 1909, 71, 72, 75, 78, 79, 92, 189

1915, 62, 103
Sickness Insurance Magazine, the, 80
 See also Sykeforsikringsbladet
Single Mothers
 expanded provisions for, 92
 financial assistance for, 110, 174
 image of, 31
 needs of, 101–102
 prejudice against, 108
 rights, 102, 175
 state support for, 112–113
Social Demokraten, 128, 156n23, 156n24, 156n26
Social question, the, 25, 31, 53n3
Stang, Fredrik, 81, 96n59, 109, 110
Storting, 4
 See also Parliament
Stuevold-Hansen, Birger, 115
Sverdrup, Johan, 32, 56n40
Sweden
 maternity policies in, 93n10
 union with, 2, 3
Sykeforsikringsbladet, 97n66, 97n67
 See also Sickness Insurance Magazine, the

T

Thrane, Marcus, 31
 Thrane movement, 31 (*see also* First working-class movement)
Tidsskrift for Jordmødre, 46, 54n18, 58n75, 58n79, 58n80, 59n87, 59n91, 60n108, 60n116, 97n73, 155n10, 160n90, 160n92, 160n96, 160n97, 160n99, 160n102, 160n104, 161n109, 161n110, 161n111, 161n112, 161n114
 See also Journal of Midwifery
Trædal, Lasse Torkelson, 87
Tveiten, Petterson Ivar, 116

U

Undset, Sigrid, 172, 197n50
Unemployment, 33, 136, 167, 177
Universal social policy, 9
Universal suffrage, 168, 169
Urbanization, 31, 56n38
Urban/rural divides, 115, 116

V

Venstre party, 3, 25, 32, 34, 35,
    56n45, 73, 85, 87, 90, 115, 116
    See also Liberal Party

W

Welfare officials, 10, 124, 131, 139
Welfare states, 2, 7–12, 16–18, 21n31,
    22n38, 22n40, 23n47, 53, 64,
    180, 192, 193, 208, 209
    development of, 2, 8–11, 16
White Ribbon Maternity Home,
    75, 107
    See also Den Hvide Baand
Widows, 7, 58n74, 113, 118, 175,
    176, 198n68
Women's agency, 12, 18, 24n48,
    115, 125
Women's Federation of the Norwegian
    Labor Party (AKF), 15, 80, 81,
    90, 126, 127, 130, 166, 169,
    173–176, 181, 182, 185, 206,
    207, 210n9
    See also Arbeiderpartiets
    kvinneforbund; Women's
    Secretariat of the Norwegian
    Labor Party
Women's health, 33, 36, 44, 62, 67,
    68, 74, 85, 118
    reproductive, 6, 12, 27, 33, 68, 69,
    103, 110, 125, 127, 164,
    171–173, 181, 205
Women's organizations, 16, 37,
    40, 43, 57n53, 75, 76, 78,

83, 109, 127, 167, 172,
    173, 178, 181, 183
Women's relationship to the state, 11
Women's rights activists, 3, 6, 11–12,
    37, 39, 40, 61, 65, 106, 139,
    164, 169, 184, 185
    See also Feminists
Women's Secretariat of the Norwegian
    Labor Party (AKF), 41, 80, 166,
    167, 206, 210n9
    See also Arbeiderpartiets
    kvinneforbund; Women's
    Federation of the Norwegian
    Labor Party
Women's suffrage, 3, 4, 19n12,
    26, 38, 40, 57n57, 118,
    131, 168, 193
Women's work
    economic value of, 205
    post-partum, 46
    social value of, 205
    wages, 65, 71, 111, 181
Worker protections, 9, 33
Workers' Commission of 1885, 32–34,
    36, 38, 47
Workers' Protection Act, 9, 166, 186
    See also Norwegian Factory
    Protection Act
Working class
    homes, 76, 113, 123, 124, 126–129
    life, 83, 129, 182
    sex lives of, 40
Working women, 6, 9, 11, 13–17,
    18n2, 26, 35, 37, 47, 48, 51, 52,
    65, 66, 70, 71, 74, 75, 89, 119,
    120n7, 139, 166, 182, 186, 188,
    206–209
    image of, 51
World War I
    influences on Norwegian social
    policy, 66, 86–87, 166,
    167, 180
    Norwegian neutrality in, 166, 193
World War II, 7, 141, 205, 207

CPSIA information can be obtained
at www.ICGtesting.com
Printed in the USA
LVHW04*0001170618
580977LV00014B/268/P